CRIMINAL MACABRE

Other books by Steve Niles:

Criminal Macabre graphic novels
Criminal Macabre: A Cal McDonald Mystery
Criminal Macabre: Supernatural Freak Machine
Criminal Macabre: Two Red Eyes
Criminal Macabre: My Demon Baby
Last Train to Deadsville: A Cal McDonald Mystery

30 Days of Night
The Nail (with Rob Zombie)
Freaks of the Heartland
Fused: Canned Heat
Fused: Think Like a Machine

CRIMINAL MACABRE

THE COMPLETE CAL McDONALD STORIES

Steve Niles

Dark Horse Books®
Milwaukie

Portions of this book previously appeared as *Savage Membrane*, published by ibooks, Inc., and *Guns, Drugs, and Monsters* and *Dial M For Monster*, published by IDW Publishing. "All My Bloody Things" first appeared in *Dark Delicacies*, published by Carroll & Graf Publishers.

Book design by Amy Arendts and Tony Ong
Cover art by ©iStockphoto.com/Ben Ryan, Chris Schmidt
Cover design by Amy Arendts
Special thanks to Shawna Gore and Jemiah Jefferson.

Published by Dark Horse Books
A division of Dark Horse Comics
10956 SE Main Street
Milwaukie, OR 97222

darkhorse.com

Library of Congress Cataloging-in-Publication Data

Niles, Steve.
  Criminal macabre : the complete Cal McDonald stories / Steve Niles. -- 1st Dark Horse Books ed.
    p. cm.
  ISBN-13: 978-1-59582-118-8
  ISBN-10: 1-59582-118-X
  1. Detective and mystery stories, American. 2. Horror tales, American. I. Title.
  PS3614.I56A6 2007
  813'.6--dc22
                          2007021263

First Dark Horse Books Edition: November 2007
ISBN 978-1-59582-118-8

Printed in USA

10 9 8 7 6 5 4 3 2 1

CONTENTS

SAVAGE MEMBRANE

It was the night after Halloween. I had vague memories of crashing a costume party with a couple of ghouls I know. I started drinking. After that I draw a blank, but I'm sure there was trouble—there always is. Besides, I could feel a hell of a fat lip throbbing and my hands were cut and bruised with the unmistakable indentations of human teeth across my knuckles. I'd hit somebody and somebody had hit back. That didn't bother me so much. I was always hitting and getting hit. What I found disturbing was my empty shoulder holster. My .38 was gone.

I was face-down in my apartment, experimenting with the adhesive properties of vomit to hardwood floors, when, of course, the phone rang. It sounded like a hammer against a steel barrel inside my skull. I groaned and peeled my head from the floorboards. My stomach lurched. It didn't like the idea of being moved very much but the phone was ringing incessantly. It was six at night so I had to get up anyway, but I didn't like being nagged. Wiping my face with one hand, I snatched the receiver violently from the cradle, choking the brain-rattling ring in half.

"McDonald Investigations. What d'you want?" I barked. My voice was gravel and phlegm.

The voice on the other end blurted, "Cal. I got something down here you might want to see."

It was Blout. Jefferson Blout is a big, bad-ass cop from the precinct I worked in for all of a year. That is, before I was asked to leave as a result of a drug test. Evidently traces of alcohol, marijuana, and crank were found in my blood. Traces, hell! At that time I was practically sweating the stuff. They didn't need to check my blood, they could've just sucked on my arm.

Blout stuck by me when everyone else on the force turned their backs. He knew why I did all the drugs, and why I still do sometimes. He knows what these eyes see. Christ. Believe me, if every time you turned around some fucked-up monster was coming down on you, you'd stay wasted too.

You see, I have this knack. Call it power, talent, what you like. I call it a curse. A fucking pain in the ass.

It's like this. Some people attract love or money and some—I think I'm one of the few—attract the bizarre. Always have, ever since I was an eight-year-old kid living in the 'burbs. That's when I found my first corpse.

I'd been tooling around the woods, playing with sticks and crap, when I came over an embankment near the creek that ran parallel with my house. There it was, tucked in the mud and leaves like a big, naked pea pod. I saw its feet first, then the torso. And that was all, because that's all there was. It was headless.

Maybe that was when things clicked, when my fate was set in stone. I wasn't scared, though—more like enthralled, so much so that I didn't bother to call the cops for over an hour. All I could do was think about the headless man. Who was he? Who killed him? And why had they taken his head?

Somehow, I knew instinctively that the head wasn't in the area, and when the cops arrived I told them my theory. They laughed, patted me on the head, and said I'd make a great detective.

That pretty much set the tone for the rest of my life: bizarre crimes, laughing cops, and me in the middle. Like I said, I'm a magnet for the weird, so I did what the cops told me all those years ago and became a detective. Now I really get on their nerves.

Anyway, Blout's supported me, helping with cases and sometimes with bail. I've tried to return the favor whenever something strange comes along that normal police investigations and procedures can't touch. And believe me, they hate to admit when they need help—especially from the likes of me.

There was this case a few years back where body parts of young boys and girls were being found all over the place—tragic, but not altogether uncommon. What was odd was that the limbs and other body parts hadn't been crudely chopped off, the norm in a hack-and-slash case. Instead, they were removed with almost surgical precision. The killer took his time with these kids, lots of time. Even weirder, the parts were rubbed with strange oils and exotic herbs. The cops waited almost six months before they came to me. If not for Blout's insistence, they may never have.

Once they showed me everything, I knew immediately that we were dealing with something of voodoo origin. The herbs and oils were commonplace in Haiti and New Orleans, even certain parts of New York. But the accuracy behind the removal of the limbs had me stumped until a day or so later. I was walking through an alley on the way to the corner liquor store, when I spotted an illegal chop shop—a garage where stolen cars are cut up for parts. It hit me like a ton of bricks, or better, a ton of bloody body parts.

I suggested the cops check the Feds' files for plastic or transplant surgeons of Haitian descent from the New Orleans area that had been fired in the past five years and had relocated to the Washington D.C. Metropolitan area. Second—and this even creeped me out—hit the files for stalking investigations on the Internet, specifically cases involving adults seeking teenagers.

On a hunch, I told them to check out a guy I'd seen on the news, name of Francis Lazar. He headed an organization that actually believed young children, and I mean young, were capable of consenting to physical relationships with adult men. The organization was called ManChildLove. I remember when I saw Lazar on CNN I quickly lost track of what he was talking about and concentrated on his eyes. In them I saw mania. The guy was a sick, twisted freak hiding behind his rhetoric.

Bottom line, boys: keep your eyes peeled for one or two twisted fucks with a penchant for teens, home surgery, and voodoo.

Sure enough, everything I told them involving the case fell into place. The cops, with the help of the Feds (who love to come in right at the end), located one Dr. Polynice, formally of New Orleans and fired from his post for "unusual practices with cadavers." In his basement, the authorities discovered the good doctor's very own teenage chop shop and Voodoo Lounge. After checking phone and mail records, it was found that the doctor had been shipping large crates all over the States. Before each shipment, a call was made from the doctor to MCL spokesman Francis Lazar.

Connection made, target hit. Bull's-eye. Dr. Polynice's network was collecting innocent teenagers, murdering them, rearranging their body parts into unidentifiable corpses, and reanimating the patchwork cadavers with forgotten voodoo zombie rituals. And it gets worse, if that's possible. The bastards were selling the jigsaw kiddies to ManChildLove members. What those twisted pricks did with them I'll leave to your imagination.

After the cops had jerked around for six months because they couldn't stretch beyond their own perception of the world, it took me less than a week to solve the case. How many kids could've been saved if they'd called me sooner? That's the question I couldn't shake.

In the end, more than sixty people were arrested from D.C. to San Diego, charged with crimes ranging from murder to kidnapping to necrophilia. Arrested were members of MCL, lonely, disturbed women, and one or two well meaning but extremely misguided couples unable to adopt or procreate.

Throughout the trial, the subject of reanimation was never brought up, nor were the zombie teens ever shown, talked about, or presented as evidence. They just disappeared, victims for all time. Nobody wants to believe in Frankenstein, but they will believe that someone mail-ordered corpses for sex.

Soon as I heard Blout on the phone this time, I knew something strange was happening. Something the cops couldn't handle using conventional methods.

"What is it? Emergency? 'Cause if it ain't, I got a lot of throwing up to do."

Blout laughed. "Yeah, I heard about last night."

I didn't want to let on I had no idea what happened at the Halloween party, so I returned the laugh and said, "It was a great party. I had a good time." I laughed again. It was one chuckle too many.

"You have no idea what happened last night, do you?"

I paused as long as I could. "No."

There was an awkward silence that happens every time Blout and I come too close to personal talk. He went on.

"You going to come down here or not?!"

I belched. Bile boiled in my throat. "Yeah, yeah, give me a couple minutes to clean up."

"Please do."

He hung up before I could retort. Bastard.

2

I took off my filthy clothes and used them to wipe up the area where I slept, then threw them out the window into the alley. It would be easier to get new stuff than to pay to have vomit, blood, and God knows what else cleaned out of them. I drew all the shades, lit a smoke, and strutted around the apartment naked until I found myself standing in front of my half shattered, full-length mirror. It'd been a long time since I'd looked at myself. What a mess; a maze of scars covered my body. I looked like a scarification fanatic, except they do it on purpose. I got mine quite unwillingly, the result of years and years of getting the shit kicked out of me.

I shook my head. Only thirty years old but you'd think I was in my late forties. Christ, fifties even! Standing there naked, I realized I looked as much like a monster as any I'd fought. I laughed a breathy, gasping-for-air laugh. Yeah, fucking hysterical.

I turned toward my trash-covered desk, head pounding. My guts were twisting so I pulled open the bottom drawer where a bottle of Jim Beam greeted me. It went down hard and connected with the craving in my bloodstream, making me queasy. The sick retreated before I returned the bottle to the drawer. Hair of the dog wins another in a long series of battles.

Kicking a trail through ankle-deep trash, I made my way to the bathroom, figuring I could catch a quick shower and shave and get down to the station within a half hour.

Just then I heard a sound from the other side of the shower curtain. Someone (or something) had shifted. I reached for my gun, but all I got was a handful of armpit. I had no weapon and I was naked, so I began to ease out of the room.

The curtain flew open and I screamed. A huge, dark figure stood in my tub.

"Ahhhhh!"

"Hey Cal, when did you wake up?"

It was Mo'Lock; sometime partner, reluctant friend, full-time ghoul. A ghoul of the lurking variety. My heart was pounding so hard I thought for sure I would die right then and there.

Yeah, I see all sorts of shit. Ghouls are actually one of the more common monsters around. They can be found all over the world, mostly in urban areas. They are the purest form of the undead, and actually the most harmless. Way back in the Middle Ages, ghouls were known for eating flesh and lurking in graveyards, but they came into their own around the turn of the century when they realized they didn't need flesh or blood to survive.

While the world was living through an industrial revolution, ghouls began a revolution of self-discovery. They were dead, cursed to live forever in a twisted form of their former human self, but they didn't need anything to survive. They made peace with the human race and began a hundred-year process of acclimating themselves into human society.

These days you can find ghouls everywhere. They tend to favor service industry jobs because they like the hours. Next time you pass a road crew, take a second look. I guarantee there's a ghoul among them. The same goes for postal workers and a wide range of people you probably never look at twice. Most people would be surprised how often they're in contact with the dead. All in all, ghouls are pretty low maintenance—that makes them all right in my book.

I met Mo'Lock on one of my earliest cases and he's been glued to me since. He has an annoying habit of creeping around, but I can't get too mad. That would be like blaming a cat for being hairy.

A slit of a grin appeared on his stark-white, bony face. "You forgot I was here, didn't you?" He looked a little too pleased with himself.

I took a deep breath. "Get the hell out of my bathroom. I got a call from Blout. Something's up."

The ghoul stepped out of the tub with long, sweeping, puppet-like motions. Two strides and he was standing outside the bathroom facing me. He looked me up and down like a ten-cent peepshow.

"Do you know you're naked?" He seemed to be genuinely concerned.

I slammed the door in his face. It hit him, and he fell to the floor cursing. He was very tall and thin, like a bone rail. Getting himself off the ground was a major pain. Teach his dead ass to mess with me. Maybe it would be a good day after all.

I showered, shat, shaved, and dressed before returning to my desk, where the ghoul was emptying his pockets onto the blotter: mace, a lock-blade knife, handcuffs, and a pair of short spiked steel knuckles—an inexpensive, but nasty cousin of the brass knuckle—covered the stained desktop.

"Hey, don't go dumping your shit on my desk!"

"This is your 'shit.' I took it from you at the party after your episode with the alien," he said, "Besides, I do not have any 'shit.'"

He wanted me to see the bloody smashed mess the door had made of his nose, but I just stared at him. His busted nose wasn't any big deal, it'd heal before we got to the precinct. The undead have amazing healing capabilities. He just wanted some easy sympathy.

"Officer Blout called again while you were in the shower. I took a message," Mo'Lock said as he lifted a piece of paper off the desk. "He said, 'If you don't get your fat, lazy-fuck, bastard-self down to the station immediately, you can kiss my black ass.'"

I loaded the stuff Mo'Lock had been holding for me into my pockets. Six-thirty PM and I was ready to start my day. When I headed for the door, Mo'Lock lumbered behind me. I stopped.

"You coming?"

"Do you mind?"

"No, not at all. You got cash?"

"Yes."

"Let's grab a cab."

The ride to the station was the usual bit of the bizarre that I've come to expect. The driver was of Mo'Lock's ilk, and the two of them gabbed on and on in a tongue that sounded foreign, but was simply regular English spoken at unbelievable speed. It's fascinating for about thirty seconds, then it works your nerves to blunt nubs. Moments like these made me wonder what the hell I was doing riding in a cab with a couple of the living dead. It was the eternal question—why me?

3

As a rule, I detest police departments, but I really hate my old precinct. Aside from the stares and nasty comments thrown my way as I pass, the place has a smell that sets my memory reeling. Walking the halls, I'm always reminded of the worst times.

The year I graduated from the academy, for instance, was a long, shit-pile of a year. I became a cop, then lost my family and nearly my mind. In the space of twelve months, my mother and younger sister were killed by a drunk driver and my father, Ben McDonald, went berserk and cut the driver's throat outside the courtroom. As usual, I couldn't do a damn thing about it because I was so loaded on smack.

My father was charged and he responded by hanging himself the night before his hearing. I discovered the body. I'll never forget the image of his corpse swinging back and forth, the sound of the rope creaking against the rafter beam, rhythmic and maddening.

All my life I tried my damnedest to be normal. I ignored the dark fringes of the world that crept toward me and if something got too close, I stomped it dead and turned my back like nothing had ever happened. Monsters? Nope, didn't see them. Werewolves, aliens, demons, and freaks? Just keep on walking. Don't look.

The police academy was an attempt at normal existence, but even there I should have known it would be impossible. I could never hide or live a normal life. No matter how hard I try, I always seem to land right in the middle of Freak Central.

The academy was no exception.

It turned out that the place was built on a goddamn burial ground. Of course, the dead decided to have their revenge the week I arrived. It was a bloodbath of possession, sacrifice, and the living dead. I don't mean living dead like Mo'Lock, soulless ghouls who can function and think; these sons-a-bitches were mindless, kill-crazy zombies.

The place turned upside down. Everyone panicked except me. The one benefit of my life is that I'm never surprised. I've had the crap scared out of me a few times, but I never panic. That day, I fought my way through the relentless invasion until I reached the little room used as the parish. I convinced the priest, who I found hiding in his confessional, to follow me to the basement where I told him to bless the water main. It took some convincing, and a slap or two, but eventually he agreed.

It was in the bag. I manned one of those riot control hoses and hosed the place down with a half million gallons of high-octane Holy Water. The dead and possessed withered and melted, screamed, and let loose the innocent. In the end, only a few dozen were dead and nobody except me and the priest knew what happened. Well, at least that was the official stand. The academy closed and moved to a new location a year later. Chickenshits.

Still, I refused to give in, to acknowledge the supernatural regions of life. To hide, I took more and more drugs, more and more drink, anything to blur my vision or dull my senses. It was a miracle I lived, let alone graduated. But I did, and everything was going great for awhile. I even made the effort and kicked drugs. It was hard, very hard, and not just because of my physical and emotional addictions. The more I stayed sober, the more horror I saw: strange things peering around corners, voices whispering in my ear in the dark. But I had to make an effort, had to make some sort of a stand against the darkness that threatened to overtake me.

I was absolutely straight the day of my graduation from the academy. My family was there (it would be several weeks until the drunk driver entered our lives) and though nobody said it outright, especially my dad, I knew they were proud.

At one point he caught me alone near a crowd of rowdy graduates. He shook my hand and in a very low tone said, "You look good, son. Nice job."

He used the pretense of the graduation to congratulate me on kicking drugs, but it was better than nothing. Then in the crowd I saw a stranger moving quickly through the crush. He moved with a confidence you don't see in a normal person. I couldn't take my eyes off him, even though my father was talking to me. He broke through the crowd, and as he passed he looked at me and raised his hand. Then I saw his palm and the strange scar burned into its center. A pentagram, the mark of the beast. I started to go after him, but stopped. I wasn't going to give in. The darkness would not consume me. I forced myself to look away. When I looked back, the stranger had disappeared into the throng of graduates.

That night I had dinner with my parents. I stayed sober despite the sight of the man in the crowd. It had been eating at me all night, though, because he seemed to take pleasure in taunting me. I knew what the man really was—a pentagram on the palm was the sign of the werewolf.

The dinner was nice despite my preoccupation. They were happy about me becoming a police officer and my newfound sobriety. Nobody said it in so many words, or any words at all, but they buzzed around, smiling at nothing, and there was a general air of peace that had been absent for a long time.

My little sister Stephie suckered me into some Nintendo after dinner and we wound up playing for hours. Finally, after I'd received countless ass-kickings, my dad asked that we turn off the game so he could see the news. I pretended to be disappointed, but it was a relief.

Everything came crashing down when the television flickered to life. The lead story on the news was a gruesome, extremely bloody multiple murder. To our horror, we found out the murders had happened nearby. A family was having a small party celebrating their daughter's graduation from the academy. Details were sparse, but at some point the party came under attack—twelve people were slaughtered.

My stomach began to tighten. I needed a drink, a pill, something. Anything to stop the feeling rushing over me.

". . . details are sketchy but police are telling us that this shocking tragedy seems to be the result of some sort of . . . animal attack."

I was numb, sick. I felt responsible for the deaths. I'd had the killer in my sights and let him go.

I suddenly felt panicked and had to get out of that house. I hastily thanked my mom for the dinner as the whole family pleaded that I stay. I remember looking back as I got into my car and seeing my parents standing in the doorway. They weren't waving. They just stood there watching me, knowing I was about to leap off the wagon. They were right—I went on a binge that would've shamed Keith Richards.

It did the trick. I felt nothing but the buzz of alcohol and painkillers in my system. Above all, I saw nothing.

Three weeks later, a drunk driver took most of my family. After that, and after I found my dad swinging by his throat, I was gone. I remember nothing from the last half of my year as a cop save for loads of crushing pain. It was then that I faced my fate, spit on it, and kicked it in the balls.

I was so much of a mess that my sergeant demanded I take a drug test. The results were bad. They didn't just ask me to leave the force, they kicked my butt and threw me bodily from the station.

It was the final straw. Still, I didn't care. I laid in the gutter until I had the strength to stagger to a liquor store. I was beaten down, twitchy, and paranoid. Faces stared, some dumbly, some seemingly loaded with malice. I had lost it all. Soon I would come apart at the seams, or if I was lucky, just collapse and die.

Then it happened. I was walking, swigging rotgut, alongside a small shadowy park off Fifteenth Street, just short of Mount Pleasant. It was a dark moonless night, yet when I glared into the park I could see clear as day. I saw the figure of a man looming over a woman. At first I thought they were making out, and I began to turn away to get back to feeling sorry for myself. Then I saw the moist glimmer of fangs.

Vampire.

I tossed the bottle, smiled, and cracked my knuckles.

I ran into that park feeling every ounce of the pain in my chest, every loss I'd suffered, and most of all, the hatred I felt for the horrible luck I had. I channeled the rage into my body, feeling strong, sober, and clear-headed. In reality, I was out of control, drunk, and over-confident.

I attacked the vampire with such ferocity that the bloodsucker seemed frightened and tried to get away. From me, a mere human! In that moment, I gave up trying to run away. If the dark wanted me, it had me.

I ripped the head from the vampire's shoulders with my bare hands, pissing on the fate that was handed to me. This was my life. I had arrived.

And that, to make a short story long, is why I hate going to the precinct. It reminds me of my family and the sorry state of my life.

Blout was waiting for us outside the door of the coroner's lab, chewing on a big sloppy cigar. Normally I dislike cigar smokers, but he pulled it off. Blout was a large, wide-framed black man in his early forties, very dark and tall. In fact, he was almost as tall as Mo'Lock. He always wore dark suits that made him all the more imposing, making me feel small and unimportant in his shadow.

He looked pissed—pretty much his natural state—and none too pleased that I'd brought the ghoul along. Nobody could quite figure out who or what Mo'Lock was. He definitely made humans uneasy, but he always wore a suit and tie, so they assumed he was okay. Funny what you can pull off with a decent suit.

Blout stood up and looked straight into my eyes. Mo'Lock was ignored with clear, obvious disdain.

"What'd you bring him for?" Blout asked in his low, rumbling voice. He stood close. I could smell the minty stink of his menthol shaving cream and the fast food taco he'd had for lunch.

I shrugged. "He's my assistant. Might be able to help."

Blout shoved a big finger close to my nose. "Just keep him the fuck away from me. Got it?"

I showed him two palms. "Okay, no sweat. What've you got?"

Blout bobbed his head sideways, indicating the door of the coroner's lab.

"In here."

The lab was cramped, bare of equipment, and dark. There were only two lights—a small desk lamp and a bare bulb dangling above the examination table in the center of the room.

There was a body on the table, head and chest cut open. The scalp had been sliced, and the flesh from the top of the head peeled like an orange. The face of the dead man was wrinkled and folded down over itself. It would have been comical if it weren't so disgusting. The ribs were sawed clean away so there was a tidy viewing window to examine the cavity. I could see the internal organs had already been removed for examination. The heart and liver were in steel trays and next to them was an array of bloody saws and surgical tools. An autopsy had recently been completed.

I stepped up to the table. The body was male. By the looks of his overgrown hair and the haggard, leathery look of his skin, I assumed he was homeless. That is, of course, when he was alive. He was dead now. Homeless and lifeless, what a raw deal.

Mo'Lock stayed behind me, close to the exit, but slowly edged toward the corner where there was the least amount of light. Blout moved to the other side of the table. He looked down at the body and sighed. He didn't have much of a stomach for an experienced cop. When he looked up at me I was screwing a cigarette into my mouth. His expression went from disgust to irritation.

"Don't smoke in here, Cal. Christ, you know better."

I put my lighter back, leaving the unlit cigarette in my mouth. "Yeah, I wouldn't want to give the stiff cancer," I said. "What's the story?"

"John Doe, homeless. He was found last night stuffed in a drainage pipe that used to dump into the old reservoir near the D.C./Maryland border."

I could see no reason why I was needed. Dead bums weren't my forté, and not the least bit strange. I chewed on the unlit cigarette like a piece of beef jerky. "What's the cause of death?"

Blout smirked. He thought he had one on me, as though the answer were so clear, so obvious. "Try opening your fucking eyes. You notice anything missing?"

I scanned the body again, stopping at the head. I leaned down and squinted into the open skull. Inside it was a clean white, as though the cavity had been scrubbed and bleached.

"I'll be damned," I said, and stood up straight.

"You see why I wanted you to come down."

From the other side of the room, Mo'Lock emerged from the shadows.

"What is it?"

Blout and I spoke at the same time.

"No brain."

The autopsy was conclusive: the skull was completely empty. There was no blood, no gray matter, and x-rays showed there were no breaks in the skull whatsoever. The brain stem was there, untouched, as though there had never been anything attached to it. The official coroner's report called it brain death, but isn't brain death when you're still alive but a vegetable? How can something that isn't there be the cause of death? I'd like someone to explain that one.

The strange thing was, I'd seen this before. Blout knew it.

"Remind you of anything, Cal?"

I nodded. This time Blout kept his mouth shut.

Mo'Lock walked right up to the table. He stood so close I could feel the cold of his flesh, his annoyance evident. "Excuse me, but I'd like to know what's going on."

I was staring at the floor, my head swimming in watery visions of distant memories.

It was one of my earliest cases, during a phase when I was doing some pretty hard drugs. I was still a mess from what had happened with my family. It had been only a few months since I'd been thrown off the force, but I decided to go into business for myself—what did I have to lose? The way I figured, if weird shit was constantly getting in my face, I might as well get paid for it. I managed to throw together enough cash to get the apartment that I use as an office, and soon after began getting a few cases.

Most of them were simple, basic demon possessions or hauntings. Other jobs were total fakes, people who thought their neighbors were Satan worshipers, vampires, and werewolves. Sometimes they were, but mostly they weren't. I didn't tell them that, though—I needed the cash. I had rent to pay and a bad habit to feed. Actually it was more difficult to cheat people than it was to deal with supernatural problems. I hated to lie, but cases involving the unnatural are pretty hard to find. It's tough making a living off something people refuse to believe exists. Things have to get way out of hand before they seek help.

That's what happened the day a guy named Edgar Cain developed a bizarre and dangerous ability. The police, at wit's end, were forced to turn to me.

Edgar lived in a huge, four-hundred-unit apartment complex. He was a lonely man, keeping to himself and hiding in his apartment for weeks on end. He was employed as an accountant for a company that did telemarketing and was thus able to work from home. It cut him off completely from contact with others, insuring his solitude. All that loneliness right smack dab in the middle of a tower of humanity was the catalyst for Cain's ability. Over the years I've found loneliness to be the source of many bizarre crimes and unnatural behavior.

One morning, residents of Cain's complex started to drop dead. Just like that. Bam! they're dead. By noon the body count reached seventy-five. And like the current stiff lying before me, their brains were gone. Not broken, splattered, or spilled. Gone.

All the while, Edgar Cain grew inside his apartment. With each death, Cain's brain increased in size and so did his skull and head. Somehow, he was absorbing the brains of everyone around him. With the brains came their intellects, memories, and ideas. In his own horrific way, Edgar Cain undid years of loneliness by making a community inside his enormous, growing head.

That was the point where I came in: scores dead and a giant head going berserk on the top floor of an apartment building. The cops had come to the right guy—it had me written all over it.

Of course, I was wasted that day, but this time it would work in my favor. I didn't know it right away but Edgar couldn't absorb my brain because of the tremendous amounts of narcotics swimming in my bloodstream. When I marched off the elevator with a shotgun, there was nothing he could do to stop me.

But I didn't just run in shooting. First I tried to reason with him. He ranted on about becoming one entity, one life, making loneliness impossible. Blah, blah, blah. After the speech, he attacked me and went airborne. The fucking head could fly! I tried to shoot him but only managed to blast his skinny little leg. He hit me hard. We went out the window, and just like that, we were flying over the city, a thousand feet up. I was clinging to his hair, ears, an open wound, anything to stay on while I punched and kicked at the wailing head.

Then I remembered the syringe in my pocket that I had shot up with earlier. I used that very syringe to stab out Cain's eyes and bring him crashing to the ground. He exploded in a massive spray of tissue and bone chips, which conveniently broke my fall. A perfect ending—I was alive and there was nothing left of the head.

"End of case. Until this," I finished. I looked from Mo'Lock to Blout and then to the body. "I thought it was a simple case of spontaneous phenomenon, but if it's happened again . . ."

Blout shook his head, "What the hell's spontaneous phenomenon?"

"I made it up," I said, "It means something that's never happened before."

Blout raised his hands. "You can't make up case descriptions!"

"Sure can," I shot back. "I just did."

Blout was about to blow his top. The fact that I smiled didn't help.

"There has to be a source." Mo'Lock said, moving the conversation back on topic.

I rubbed my eyes. "Exactly."

Blout looked at Mo'Lock's pale flesh and deep sunken eyes. The ghoul bothered him in a way he'd never admit. To even entertain the thought of the walking dead would drive a normal person over the edge. For a cop like Blout whose entire existence is grounded in fact, the truth would kill him.

Blout started to say something, but before he got it out, the door of the lab was knocked open by someone pushing a cart. It was a young woman with a serious face and hair pulled in a tight bun wearing a dark blue coroner's office windbreaker. On the cart was a bagged corpse, and behind it another.

"You Blout?" she demanded as much as asked. "On the John Doe case?"

Blout nodded quickly, flustered as a third and fourth cart were rolled in. "Yes to both questions," he said. "What the hell's going on?"

The woman handed him a clipboard. "We've been trying to reach you. Beat cops found a dumpster full of bodies alongside the water treatment plant near Georgetown. Sign please."

Blout grabbed his head and shot me a look. "All homeless?"

"Near as I can tell." She stopped for one quick moment as she caught a glimpse of Mo'Lock and was out the door.

In the hall, they had begun to line the walls with carts and bodies. There wasn't any room left in the lab.

Seconds turned into minutes at Dead Body Central. We all did a lot of head shaking, muttering, and heavy sighing. Everywhere we looked was a cart and body bag. The place was a cadaver parking lot. I waited for Blout to say something, but when at last he spoke, it was anti-climactic to say the least.

"I better get back to the office to start sorting this shit out." He eyed me sharply from across the table. "Got any ideas?"

"A few. I think the first thing I should do is get ahold of the Edgar Cain files. Can you get them for me?"

Blout shook his head. "Whoa, whoa, whoa! Don't go running off on one of your tangents. That was a nice story, but I need to investigate on planet Earth first."

"Would it hurt you to humor me before it's too late just this one time?" I said and smacked his shoulder.

Blout muttered something under his breath, then, "Give me an hour."

"What about Cain's phone records?"

"Oh, come on, Cal. Why do you want phone records? You know what a bitch those are to get." Blout looked irritated.

"Just a hunch. I'll fill you in if anything pans out."

I turned to Mo'Lock. "One thing's for sure, if John Doe was found outside a drainage pipe and this crowd was near the treatment plant, we got one place we have to check out."

The ghoul bobbed his head. "The sewers."

"Right. Grab some of your buddies and check it out."

"I'm on it."

Out of the corner of my eye, I saw Blout shudder as the ghoul left. I chuckled.

"That freak gives me the creeps," Blout said with a little extra gravel in his throat.

"Be glad he's on our side. You'd cry like a baby if you knew what he was capable of," I said. "Besides, he's saved my ass more times than I care to admit, so in my book that makes him a lifetime pal."

"The two of you make a lovely couple. Let's get out of here. These stiffs got a meeting with the butcher."

Right on cue, the medical examiner came in with a couple of her assistants following like little bloodthirsty ducklings. I was halfway down the hall when Blout stopped and went back to the door.

"Wilson? Would you mind starting with the head examination first? I need to know what you find."

"Sure. It's your show."

Blout caught up with me as I was heading out the front door. "Hey Cal, want your gun back?"

I stopped outside, bit the inside of my lip, and turned. Blout was grinning. My stomach sank. "You have my gun?"

He nodded slowly.

"You were at the party?"

"After the police were called in."

I threw my hands up in the air. Fuck it, I had no idea what I'd done. The jig was up. "Okay, you got me! What the hell happened?"

"First," he said reaching into his coat pocket, "here's your piece. Try to hang on to it."

I took the gun and put it into the empty holster. "Go on. I can see you're enjoying the shit out of this."

"Well, it seems you took it upon yourself to break some kind of world record for most drinks consumed in an hour—"

"Skip the embellishments."

"You got blind, piss-drunk, and seemed to forgot it was Halloween and you were at a costume party. Evidently, you spotted this dude in a real convincing alien costume and you . . . went . . . nuts." He rolled the last word off his tongue by touching it to his teeth, causing an irritating hiss.

"Did I hurt the guy?"

"Oh yeah."

"I didn't shoot him or anything, did I?"

Blout shook his head. "No, no. Luckily your buddies disarmed you while you were getting riled up. All you managed to do was smash a forty-gallon punch bowl over his head and beat him with a table leg. It wasn't pretty."

I slapped my hand over my eyes. "Is he pressing charges?"

"I'd be expecting a large lawsuit in the not-too-distant future."

I waved off the whole mess. "Fuck it. I don't care. I'll think of something."

I started down the front steps. The night air was breezy and the first hint of cold tickled the surface of my skin. Fall was in full swing.

"Let me know when you find Cain's case file, and about the autopsy results."

Before the door closed I heard Blout laughing, saying "I'm on it," in his best Mo'Lock impression. It was horrendous.

Walking back to my apartment I snagged a pint of rotgut from the liquor store and swigged. The bottle was empty by the time I reached my building, and I was feeling fine. A little bleary, but better.

I reached for the door handle but it wouldn't budge. I gave it another tug. Nothing. It was stuck.

"Goddammit."

After one last yank I leaned in and inspected the door closely. The space between door and frame was clogged with hardened opaque crud. Some punk had super-glued the door shut. I was about to curse everyone under thirty, when I suddenly stopped. There was a sharp noise over my shoulder—a click.

The small hairs on my arms stood on end. Instinctively I dove sideways. At that exact moment, the door exploded in a hail of automatic gunfire. I hit the ground hard and rolled, but the barrage followed me like a swarm of angry bees. I rolled as fast as I could and jumped to my feet, diving for cover into the alley. Not fast enough: I felt the sting of a bullet graze my shoulder.

Then, as suddenly as it began, it was quiet again. I was lying in a pile of rancid garbage and pigeon shit, bleeding and trying to stay as still as possible while a car screeched away. When I ran to the curb a smoke cloud from the tires still hung in the air. I could see the car ahead and a figure hanging out the window, throwing away the gun. He was wearing a ski mask, no gloves, and wrist bands. I reached for my revolver, but the shoulder wound tore wider and stopped me cold.

The street looked like the set of *The Hound of the Baskervilles*. Smoke was everywhere. I pushed through the haze toward the receding car until I found the gun lying in water and leaves. I don't know a hell of a lot about guns but I was pretty sure it was an Uzi.

That in itself was scary enough. To top that off, painted along the side of the gun were the words, "Cal McDonald."

Venturing a guess, I'd say it was meant as a threat. Rank amateurs. That out-of-control hail of bullets could have just as easily hit me as not. Some warning. And writing my name on the weapon? That was just plain stupid.

Then I noticed the entire door to my building was gone, blown completely apart. At least I could get in now.

My shoulder was bleeding, but not bad. I'd be able to sew it up myself.

6

Blout sent Cain's file to my apartment by courier. No phone records, and the rest I already knew. The evidence list, though— that I found fascinating. Most of the stuff was pretty standard, but I was surprised to see that an accountant who worked out of his home owned no calculator, computer, fax, or answering machine. His life seemed oddly devoid of modern conveniences.

About ten minutes after the courier dropped by, Blout called with the preliminary autopsy results. The heads of the first three victims were empty and sparkling clean. I was sure the rest would turn out the same. What did surprise me was what Blout said next.

Some of the corpses had been dead for more than five months.

I was getting the unsettling feeling this case was going to be a bit more difficult than my usual day-to-day monster-in-the-closet case. As far as I knew, Cain was the only loon to suck brains telepathically, and that ability died when I killed him. This was something new, something bigger, and something much, much deadlier. I wasn't sure if that case had anything to do with this one, but it was all I had to work with. I needed to establish a timeline of Edgar Cain's activities the day he started absorbing people's brains.

"By the way," I said into the receiver as I reached for the bottle, "someone tried to turn me into a greasy smear outside my apartment earlier. I got the gun. Can I drop it off for dusting and ballistics?"

Blout sounded amused. "Any idea who it was?"

"Zip. All I saw was a dark '65 Mustang, speeding away with three people inside."

"Why don't you run down here in a little while? I'll run the weapon, and we can grab some food and talk about the case. Suits upstairs are nervous that the press might catch wind and turn the thing into a circus."

"Give me half an hour. I took a slug in the shoulder. I gotta stitch myself up." I took a big swig of Beam.

"Christ, Cal. Go to the fucking hospital!"

I swallowed. The burn felt great. "No. I've been there a thousand times this month. It's nothing. I'll take care of it."

"Fine," was all Blout had to say. He hung up.

I chuckled. "What a granny."

I removed my dress shirt and did some sewing.

By eleven o'clock that night, I'd polished off the bottle, popped some speed, and was at the station with the gun. The precinct was quiet. The only two people in the front office were me and the desk sergeant, an old-timer named Potts. He plastered a fake welcome smile across his bored, withered face.

"I'm here to see Blout."

Potts made a face like bile had just shot the length of his throat, picked up the phone, and paged Blout.

I was about to take a seat when the front doors banged open. Two uniforms came in, noisily hauling an unruly who looked to be drunk and disorderly. I knew one of the cops, Dan Stockton. He was a major prick, disliked by more people than just me. He was pissed because he was still in uniform while everybody else made detective or better, bitter because he knew he was a nasty fuck that everybody hated, but mostly because it was just his nature. He was what you'd call a bad egg.

Stockton let his partner take the prisoner, and stopped—facing me. He was way too close. I was torn between a short lecture on personal space and jamming the cartilage in his nose through his brain.

"Well, well, if it isn't Cal McDonald," he sneered. "What the hell are you doing here? This is a police station, not a junkie detective station."

He stepped even closer. I stood my ground.

"I got plenty of business here, Stockton. And all of it's none of yours, so why don't you just back off," I growled, curling my mouth into a nasty scowl.

Stockton's eyes blinked and stuttered. I'd got him. He wasn't so sure I'd back down. I could tell he was searching for something snappy to say, but all he could muster was, "Why should I back off?"

"Because I have an aversion to halitosis," I shot back.

It was a dud. He didn't get it. Instead of being offended, he was confused.

"What?" he sputtered.

I sighed. "Bad breath." I was disappointed that the fire had puttered out. But Stockton snapped and went for his baton screaming "Motherfucker!"

I backed away fast and threw my bag down. If I was gonna fight a cop in the damn precinct, I didn't want to have a loaded Uzi on me. They'd just love that.

Stockton had his nightstick at the ready, violence flaring in his eyes. He could beat the crap out of me and get away with it. He was a cop, after all! If I fought back, he could slap me with charges and a free beating. I didn't give a shit. I had every intention of mopping the joint with the nasty little prick's face.

Before any blows could be exchanged, Blout came out of a side door. "Stockton, what the hell are you doing?!"

In the end, I was relieved there weren't going to be any punches thrown. I would have come out on the losing end of that particular stick any way you looked at it. Cops don't look kindly on flatfoots beating on uniforms in the hall of the precinct.

"Get the hell out of here," Blout spat.

Stockton gave me a nasty look and promptly left. It wasn't over. Blout was looking at me, pissed again.

"Do you think you could stay out of trouble for two seconds?"

I shrugged. "I'm willing to try," I said, picking the bag off the seat. "Here's the Uzi someone tried to kill me with."

Blout laughed a jerky, breathy laugh.

We left the Uzi with the lab to dust for prints and run ballistics, and left the precinct at around eleven thirty. Blout was hungry, but I had other plans.

7

By midnight we arrived at the deserted apartment complex where Edgar Cain had lived. The place couldn't have been creepier. The streetlights were dead, but it didn't matter since four looming high rises would block out any moonlight. The way the buildings were laid out gave the impression that the architect had simply thrown blocks into the air, and the way they landed was how the apartments were built. It was planned chaos that created shadowy corners, blind spots, and black canyons even the bravest thug would be wise to avoid.

The complex was called Whitney Green. In some ways it could be compared to the gigantic, soulless projects in New York and Chicago, with two major differences. It was condemned, for one. But what made it ominous was when you looked around Whitney, you saw nothing. No graffiti, no gang signs. No homeless, no squatters. Not so much as a broken window since the day Cain slaughtered the tenants with his mind. The compound imprisoned the troubled memories of over a hundred dead.

Nobody, not even the lowest of lows, dared penetrate its boundaries for shelter. It was truly a haunted place.

Blout was not at all pleased to be there.

"This is ridiculous, Cal. There's nothing here!"

We each had a flashlight. I flashed mine forward into the pitch-dark courtyard leading to unit number four, Cain's building. My footfalls echoed around our ears. Behind me, Blout's breath was heavy and labored.

"I have to make sure. I got a feeling something's here. Something that can help us," I said, and started walking away from Blout. "I'm going in. You can stay here if you want."

Blout didn't need to think it over. "Just wait up, goddammit."

The flashlight did little to light our path once we were inside the building. The darkness had a texture like smoky tar that seemed to fight the light, only allowing it to penetrate a few yards ahead of us. I was looking for the staircase.

"This is crazy. Why don't we come back during the day?" Blout whined behind me.

My light landed on an exit sign above a red steel door. "Because you can find things at night that aren't there during the day."

"Listen to yourself, McDonald. You're nuts!"

I ignored him. Some people need to whine when they're frightened. I know I do. "This way," I said, guiding him to the red door as I gave it a shove.

Inside the stairwell a gust of rotten air greeted us. An echo gave voluminous dimension to the corkscrew tower as we stepped inside. The door creaked shut slowly and closed with a small but definitive click. Blout swallowed. Like it or not, we were in.

"Which way?" he asked.

"Up," I said. "Cain's apartment. Top floor."

I took the first step. Then, above us, we heard a door slamming.

I jumped back. Blout threw himself against the exit door.

"W . . . what the fuck was that? Wind?" Blout hissed. I could hear the dry crack of his throat.

"Probably not. Come on."

Hearts pounding, we went up the first flight, then the second and third. By the fifth floor we were both calm.

Bang!

This time it came from below us. My eyes had adjusted somewhat and I could see that Blout was covered with sweat.

"You okay?" I whispered.

"No," Blout croaked. "You realize that in high rises like this, it isn't really the fourteenth floor. It's the thirteenth."

"Yes, I thought of that."

"Does that figure into your case?"

"Everything does." We had reached the eleventh floor. I stopped and pulled a flask out of my jacket, took two short swigs, and offered it to Blout.

He grabbed it, took one mini-swig, washed it around in his mouth, and spit it out. "Christ, what is that crap?!"

"You heard of 'premium'? That's 'sale.'" I took one more drink and then pushed on.

Cain's floor was as I'd left it years before—completely destroyed. The walls and ceiling were ripped away. Plaster and tile littered the place, forming piles of dusty white. At the far end of the hall I could feel a breeze coming through the hole we'd made when we went airborne. I could see the shattered wall and the dark blue, star-flecked sky that filled the vacant space.

Exactly halfway down the hall was another hole where Cain had smashed through from inside his apartment. That was where we stopped.

"This is it," I whispered and shot Blout a glance. He was looking behind him and wasn't listening to a word I said. "Blout?"

He turned. "What?"

"In here. Cain's apartment."

The hole was large enough so that the two of us walked through side by side. For me, walking into the apartment brought a rush of memories. Because of the massive amounts of drugs I was on at the time not all of my memory is available for recall, but standing in this room where so much violence had taken place brought it all back to me.

Cain had first attacked me when I was still several floors away. His strange power pulled at my brain, but he couldn't take it. The pain was unbelievable, like nothing I'd experienced before, like fingernails grinding along the base of my brain. It made a migraine feel like pure pleasure. Cain pulled, pushed, tugged, and squeezed my brain. I was so determined, or so wasted, that I kept moving until I was standing square in the doorway.

I had a shotgun trained on the floating head, but it wasn't afraid. I remember that we spoke.

"Why won't you leave me alone?"

"You killed all those people."

"I didn't do it," he said. "Didn't really kill them. Only absorbed their brains. They were unhappy, all of them. Leading empty, pointless lives . . ."

The floating head paused, and swayed. I shot off one of his legs, and he hardly noticed.

". . . like everyone else." He went on, "I simply combined them into one big pointless life."

Then Cain stopped talking and attacked. The fight wasn't over until I stabbed his eyes out high above the city and sent him crashing to his death.

"Cain had no remorse," I said.

Blout was at the window shining his flashlight along the shattered frame. "What was that?"

I shook my head. "I remember Cain talking like he did the dead a favor by taking their brains."

"He was a homicidal maniac. You were expecting logic?" Blout said. Then, as though suddenly annoyed, he turned off his light and raised his arms. "Would you please tell me what I'm supposed to be looking for?"

"Not really sure. I just needed to come here . . . to feel it."

"Well, are you done feeling it yet?"

"Look, Blout, I don't knock your methods. Don't knock mine."

I was getting pissed. I turned off my flashlight and waved him over to my side of the room. "Let's take a break."

As we pulled up boxes and sat, I took out my pack of cigarettes and the flask. I swigged and handed it to Blout. Before drinking he held it up to the moonlight coming through the window.

"Checking for germs?"

"No, just seeing if there was any left," Blout said and this time took a big-ass mouthful and choked it down. "Ahhhhh ahh! Damn, that's awful." He coughed, then took another pull.

I smiled, thinking how odd it was that the two of us tolerated each other. We couldn't have been more different. He was successful, together, and completely on the up-and-up. And me? I was in as much, if not more, trouble than I was in my teens. What a pair we made.

"You know, you have a name that should be in a Frank Capra movie. *Jefferson Blout Goes to Washington*." I displayed the marquee in the air with my hands.

Blout laughed. "Yeah, Capra made a bunch of films about black cops."

I took a drink and swallowed hard. "Can I ask you a question?"

Blout just shrugged. The last mouthful was his.

"It's what, two, three o'clock in the morning. Doesn't it bother your wife that you don't come home?"

Blout looked away and sighed. "Jessica left me last month. So yes, I guess it did bother her."

"Shit, I'm sorry. I wouldn't have brought it up if—"

"It's all right. We were married a long time, a lot of good years. I don't have any regrets." He was fumbling in his coat. His hand came out holding two of those jumbo cigars he smokes. "Want one?"

I was about to agree when I had an idea. "I'll be right back."

I got up and darted to the right where there was a small efficiency kitchen. I opened the refrigerator and smiled. I love it when hunches pay off.

"What've you got there?" Blout asked at my back.

I turned and showed him. "I present to you, one six-pack of the finest ten-year-old Black Label for our consuming pleasure. Warm, of course."

I planted the six-pack on the floor between us, broke one from the ring, and gave it to Blout in exchange for the cigar. When I popped open my beer, it foamed. I took that as a good sign.

Blout was staring at his can. "Is this safe?"

"Only one way to find out." I swigged and was surprised to discover that it tasted as crappy and watery as a new Black Label.

Blout sipped, testing. Finding it normal, he swigged away.

"What about you, Cal? Why haven't you ever settled down? I've seen you with some young women that weren't completely out of their minds."

"Thanks," I laughed. "The way shit comes flying at me, it's impossible. Nobody can take a life like that, and I wouldn't wish it on them."

"Come on. You're exaggerating. It can't be that bad."

I looked him square in the eyes. "My best friend is a fucking ghoul. It's that bad."

Blout stared at me for a full minute before he spoke. His voice lowered. It was serious time. "It really boggles me that you buy into all this crap."

"When a brick lands on your head, you start believing in

bricks or you get your skull bashed in." I paused, feeling a speech coming on. "Don't you see, Blout, nothing is true if you don't believe, but if you do believe, really believe, you can create the impossible. The power of belief—Braaappp!—is a potent force."

Blout opened his second can and tossed me one, but I was already on my third. "Then explain this. How come you're the only one who ever sees all this spooky bullshit? Can you tell me that? I never see any of it."

"It's right there in front of you. You just don't accept it. I see it because I believe. Ain't it the shit?" I stopped and gave a smirk. "But mostly because you're not looking. You've seen it. I've seen you see it."

"Bullshit."

I looked around at nothing in particular. "Maybe, maybe not. Ignorance is bliss, right?"

I stood. This conversation could only turn ugly. It was time to get back to work. I looked around the room. My eyes were more or less adjusted to the cool light of the moon. I could make out the corners and some muddied colors.

Blout stood as well. "So what aren't I looking for now? I know you're after something here."

"I'm trying to figure out where it began. Where was Cain when people started to die?"

Blout perked up. I'd finally given him something to work with. "In the report it said that the deaths started early, before noon."

I snapped my fingers. "The bed."

It was in the farthest corner from the front door, away from the window. The bed itself was crushed.

"It started in the morning. Cain started absorbing early and grew until the bed couldn't support the weight."

Blout had moved to the foot of the crushed bed, where he stood pushing debris away with his feet. "What do you make of this?"

I stepped to the end of the bed where Blout was looking down at the floor. There was a pentagram carved into the floorboards. I flashed my light on it as Blout kicked away more of the plaster and dust. Carved around it, smaller but no less prominent, were several other symbols: a Star of David, a pyramid, a cross, and several that were so badly carved I couldn't venture a guess.

"Well?" Blout said. "How does this fit into your conductor theory?"

I shrugged. "It doesn't, but it doesn't discount it either," I replied, lamely trying to cover my ass. "It just means Cain wasn't getting his security deposit back"

Blout didn't laugh. "I'm outta here," he said and headed for the exit hole.

"Blout, wait. Just one more thing."

I got his attention. He stopped and turned. "One more?"

"One more, then we get breakfast."

"What is it?"

"I want to check out the basement."

"See ya."

I chased Blout halfway down the stairwell. He finally stopped on the ninth floor, not because I was pleading with him to stay and help, but because we were both horribly out of breath.

"You ask too much, Cal."

"I know, but you want to solve this thing, right? You've got a morgue full of people who died under very strange circumstances. It stands to reason that the solution is going to be as strange as the crime."

Blout laughed. "You're the only person I've ever met that talks in circles and comes out makin' sense."

"Basement, then breakfast?"

"Deal."

We started back down the stairs to check out the basement, but somebody had other plans. All at once, above and below us, the sounds of doors opening and slamming filled the stairwell.

Slam!

"What the hell is that?!" Blout yelled. The sound was deafening.

Slam! Slam!

We both had our guns drawn, cocked, and waving at darkness.

Slam! Slam! Slam!

"Screw the basement!" I screamed. "Let's break for the first floor and get out of here!"

We got nowhere. I heard a rasping sound, and a stink passed beneath my nostrils, making me gag. Then a board hit me flat on the back of the head and I went down hard, feeling my neck doused with hot blood. The hall was filled with attacking bodies. Blout was yelling and firing off rounds, but I couldn't do anything to help him. I was being beaten on every inch of my body.

There were so many attackers I couldn't breathe. When I gasped for air, all I got was a lung full of dusty, death-like stink.

I fell, gagging and trying to go limp, but there were a dozen fists and two dozen kicking legs waiting to meet me. It was too dark in the stairwell to see our attackers, and I was being hit too much to focus. The last thing I remember was hearing Blout screaming my name. As I began to lose consciousness, I reached out for support, but instead my right hand fell upon what could only be a face. I scratched where the eyes should have been but my fingers found nothing but dry empty sockets.

Then, mercifully, everything went black.

8

I was out cold, drifting in a state that would have been pleasant had it not been forcibly induced by a beating. I had a vague awareness of being dragged, surrounded by loud static noises, heat, flame, and smoke. Voices barked and grunted, and as time passed I felt the presence of fresh air. Then more screaming and a sound that could have been the pounding of feet on concrete.

It all ended with a jolting blast of pain erupting in the back of my skull. I woke to the sights and sounds of the chaos I had been distantly experiencing while unconscious. It wasn't what I expected.

I saw daylight, early morning daylight. I was on my back, lying in the parking lot of Whitney Green surrounded by emergency medical personnel. They were looking down at me, poking and prodding my body, and talking like I was an idiot. I tried to sit up, coughing, pushing them away. Every millimeter of my person hurt. I felt broken ribs, a multitude of bruises, and a gaping gash on the back of my head.

"Get off me!" I yelled at the medics, and stood with great effort. It was then that I saw what had happened.

Cain's apartment building was an inferno. From the ground floor to the roof, fire tore away the structure. Flames shot from every window. Smoke billowed thick into the clouds overhead. Trying to stop the blaze would be useless. The best bet was to contain it, and judging from the lackadaisical efforts of the firefighters, I guessed that was the plan.

Let it burn, let the haunted halls crumble. I'm sure that was what everyone was thinking. Erase the horror once and for all. I could see it in the eyes of the onlookers—they were watching a monster die.

I shook my attention away from the fire. I had to find Blout so I headed toward the nearest squad car where I found some medics working on a nasty swelling beneath his left eye. When he saw me, his eyes went wide. I had a pretty good idea what a bloody mess I was.

"Jesus H. Christ, Cal! Are you okay? My God, they really worked you over!"

"It's a karma thing, no doubt." I touched the back of my head. My hand came back soaked with sticky red. "Can I get a goddamn bandage here?!"

I finally allowed a pesky medic to bandage me up. They wrapped my ribs and put in a couple of butterfly stitches, including a few in the bullet graze that I'd stitched earlier. They doused each wound with antibiotics, which hurt worse than the damn beating, then finally backed off.

Meanwhile, Blout gave a very abbreviated report to his captain.

". . . there was every reason to believe we had a connection between the bodies discovered early yesterday and the events that took place here ten years ago. We decided to check it out, but instead came across a bunch of crackheads. They attacked us, and I guess that's who set the fire."

Luckily, the captain was too concerned with the arriving TV crews to notice the huge holes in the story. He wasn't even looking at Blout during the last half of the spiel.

"Um, okay . . . I want it on my desk by this afternoon," the Captain said, and was gone.

Blout rolled his eyes in my direction.

I winked, blew him a kiss, and re-split my lip doing it. "Fuck!"

All I wanted to do was get back home. I needed to shower. I needed to sleep. But before that, I needed many drinks and smokes. Unfortunately, Blout wasn't finished. I tried to walk away from the rapidly burgeoning media circus when he came stomping up behind me.

"What the hell happened in there, Cal? How'd we get out? Did you do it?"

I kept on walking. "Last thing I remember was being in the stairwell getting the shit kicked outta me."

"Cal, stop. We'll take my car."

I fell behind him as we walked. He was asking too many questions too soon. My head was spinning and I guess his was as well. After all, he wasn't used to this kind of thing.

I caught up to him at the car. It was one of those bland blue jobs that looked like a giant Matchbox car. "Is this thing for undercover?"

"Why?"

"Wouldn't fool a blind man. Why don't you just write 'COP' on the doors."

Blout wasn't amused. "I'll inform my superiors."

I got in. Blout stared ahead with a sleepy blank stare and then turned to me. "Any idea what we just got out of?"

"I'd bet that our attackers were also our saviors."

"What?! That makes no sense. What possible purpose would that serve?!"

"A warning, maybe," I said as the car jerked and rumbled to life, "possibly a diversion. All I know is those things could have offed us easily, and didn't. Hell, they could've just left us inside.

But they did destroy the building. We were close to something, that's for sure."

We pulled out of the lot, waved on by a uniform guarding the exit, and drove for a while without saying a word. I sat there feeling every cut and bruise throb, and thought of morphine. I missed it, but I wouldn't fall into that trap again. I'd have to settle for some Percocet or something equally tame. Fuck.

9

After a large and much needed diner breakfast, Blout dumped me off at my place just short of noon. I felt bad for him—while I was planning to lapse into a painkiller-induced coma, he had to go back to the precinct and do paperwork.

Blout caught me looking at him as I pushed open the door. "I'll call you if anything happens," he said. "Get some sleep."

I slammed the door, then leaned down to the open window. "Let me know how the ballistics and crap turned out on that Uzi."

"Will do."

He pulled away with a screech and was gone.

As I turned toward my building, I noticed the door hadn't been fixed, just boarded up. It was a sloppy, erratic job with dozens of holes and jagged slits and it sure as hell wouldn't keep anybody out. Pull one nail and the whole job would fall apart.

Even worse, there was a little man in a suit waiting right beside the boarded door. He had a stained manila envelope tucked under his stubby arm. No doubt about it, he was here to serve me papers.

I thought briefly about running, but he'd seen me, and really, what would be the point? Sooner or later those little rat bastards manage to slip you the notice. So I just walked right up to him, stood a little too close, and stared down at him.

"A . . . are you Mr. Calvin McDonald?" The little weasel shook and broke a sweat.

I leaned in. "Yes."

As cowardly as the creep looked, he was quick. Without saying a word he crammed the envelope into my hands, scurried sideways, and was walking away toward a hot little sports car when I heard him say without a shake in his voice, "You have been served."

I didn't open the envelope. I rolled it and shoved it into my back pocket, pulled the door open, and went in. Everything hurt, as three flights of stairs painfully tugged, pulled, and stretched each gash and bruise. And I don't mind telling you, I bitched and moaned every step of the way.

I stopped cold on the last step. My place was the first door on the left and I could see the door from where I stood. It was open. Just a crack, but open just the same. I took out my piece, planted my back against the wall, and began edging along the flaking plaster until I was right beside the door. I held my breath so I could hear over my raspy, pained breathing. There was movement inside, drawers opening and closing, paper rustling. It didn't sound like a shakedown. They don't close drawers.

"Mo'Lock? Is that you?" I said low, almost a whisper. Ghouls have excellent hearing.

There was a second of complete silence. I lowered the gun at the crack in the door. Another second passed.

"Yes, it's me, Cal." The voice was Mo'Lock's unmistakable low rumble.

I jammed the gun back in my armpit and stepped through the door. The ghoul was at my desk, bent over, looking for something. He straightened and I saw that he was filthy, almost completely covered with grime and soot.

"Are you looking for a moist towelette?"

Mo'Lock bobbed his head. I'd confused him. Any sort of modern reference tends to throw off a guy who's been dead for over a hundred years. "Well," he said "something of that sort. I didn't want to muss up your cloth towels."

"Ah, go ahead. Just leave one for me."

That was all the ghoul needed to hear. He turned and trucked out of the room while I gingerly began removing my jacket and tie. Lastly, I kicked off my shoes and untucked my shirt and threw the envelope on the floor. I retrieved the bottle from the desk and several quick swigs later began to feel fuzzy and light. To add to the haze, I threw down a couple of painkillers. By the time the ghoul came back all clean and sparkly, I wasn't feeling a goddamn thing.

"So what happened? Did you find anything?"

Mo'Lock stepped up to the front of the desk and bent forward. "I assembled a couple of my friends as you asked—"

I interrupted him. "Please, for God's sake, sit down. You make me crazy."

The ghoul did as I asked, which brought him to just above eye level.

"My friends and I went to the drainage pipe where the first body was found. But first, I searched the area where the dumpster was located. We found an entrance to the sewer, but didn't go in. It was too small and smelled terrible. Instead, we doubled back to the larger drainage pipe and entered." He nodded at the end of the speech, as though some point had been made.

I shook my head. "And that's how you got dirty?"

"Let me finish."

"Sorry."

"After walking through the pipe for an hour, we came to an intersection. I believe it was somewhere below Dupont Circle."

The ghoul spoke slowly and carefully, rolling out each word for maximum effect. Sometimes his speech patterns reminded me of a drunk trying to sound sober, but with an air of elegance that belonged only to the undead.

"Dupont? That's like five miles from the drainage pipe!"

"Yes, I'm aware of that. Anyway, that was where we found the hole."

I sat forward. "Hole?"

"Yes, and it was not city work, I can tell you. The pipe had been cut with a blow-torch and was very uneven, like the cutter started out trying for a circle, but settled for a square."

"Where'd it go?"

"For the first several yards it went east, maybe north-east."

I nodded. "Toward Whitney Green." I took another drink. My gums were numb and my scalp felt like it was swarming with ants.

"Possibly, but after those several feet the tunnel turned into an incline, and after that there was an unexpected drop . . . straight down."

I was getting a little impatient. At times he could be too efficient. "Did you go down?"

Mo'Lock looked away. "We had no choice . . . we slid."

I laughed. "And you got dumped into the pit!" I was feeling good.

I offered the bottle to the ghoul as a peace offering. He waved it off. "No, thank you."

"Come on, it won't kill you," I urged.

He looked back toward me. "No, it won't kill me. It tastes bad."

The drink and drugs were making my thoughts wander. "When was the last time you ate or drank anything?"

He thought about it for a second. "Just a little over a hundred and ten years. Not counting the occasional mouthful of rainwater."

"Or a chunk of that guy's neck! Remember that?!" I was having fun. It was the best I felt all week. You gotta love painkillers.

Mo'Lock stuck out his tongue. "How could I forget? That tasted very bad."

We fell silent for a moment as Mo'Lock worked the memory of biting that guy through his mind. I lit a smoke. "So, you and your buddies fell in the pit . . ."

Mo'Lock looked up slowly. "It was a short fall into another tunnel. We found that it went in two directions, so we split up. I went east by myself. The other two went west."

"What was the tunnel like?"

"Big, wide. I'd say twice the size of the drainage pipe," he answered, then continued. "I walked for a while. Didn't see much of anything. The tunnel was clean and quiet, like a spotless mining shaft. Very odd."

I laid my head on the desk.

"Then I started coming across exits. They were above me, and near as I could see they were normal manhole covers with these strange clamp locks welded to them. You know, like on preserve jars. There was one about every five hundred yards."

Tunnels and exits heading toward and away from Whitney Green. A web. Something solid was beginning to form, connections were being made. I just wasn't exactly sure where it all led.

Mo'Lock went on. "After another hour I began hearing noises ahead of me. I walked faster until I was running. The noises got louder as I got closer. At first it was just a banging sound, then voices."

I raised an eyebrow, but stayed head-down on the desk blotter.

"As I got closer to the voices and the banging, the tunnel was no longer smooth. It was rough dirt with rocks, rats, and trash everywhere. It was when I stopped running that I heard your voice."

That got my attention. I raised my head. "My voice. You heard my voice? Are you sure?"

"Yes, and Blout's as well. You were arguing. It was high above me and there was an echo."

I nodded for the ghoul to continue his story.

"I moved cautiously toward the sound of your voices when suddenly it changed to yelling and screaming. I thought you and Blout might be under attack so I ran, but unfortunately I was blocked by a large steel door. I pulled and kicked at it, but it was too strong. So I did all I could. I listened."

"Meanwhile, I was getting my ass kicked."

Mo'Lock ignored me. "A short time later a thunderous stampede came from the other side of the door. There was a great grinding noise, and then the door unlatched and flew open. I was face-to-face with your assailants. At first they didn't see me, but when they did, they started screaming and crying, cowering against the wall. They were terrified of me."

"What were they? Did you get a good look?"

"Undead of some sort. Nothing I'd ever seen before. They were mummified, dried skin tight against their skulls, with empty eye sockets."

I nodded. "That's them."

"I approached one that was near me. It screamed and carried on. I didn't mean to, but in trying to calm the thing, I accidentally grabbed a necklace that was around its neck, and it came off." Mo'Lock stopped talking and looked down at his feet. "It was terrible."

I didn't say a word. He'd go on when he was ready.

"The thing just turned into dust at first, but then it liquefied and became blood. Just like that, there was a pile of clothes soaked in blood." The ghoul shook his head. I guess it was a little too close to home for him.

"What happened next?" I urged.

"Chaos. The other things started running away, back the way I'd come. I was about to give chase when I remembered you were somewhere on the other side of the door. As I started through, I was overcome by black smoke and intense heat. I tried to push on, but it was too much. I ran to one of the sewer covers. It was melted shut, so I had to break the concrete to escape. I could see the building on fire, but when I saw you and Mr. Blout were all right, I came back here."

"Did you say you broke the concrete?"

"Yes."

"With what?"

"My hands."

"You can break concrete with your hands?"

"If need be."

I smiled, recalling when I first met Mo'Lock. He was just your standard ghoul doing what ghouls do best: lurking in the shadows, wandering the earth soulless and aimless. He'd helped me out on a case because he thought I was a monster as well. He said it was a vibration I gave off. Sort of the supernatural equivalent of a butt sniff.

When I met him, he barely spoke. Now he could recount events as well as any detective I'd ever known. Better, really, with his heightened senses and all.

"What about your two partners and the necklace you nabbed?"

"I haven't seen them since. I'm a bit worried." He fumbled in his pocket and then held up an object. "This is what I pulled from the neck of your undead attacker."

He held up a simple homemade necklace. I took it from him. It was a plain strip of brown leather with a pendant attached, a small glass vial. Inside was what I took to be blood. That seemed to go along with the ghoul's description of what had happened.

"Amulet?" the ghoul asked.

I shook my head. "More like a talisman. Amulets protect, ward off evil and things like that. Talismans make things happen."

I held it up to the light, turning it in my palm. No inscriptions or marks of any kind. Nothing that told me what it was, or where it originated. I had two facts: the object was a talisman, and the wearer had been a reanimated, mummified corpse. Its origins could range from Haitian voodoo priests to Egypt or South America. Every culture had some sort of reanimation ritual, but which one fit the tiny vial?

It was just another mysterious piece to the puzzle. I still had no clue what the big picture was.

I held the vial up to the bulb of my desk light again. I wasn't sure, but there seemed to be something else inside, floating in the blood. Probably a clot or a maggot.

I stared at the vial and shook my head. When I looked up to say something, Mo'Lock was gone. He was pinned against the wall, staring out the window—trying not to be seen from the outside.

"What is it?"

The ghoul turned to me. "Are you aware that someone is watching the apartment?"

"Dark-colored sports car?"

"Yes. How did you know?"

"Lucky guess." I swallowed a huge mouthful of whiskey.

10

I told the ghoul to shut the blinds. I'd had enough for the week. Some downtime was needed or I was going to fall apart. The vial was stashed in a compartment inside the top drawer of my desk. It would be safe there until I wanted to deal with it. I took another Percocet, stood from the desk, and zigzagged over to the couch. It was buried in trash. I cleared it off with a swipe of my aching arm, while Mo'Lock watched me curiously.

After I had the couch cleared, I opened the closet near the unused kitchen. I dug around in there until I found a small black-and-white television which I put on a chair in front of the couch.

Lastly, I went to the fridge and snagged a six-pack, grabbed the ashtray, whiskey, and smokes. Then I did something I hadn't done for years. I just sat my ass on the couch, turned on the idiot box, and stared like a goon.

"Ahhhhhhh," I moaned in relief. Each and every wound on my body purred and tingled. The painkiller was working its magic.

I immediately began to nod off. Mo'Lock shuffled his feet, bored. I suggested that he check out whoever was watching the apartment, and he was out the door.

Then the phone rang. I started to answer it, but decided to let the machine get it. After the tone I heard Blout's voice.

"Cal, are you there? Pick up."

I shook my head and yawned.

"Well, listen. The test on the Uzi came back. Whoever shot at you had no fingerprints. They were burned off. The rest of the test came back empty. They couldn't trace the weapon."

I started into the bedroom, but Blout went on.

"Another body matching the others was found. This time it wasn't some homeless guy. It was a history professor from George Washington University."

I ran over and picked up the phone. "I'm here! What kind of professor was he?"

"Like I said, history . . . uh, it says here something about folklore and myth. Sounds like he might be a friend of yours."

"Where was his body found? Sewers again? Because—"

"No, get this. The guy had been in a bad car accident about six months ago and lapsed into a coma—"

Lucky stiff, I thought.

"—and he stayed that way until this morning when he was found dead. When they cut him open, no gray matter, nothing."

I stretched and felt some of the butterflies tighten. I was close to passing out. "Look, Blout, we found dick in that apartment. Can you find out what happened to Cain's personal belongings? I noticed on the evidence list there were some books I'd like to take a look at." I yawned right into the receiver.

"Have you slept yet?"

"Nope."

"Neither have I. What say we check in with each other tomorrow?"

"Sounds good."

I dropped the phone into the cradle, turned, reeled into the closet I call my bedroom, and was out cold before I hit the mattress.

11

I woke up on the floor the next morning. I was groggy, but felt pretty good. It was Sunday, just before eleven AM—an eighteen-hour sleep. Eighteen hours of drug-induced, body-healing bliss. But soon enough my thoughts turned to the case. Something had been eating at me that I needed to check out.

Mo'Lock was waiting for me in the office. I had locked the apartment door and the front door and he had no key, but he still managed to get in somehow. I never asked how and he never offered the information. In the past, I would have been startled, but I was beginning to get used to it. It was just another ghoul thing, another of the seemingly endless talents acquired by those caught between life and death.

"Morning Mo'," I said, doing a beeline to the desk. I called Blout at the precinct. After a couple of holds and transfers, I got him on the line.

"Something's been bugging me," I said.

Blout didn't say anything, waiting for me to get on with it.

"Medical autopsies aren't usually performed on John Does and homeless, are they? Why were they performed on the ones we got?"

Blout wasn't impressed. "Well, the first one looked like he was thrown in the ditch. Possible homicide. The dumpster full I think you can figure out."

"But my point is, usually medical autopsies aren't performed on homeless found dead, are they?"

"Not if it looks clean," Blout said. "Dental records are checked for identification and then cause of death is determined. Most of the time there's no reason to open the chest, let alone the head."

"What about senior citizens who die of natural causes in retirement homes and hospitals?"

"Same. What are you getting at?" Blout sounded a little upset, possibly because he thought I was ahead of the game and holding out.

"What about people who die of a chronic illness—AIDS, cancer, and the like?"

"There's no reason to do an autopsy. The cause of death is presumed known by the circumstances of the illness." Blout paused. "Look, are you going to tell me what this is about, or am I going to have to hang up?!"

"It's just that I think we should consider the fact that deaths like these could have been going on for awhile, months or even years. We just lucked out because whoever or whatever is behind this got sloppy." I was pleased with my coherent argument. "Is there any way we can get confirmation?"

Blout sighed hard. "I think you've got something there, but it would be next to impossible to find out. Usually John Does are cremated by independent funeral contractors. The rest could be anywhere. Besides, I can guarantee there's no way I'd get clearance to exhume any bodies."

I thought about that for a second. "I think it's enough that we consider the chance that this might have been going on for awhile. Maybe a very long while."

"I agree," Blout responded reluctantly. Maybe he was doing the math, like I had. The possible body count was daunting.

Blout went on. "Cain's personal belongings are stored in a warehouse next to the sixth precinct. I told them to expect you, so bring some ID and leave your freaky friend home."

"Thanks. Anything else?"

"No."

We hung up without good-byes.

The ghoul was standing by the window as usual. He was pulling up the shade I had asked him to close yesterday. Without looking my way, he spoke. "I tried to check out the subjects watching you, but when they saw me coming, they drove away."

"Did you get any kind of look at them?"

"There were three of them. They appeared to be fairly young, late teens, maybe early twenties. Two male, one female. What I found odd was that they all were wearing wrist bands and scarfs of some sort around their necks."

"Ascots?" I laughed. "No accounting for taste."

Mo'Lock's brow wrinkled as he squinted out the window. "Well, I'll be."

"What?"

"They're outside the apartment again," the ghoul said and looked my way. "One of them has a rifle."

"What the fuck are they doing?!" I started toward the ghoul and the window. Enough was enough.

Mo'Lock went on, "He's pointing it up here and—"

Blamm! Blamm! Blamm!

The window shattered and the ghoul's upper back exploded in three places. He flopped in the air like a marionette cut loose, then collapsed hard to the floor. I threw myself against the wall. Mo'Lock was spread-eagle on the floor. No blood seeped from the three big holes in his shirt.

"You okay?" I reached out with my leg and gave him a little nudge with my foot.

"I'm fine," the ghoul said from the floor. "Don't kick me."

Nobody shoots my friends, even if shooting them doesn't hurt. I was pissed. I dove past the shattered window and grabbed my pistol off the desk. I was out the door before Mo'Lock could get to his feet. Taking the stairs by twos, I was outside in time to see the three fashion casualties getting into their Mustang. I wasted no time in raising the gun, and quickly squeezed off a few shots.

"Freeze, you sons-a-bitches!!"

My first shot shattered the back window of the car. The second and third went stray. The last three were anybody's guess. A .38 caliber crap-shoot.

The Mustang's rear tires spun. The smell of burned rubber wafted across my face as I ran up to the curb, but the car was already gone, speeding away down the street and very nearly hitting a commuter bus. That would have been perfect, but they steered clear. For the second time, they had gotten away with shooting at me. But this time there was a silver lining. There was blood on the sidewalk. At least I'd hit one of the bastards.

It was then that I realized I was standing in the street holding a smoking gun—wearing only my boxers.

12

The sixth precinct police evidence warehouse was little more than a bunker sitting in a corner of the parking lot. It was a flat, one-story building made of cinder blocks and those god-awful green glass cubes. The chain-link fence surrounding the warehouse had rusted barbed wire running along the top, but it and the fence were in such bad shape they would probably crumble at the slightest touch, and besides, the gate was open. The steel door of the warehouse was protected by a large but far from unbreakable padlock—nothing that couldn't be snapped with a decent crowbar.

Point being, it would've been easier to bust into the joint than go through all the usual procedural bullshit, but I did it anyway. I knew they had my name and didn't want to get Blout in trouble.

A uniformed flunky unlocked the door, removing the padlock with a lazy yank, then handed me a large ring with one key dangling pathetically from it like a tiny hanged man.

"Lock up when you're finished. The boxes are alphabetical by last name of victim or perp. If you want to take anything, clear it at the desk," he drawled and walked off, lazy and slack-jawed.

I watched him walk away. He was more dead than any zombie I'd ever encountered. "Thanks a lot, sparkles," I muttered. I was pretty sure he didn't hear.

The big metal door gave me a little trouble at first. I had to push against it with my bum shoulder, but that wasn't enough. So this was the master security system, I thought. How diabolical. The hinges were rusted, so I resorted to kicking. The first two kicks did nothing but send shooting pains up my leg. The third did the trick. The door swung open, sending a cloud of dust billowing into the air.

I coughed and fanned my arms through the soot. The warehouse was dark and smelled of grime, mothballs, and that smoky smell you can only get from old books. I let the door swing shut behind me while I fumbled for a light switch. The low-ceilinged rectangle filled with brownish-yellow light. The place was jam-packed to the roof with rotting cardboard—a total mess.

I doubted anyone had been in here for a long time. I was equally sure the place had been ransacked, with anything even remotely of value stolen. That happened all the time with police evidence. There are cops who use these warehouses as their own personal K-Mart. Luckily, I was looking for books. I was willing to bet that the type of cops who stole police evidence weren't big readers.

The evidence had been stored in alphabetical order as the flunky had said, but only in the most general sense. There were letters of the alphabet painted on the walls, like an underground parking lot. I was amazed at the idiocy of the system. Fortunately, the boxes themselves were labeled, but it was still going to be a major pain in the ass. I took off my jacket, rolled up my sleeves, and set about digging into the area around the letter "C."

It took over an hour for me to locate five small boxes labeled as Cain's property. All of the seals were broken, but it didn't look like much had been stolen. I sat down near the door encircled by the boxes, lit a cigarette, and took out my flask. After a long satisfying gulp, I dug into the clutter.

I found something curious as soon as I saw the first book title. The rest were much the same. It seemed Cain and I had some shared interests. There were editions I owned myself, titles like *Monsters, Myths and Folklore; The Big Book of Spells; Modern Witchcraft; Ceremonies of Haiti*; and *ESP and Telepathy Today*.

Each of the books was littered with papers marking spots in the pages. On several of the papers, Cain had written notes. It was better than I could have imagined, a friggin' Clues 'R' Us. It seemed odd that the original investigators didn't take notice, but I assumed any further probing might have brought out facts the authorities would rather not know. Besides, who was I to point fingers? I dropped the case as soon as we smashed into the pavement.

The first book I looked over was *ESP and Telepathy Today*, an outdated and sensationalist volume published by a company specializing in books on Bigfoot and UFOs. The paperback was packed with black-and-white photos and crude drawings that claimed to prove the existence and validity of telepathy, telekinesis and ESP. There were photos of people floating in the air with no visible supports (obviously airbrushed), a man with horned-rimmed glasses and a goatee straining to lift a person with the power of his mind, that sort of crap.

I actually found myself enjoying flipping through the junky, dog-eared book, just like when I was a kid. True or not, these books had a kind of charm about them that I still found fascinating. Cain seemed to have been especially interested in a section of the book showing a man bending spoons with mind power. The pages were marked and several photos circled, but nothing seemed overly important, so I closed the book and shoved it into my coat pocket.

Next was *The Big Book of Spells*. Most of it was clean except for a chapter on voodoo which Cain had highlighted and underlined almost completely. The text was very simple, obviously intended for young readers with overwritten, dramatic passages and outright silly chants purported to evoke the spirits. Cain had circled several of the spells in red.

Early in *Monsters, Myths, and Folklore*, Cain had marked off a two-page spread discussing the Egyptian god Anubis, the jackal-headed god of death. Anubis was often associated with the creation of the art of embalming and was sometimes called the conductor of the dead.

Most of the underlining seemed to revolve around gods of death, reanimation, and resurrection. When I came across the last marked page, the pieces began to fall into place. The passage described the Norse legend of the Yimir. On the edges of the text, Cain had scrawled the words "the first giant," and had underlined "legend says that the clouds are made from the brains of the Yimir." At the bottom of the page he had written incantations from the voodoo book. Next to some of the spells were page numbers.

I opened the spell book Cain referred to and turned to the indicated pages. The underlined section read "in voodoo, the brain is the seat of animate spirits."

On a Post-it note stuck to the page, Cain linked the passages:

The brain is the seat of the animate, the soul of all spirits.

Clouds are made from the brains of the Yimir.

The Yimir was the first giant.

The mind is the soul.
The heart is life.
Never shall they cross.
Never will we die.

I had no idea what the hell this all meant, beyond the fact that it was pretty clear he'd been obsessed with witchcraft, voodoo, and resurrection. I began to rethink my earlier deductions about spontaneous phenomenon: there may be a source other than Cain, and he may have even created it, but Cain was dead, definitely dead. I had sat covered in his splattered remains. There was nothing left of him that could even be collected. That final fall we took together had reduced him to a pool of splattered, slimy slop.

I found what I came for. Not a lot of answers, but a whole lot of clues, and one or two flimsy concepts. I threw the books back into the boxes, keeping all the scraps of paper for myself. Before I left, I rummaged through the boxes one more time.

Good thing too, because I came across something interesting. It was a pair of brown corduroy bell-bottom pants. The fact that somebody actually wore them was amazing enough, but in the back pocket I found Cain's wallet, complete and untouched. The pocket had been snapped shut with those little pocket snaps that they only use on kids' slacks. Thank God for small miracles and inept police work. I did wonder how the cops could have possibly missed the wallet, but the reason became immediately clear. There was a skid mark the size of New Jersey that started on the inside of the pants and seeped all the way through to the outside. I dropped that foul shit and prayed my hand hadn't gone near the stain.

Inside the wallet there was, briefly, seventeen bucks. I found Cain's driver's license, but the photo didn't ring any bells. The only time I'd seen him, his head was huge, features stretched and distorted. When I felt along the inside seam of the wallet, I felt a small hard object sewn inside. The seam tore easily and a tiny manila envelope fell out. It hit the cement floor with a muffled clink.

The envelope had the Riggs National Bank logo stamped on it. Inside was a key on a tiny cardboard tag, "G454" written on it. I couldn't help but grin.

13

It was Sunday, so going to the bank was out of the question. Instead, I had another plan. I called my apartment, and after a few rings, Mo'Lock picked up. In the background the TV was blaring so loudly that I could hardly hear the ghoul say hello.

"For Christ sake, Mo'!" I yelled. "Turn down the TV!"

I heard him drop the receiver. Fuckin' ghoul.

The noise cut off abruptly and a second later he was back on the line. "Yes, Cal. What is it?"

"How're you doing?" I asked, "Gun wounds all right?"

"All healed up, but I need a new shirt."

I grinned. "I got a plan. It looks like we've got a little down time on the brainless case, so I thought we could go after the gun-happy punks who shot you."

"They're outside again. A little farther down the block, but I can see them."

"Persistent little bastards, aren't they?"

"And not too bright, I'd say. Tell me the plan." He sounded more like a cop than I ever did.

"Simple, get a couple of your friends together. Not a crowd, just one or two—"

The ghoul cut me off. "Since the disappearance of the last two volunteers in the tunnel, I don't think anybody will be up for another mission."

"They're goddamn dead already! What the hell have they got to be scared of?!" I was pissed, and a little embarrassed. I couldn't even get dead guys to help me.

"That's just it, Cal. They have nothing to be afraid of, but they are afraid. We still have gotten no word from the last two and nobody wants to go down there to find out why."

"Pussies. When I get the chance, I'll do it myself. Right now, let's just stop these punks before they get lucky and put a slug in my brain. Are you with me?"

Mo'Lock sounded insulted. "Of course."

"I need you to distract them. Walk by the windows, rustle the shades. I don't care what you do, just keep 'em looking at the apartment. When you see some action, come down and give me a hand."

"I'm on it."

It took me a few minutes to walk from the Dupont Metro station to the street where I lived. I stopped about three blocks back, careful to check everything in my line of vision. Since it was Sunday, the streets were deserted. If bullets started flying, I didn't have to worry about bystanders.

Everything was clear. When I was a block away, I flattened myself against the wall of the building to my left. If Mo'Lock was right, my ascot-wearing would-be assassins were right in the courtyard, near the entrance.

I took out a can of mace and my favorite blackjack. I wanted them alive, if possible. Well, at least one of them. For questioning. If they were working for someone else, I needed to know who it was. If they were operating on their own, I wanted to find out why. After that, I was just going to beat the living crap out of them for fun.

I peered, one-eyed, around the corner. They were there, all three of them, staring up at the window of my place. I started moving around the corner, edging slowly so as not to catch their attention. I made the mistake of following their gaze and almost laughed out loud.

Mo'Lock was thrashing wildly from window to window. It looked like he was doing a super-charged dance of the veils. I forced myself to look away and focus on the perps.

They wore the same clothes as the day before, with one exception—the female had a bandage around her head. I could see a spot of blood where one of my shots must have grazed her.

I crept up until I was right behind her, but she turned quickly. The look on her face when she saw me was reward enough, but I popped her anyway. One swipe with the blackjack and she hit the ground like a wet tea-bag. Her two buddies spun around and I was in trouble instantly. Caught with no room to move and no time to reach for my piece, I did what seemed to be the only thing that made any sense.

I screamed for the ghoul to back me up.

"Mo'Lock!"

Yelling stalled the two boys for half a second. I was about to mace them to hold them at bay while I awaited Tall-Dead-and-Ugly, but the sight of their faces made me hesitate. They were beyond strange, like plastic or wax, but very, very pretty. Like models straight out of a glossy advertisement, every feature was carved perfection. I began to realize who these oddly beautiful teens might be.

One of the lovelies broke my reverie by pulling a small silver pistol. The look on his face was anything but attractive as he lowered it and fired. I dodged but the bullet hit the exact spot of the first bullet wound, an unbelievable bull's-eye. To describe the pain would be impossible. Suffice to say, I screamed.

The kid never got off a second shot. Mo'Lock had arrived via the window. He was on the armed kid like stink on shit, a flailing angry marionette, hitting the shooter while kicking the other male, the only blond of the three, in the lower back. Blondie hit the ground, and I followed up with a smack from the blackjack, hitting him square in the mouth. His teeth blew apart like china teacups, raining on the street with a hundred gentle tinkles. It was incredible.

Mo'Lock was out of control. He had the kid over his head. I wanted to say something, but it was too late. The ghoul threw pretty boy through the Mustang's windshield and the brief skirmish came to a sudden and resounding halt. All we needed to do was get the three of them up to my place for a little chitchat. I grabbed the girl and Toothless and left Mo'Lock to deal with the one wedged in the windshield.

The trio slept for awhile, giving us time to tie them to chairs after patching them up. Mo'Lock played nurse, applying cold packs and bandages to their bruises. As they began to stir, I removed their ascots and wrist bands. What I saw underneath, just below the neckline of their shirts, cleared up a mystery I had been trying to resolve for years and confirmed the hunch I got when I first saw their faces.

Wrapping all the way around each of their wrists and throats were very faint but visible stitch scars—scars from where the body parts had been grafted together by Dr. Polynice at the request of Francis Lazar, founder of ManChildLove. Tied to chairs in my apartment were the mail-order Voodoo Love Teens, kids that those two creeps had created. I'd broken the case wide open and sent Lazar, Polynice, and all those involved to prison, including anyone who had ordered a love slave, but not a trace of the teens had ever been found.

Until today.

I stared at their chiseled features. If you looked very closely you could see faint signs of plastic surgery. It was very important to Lazar and the good doctor that the love dolls could never be traced to the original victims. Their entire bodies, including their heads and facial features, were a jumbled mishmash of dissected, murdered young men and women, complete with burned-off fingerprints and brittle teeth.

The teeth were a nice touch—you've gotta admire attention to detail. Fake teeth meant no dental records. They must've used porcelain for that perfect white color. Evidently, being smacked in the mouth with a blackjack wasn't in the plans.

Windshield was the first to come around. He shook his head, blinked, and blew his dark hair away from his eyes which were a deep, unnatural navy blue. They locked on me immediately. The look was pure hatred.

"You got a name?" I asked, indifferent to the boy's glare. I was standing with one foot up on a chair, interrogation style.

"Randy."

I was surprised. The kid gave up his name easily. I suspect that was part of the conditioning they went through before they were sold off. Nobody likes a difficult love doll.

The whole thing made me sick to my stomach, and it wasn't just me. Mo'Lock seemed uneasy around the kids. He muttered under his breath about tormented souls before retiring to his corner and staring out the window. I didn't have that luxury. I got on with it. "You know who I am?"

Randy nodded, with his glaring blue eyes fixed on my face. "Cal McDonald," he said. "You took my father away . . . took away all our parents. Took away Lazar and everybody!"

I shook my head and paced a small circle. This was going to be tough. "What your 'parents' did was wrong, not to mention illegal and highly immoral. Lazar was a bad person who had to be stopped."

"He never hurt anyone! He took care of us when nobody else would, and he found us homes!"

The other two had begun to stir. The female was muttering and her head swayed from side to side.

This was going to be difficult. Very, very difficult. The kids probably had no idea what they were or where they came from. I had to be careful. Mo'Lock turned to me and shrugged his wide bony shoulders, offering me no help. I couldn't determine whether the ghoul couldn't or wouldn't. He seemed edgy about the whole thing, edgy and distant.

I paced a little, then went back to Randy and stood in front of him holding my hand on my chin.

"Can you tell me how old you are, Randy?"

The kid dropped the glare and thought about the question.

"I think . . . yes, I'm sure. I'm five years old." His face lit up with pride.

I shook my head. "Don't you think you're a little big for a five-year-old?"

Randy looked at me, incredulous to my query. "No," he said, "all of my brothers and sisters are five."

By now the other two were conscious and listening. Neither had the rage in their eyes that Randy had. Just the opposite, actually. They seemed scared of me. I counted myself lucky for that. It meant if I could get through to Randy, the others would most likely follow. I scrambled for questions.

"Can you tell me how you were born?"

The boy looked at me like I was the dumbest thing he'd ever laid eyes on. All three smiled, enjoying their little in-joke.

"In the lab," Randy said sarcastically, "Where else?"

Blondie and the girl suppressed laughter.

I nodded. Lazar and Polynice had done a real job on these kids. They had no concept of the real world, just the twisted reality created for them. In desperation, I looked at Mo'Lock again—I was out of ideas. "What do you think, Mo'?"

"They are very scary, Cal. Do you realize between the three of them, they share the fragments of over one hundred tormented souls?"

"Fucking-A. What we can do? How can we make them see what's really happening? They don't even know what they are!" I could hear the desperation in my own voice.

Mo'Lock turned and stared at the three teens who were whispering to each other, seemingly unaffected by the fact they were tied up.

"They're not stupid, Cal. Show them the file, the articles, the whole mess. Let them see for themselves."

He was right.

I told Mo'Lock to untie Randy's arms so he could flip freely through the files, but to make sure his legs were secure. I didn't want the little punk running off on us. Meanwhile, I ransacked the file cabinets for everything I had on the Lazar case.

While I was rooting around, I glanced over and saw Randy staring fascinated at Mo'Lock. Mo'Lock met the kid's eyes and did something that was all too rare for a ghoul, and truly gave me pause. He smiled. Slight, but distinct. His dead lips parted, curving slowly upward. His eyes, usually stone cold, opened wider and brightened.

I was a minority in the room. The others were cousins in a very large and odd clan—the family of the living dead.

When I'd gathered all the Lazar/Polynice files, I dropped them in Randy's lap. He no longer glared at me. In fact all three seemed much less hostile. They were like putty, instantly impressionable, easily swayed. Nonetheless, I wasn't about to untie anybody until after they'd read the files. I had no idea what the reaction would be, but it was reasonable to assume a violent one.

All eyes were on Randy. He began reading the police report, slowly scanning the pages. At first he seemed calm seeing the photos of the men who had created and sold him for a profit. He almost had a look of love in his eyes. But as he began to soak everything in, his features hardened. Word after word, paragraph after paragraph, page after page had a visible effect on him. He began to shake as pages turned. Finally the tremors were so bad he could no longer hold onto a file. I stood by uncomfortably. Mo'Lock rocked from foot to foot behind me. There was nothing we could do but wait for the reaction, the inevitable explosion.

When it came it was fast and loud. Randy's eyes began to well. He looked up at me first, then shot quick glances at Mo'Lock and me, eyes overflowing with tears. It was as if his soul were bleeding out his tear ducts.

"Who am I?" he asked.

For that, I had no answer . . . but Mo'Lock did.

Mo'Lock stepped past me, stopping close to the weeping boy. The other two had started crying as well, but I doubt they knew why. Fuckin' puppets. Mo'Lock got down on one knee and addressed his distant cousin.

"You are many people and many souls. You are bound by the bodies that have been assembled for you. There is no changing this. You must accept what you are . . . as I have."

Randy stuttered and stammered before finally collecting himself enough to speak. "You . . . you're like us?"

The ghoul nodded. "In a sense. I too used to be mortal, but then I died. Though my soul departed, I remained. Now I am undead. What happened to all of you was brought on by the magic of a conjurer, and now you too are undead. Trust me when I tell you . . . being dead is not at all a bad thing to be."

He spoke in such a confident manner, oddly poetic in a scary sort of way. His voice was soothing, gently guiding the zombie youth to the realization that although they were created from evil they did not have to follow its twisted course. That was the great lie to which too many monsters, past and present, had fallen prey.

They were quickly convinced, maybe because they were made that way, maybe because we offered them an alternative future. I wasn't about to question it, though. I'd expected much worse.

I was still uneasy, but Mo'Lock assured me they were okay now, so I reluctantly loosened their bindings. Sure enough, they'd been defanged.

Randy introduced the others. Blondie was Scott, and the girl was Miriam. I shook each of their hands as they apologized for trying to kill me.

"Don't sweat it," I said. This whole situation was fucking surreal. I grabbed the bottle from my desk and took several large mouthfuls until it was empty. I hadn't eaten, so I felt instantly buzzed.

Twenty minutes passed without anyone saying a word. Mo'Lock and I realized the poor kids had spent so long tracking me down that they had no other experience whatsoever. The three of them sat there, free of the ropes, but with no reason to stand and nowhere to go.

"What do we do now?" Randy said.

Maybe it was only a drunken brainstorm, but I had an idea. I weaved out of the room and came back a minute later with the Yellow Pages. I tore a page out and handed it to Randy. He was confused at first, but a smile soon grew across his lips.

"What do you think?" I asked.

He showed Scott and Miriam the page. They all smiled.

Miriam looked at me. "That would be fun. Do you think we can?"

"I think you'd be perfect."

The beautiful voodoo teens were absolutely giddy. Mo'Lock was confused.

"Mo'Lock, how much cash do you have?"

He shrugged. "Couple hundred."

"Can you get these guys set up someplace? One of your ghoul flophouses or something?"

Everybody was happy. Mo'Lock agreed to leave with the trio and find them a place to crash, but after ushering the group out the door he popped his head back inside as I was taking a seat at the desk.

"What was on that page, Cal?" he asked peering around the door.

"Modeling agencies. I figured once they healed, they'd clean up pretty good as models," I said. "Always attractive. Never age."

He mulled it over for a minute, then nodded. "Good going, Cal. Good for you," he said and was gone.

I admit that I felt pretty damn good after that. For once I didn't have to kill something to solve a problem. It's not often in my line of work that there's a happy ending. I celebrated with a Vicodin, a pop of crank, and a big sloppy gyro I had delivered, along with a huge, heart-stopping pile of cheese fries.

14

The good feelings lasted for as long as it took the phone to ring—four blissful days. Then on Thursday Blout called and broke the spell.

"Big trouble!" he yelled. I'd never heard him so agitated.

"Calm the fuck down! What's up?"

"Tourists are dropping like goddamn flies down on the Mall. We've got ten down in Natural History and the 911 switchboards are lighting up! I'm heading down there."

Christ, I thought, it was just like Whitney Green all those years ago. "Here we go again. I guess whatever is behind this is up to steam. Listen, do you have any painkillers or some liquor there with you?"

"Yeah, sure . . . why?!"

"Do me a favor, before you go down there, have a drink or a pill or sniff some glue. I don't care, just do something that clouds your mind. It won't take you if your brain is damaged."

"Please, Cal, shut the fuck up. I called for help."

He wasn't buying it. "Think of the dope as a Kevlar vest for your brain."

Blout paused. For once he didn't argue. "Whatever."

I told him I had an errand to run, that it was important to the case and that I'd be down as soon as I could.

Speed and a pot of black coffee got me to work making some changes on Edgar Cain's driver's license. I altered the expiration date and popped in my photo. Kid stuff really, and when the job was done it looked damn convincing. There'd be no trouble at the bank.

As I was about to leave, Mo'Lock came through the door.

"Good," I said, "I'm glad you're here. We got bad news."

"I know. My brothers and sisters are fleeing the city. There's a major disturbance. Any leads?"

"Leads I got. Answers, not a one." I rubbed my face. "Everything points to Edgar Cain, but—"

"He's dead," Mo' said and then, "He is dead, right?"

I looked up. "That's the one thing I am sure of. There was nothing left of him, not enough to even collect for evidence. The fire department had to wash the gunk off the streets with their hoses . . ."

I stopped. If my head could have turned into a jackass head, it would have. Mo'Lock finished my thought.

"Into the sewers."

I rubbed my eyes. "Why do they always go in the sewers?"

I had what I thought was a decent plan, but first, I had to get to the bank. I had a pretty good hunch what was in that safe deposit box, and we'd need it to survive what was to come. After that, there was no avoiding it. The ghoul and I had to go down into the sewers.

Mo'Lock and I agreed to meet at the drainage pipe a few hours later. After he left, I checked to make sure I was properly armed. Fuck yeah, I must have weighed an extra ten pounds with all my extra baggage. I made sure I had the safe deposit key and the talisman Mo' had found.

As an extra precaution, I slipped a small leather case that I'd kept for years into my sock.

Everything was in place. I was as ready as I'd ever be. But before I could get out the office door, I had company.

Dan Stockton, that huge prick of a cop, was standing there blocking my exit, with two other uniforms behind him.

I motioned to push past. Stockton blocked my way.

"I don't have time for this shit, Stockton. Get out of my way. We can fight later." I made another move, he countered. This time he held up a folded document.

"This ain't personal," Stockton said, waving the papers in my face. "This is straight-up official. I've got a warrant for your arrest."

I stepped back. All three pressed forward. I could see that the two backups were taking out their batons. One had handcuffs ready for me.

"Arrest? What the hell for?!"

Stockton smirked. "You had a court date yesterday with some guy you pummeled on Halloween, and you were a no-show. That, my asshole friend, is against the law."

"Moving a little fast, aren't they?" I said.

Stockton's smirk widened to an outright obnoxious grin. "That's the personal part. I did the paperwork myself."

"Gee, thanks."

The scene froze while everybody waited for something to happen. I made it happen by bolting for the door. I broke the blue-boy wall, catching them off-guard. Stockton made a stupid choking sound as I brushed past, as though he couldn't believe he'd lost control of the situation. Idiot.

I was at the door, almost to the hallway. Once there, I could really haul ass. "I told you I don't have time for this sh—" That was that.

For the second goddamn time in under a month, I was knocked cold.

16

I woke in a small room that reeked of body odor and cigarettes, handcuffed to a loop in the wall. I was kneeling, facing the loop, with my back to the rest of the cramped room. The only way in or out—a heavy, industrial-strength door—was behind me. The brick walls were spotted with traces of blood that had been lazily wiped off and covered by a thin coat of off-white.

Standard interrogation procedure. They wanted you to see the blood so you'd start shitting yourself before they even hit you. I'd been through it before, but had a bad feeling about this. Something felt very wrong.

My wrists were bleeding from the cuffs that supported most of my weight and the back of my head stung from where Stockton had planted his nightstick. It made me think of those kids and how I'd walloped them with my blackjack. I was about to feel bad about it when the door behind me opened. I didn't twist around to see who it was. I already knew.

"Thought you'd never wake up," Stockton said behind me.

"Gotta get my beauty sleep."

I heard him shut the door, then a hard clack as the lock slipped into place. "You're gonna go out smart-assin', huh?"

Go out? What the hell was he talking about? I mean, we didn't like each other, but this was out of left field. Years of unfriendly snipes, the occasional fisticuffs was one thing. This was beyond bitter dislike. This was nuts. I began to feel scared for the first time in a long while.

"You know, Stocky," I said. "This kind of thing is frowned upon these days. I could sue." I was half telling the truth, half fishing. I heard my voice shake.

He grabbed me by the hair and jerked my face around to his. He was red-faced and spitting. "Not if you're dead, funny man!"

"Have you considered an anger management course?"

That was the last thing I remember saying. The next twenty minutes were a blur of kicks and punches. Stockton was good at it. He knew all the places to hit and just how hard to strike for maximum pain. I just went limp and tried not to make a sound. I figured even a raging psycho like him would get sick of beating on a wet sack of mud after a while.

But he just went on and on until my face was puffed like a bloody bundt-cake and my body was tender to the touch. What amazed me even as I was being beaten was his skill at keeping me conscious. He wanted me awake, and awake I stayed. Finally he tired of hitting me and pulled a blade from his back pocket.

I spat a wad of thick blood. "Come on, Stockton. You made your point."

He ignored me. "You ever hear of hamstringing? It's supposed to hurt a lot."

I shivered. Nobody walks after having the backs of their knees sliced. If he truly meant to hamstring me, I was through.

Luckily, I have a merciful angel that watches over me. That angel happens to be a big cop named Jefferson Blout.

My eyes were nearly swollen shut, but I heard him come crashing into that room like a diesel. I had the pleasure of hearing

Stockton give a little baby yelp right before Blout shattered his jaw with a roundhouse punch that would have made a Viking weep. It was beautiful.

When it was all said and done, I was banged up pretty good, but I could still walk. Blout talked me into going to the hospital where I got a couple dozen stitches and a jumbo Band-Aid or two. I made sure to whine until the doctor ordered some painkillers, so in the end I came out okay. Shit, I'd gone through a lot worse to get drugs before.

Blout was waiting for me outside.

"So how the hell did you know Stockton had me dragged in?" I asked. His appearance had been nothing short of miraculous.

"A rookie tipped me off. He wasn't too keen on losing his badge so Stockton could waste some lousy gumshoe."

"Thanks."

"His words, not mine." But he enjoyed telling me. I could see it in his face.

"So what's the word on the deaths at the Mall?"

"Not as bad as I thought. Eight, maybe nine."

"Skulls?"

"Clean."

I nodded. "It's revving up for the big strike."

Blout rammed one of his cigars into his mouth and lit it. "What are you talking about now?"

"What we're dealing with here played it safe for a few years. It plucked the brains out of people who never went through full autopsies, like chronic cases and the elderly. Then it moved on to the homeless."

I paused and lit a cigarette of my own.

"Now it's getting up some speed and hitting tourists, and soon it's going to bust loose and then . . . the whole city's fair game."

I thought Blout was going to bust my chops, but instead he shook his head. "Christ. What are we dealing with here? Do you have any ideas at all?"

"It's Cain," I said.

"The dead man?"

"The dead man."

"You want to tell me how?"

"Would it matter?"

Blout thought about getting pissed, but he didn't have the strength. He just nodded a sad little nod and bit his lip.

As we got to Blout's ugly car, he gave me back all the stuff the cops had confiscated—gun, blackjack, fake ID, and safe deposit key. Asshole held back two items, though, wanting answers before he'd hand them over. I was in no shape to fight, so I played his little game.

He opened one of his big hands, revealing the leather case I'd stashed in my sock. It was my old friends: syringe, spoon, and smack. I couldn't believe Blout had retrieved it for me. In the other hand he clutched the talisman Mo'Lock had ripped off the tunnel zombie.

"Where do I start?"

"How about the works?" Blout said. "Don't tell me you're doing shit again."

I shook my head and spoke, praying my voice didn't slur from the painkillers. "Remember what I told you? That last time I dealt with Cain? It didn't absorb my brain because it disliked the pollution. I just have it on me as a precaution. I swear." My hand was raised like a boy scout, and I tried to force a brown-nose smile across my beaten, puffy face.

He seemed satisfied enough and tossed me the case. "Thought you'd say that. Only as a last resort, you got it?" he said. Then he held up the talisman. "And this?"

"Mo'Lock found it in the tunnels beneath Whitney Green." I looked down at the ground.

"Tunnels beneath Whitney Green? Hmmm, I don't recall you mentioning anything about tunnels," he spoke in mock tones of mystery. Then he screamed, "YOU FUCK!" and rammed his palm right into my wounded shoulder.

I yelled out.

"What else aren't you telling me? Goddammit, Cal! Stop keeping me in the dark! What good am I if I only know half the story?"

I looked up, rubbing my shoulder. "Sorry. I'm not used to letting cops in on this kind of stuff. I think you'll recall what happened the few times I did. I got laughed right off the case."

Blout took a couple of angry puffs off his log of a cigar. "Well that was them, this is me. Cough it up."

He was right. Where would I be if he hadn't informed me of the mysterious deaths when he did? I told him everything I knew, about Mo'Lock and the crusty tunnel zombies who had attacked us, and about the missing ghouls. I filled him in on Cain and what I found in the evidence room. When I was finished he tossed me the talisman.

"What about this, then? How does that fit it?"

I looked at the charm. "Considering the thing wearing it turned into a pool of blood when it was removed, I'd say it's a resurrection talisman. Black magic, voodoo maybe. I can't say for sure."

"Did you notice something floating in the liquid?"

"Yeah, but I couldn't make it out. Probably a piece of bone." I stuffed the charm into my pocket considering the issue closed and moot.

"It's an Egyptian symbol," Blout said plainly.

"Huh? How'd you know?" I was stunned.

"My wife collects all kinds of that ugly crap. The house was full of it. The living room looked like friggin' King Tut's tomb. That shit was gone the moment she left."

I had to laugh. "Any idea what it means?"

"The perp shops at the same place as Jessica?"

"Now who's the smart ass? So what we're left with here is a mix of black magic, monsters and myth, voodoo of several varieties, and now Egyptian symbols. That's the oddest, because the Egyptians weren't into reviving dead. All their ceremonies revolved around surviving the afterlife. Even this talisman's a little bit this, a little bit that—a goddamn potpourri of evil." I scratched my aching head. "Oh yeah, and we have a giant brain-sucking head that should be dead but somehow isn't."

I needed to get moving to clear my head. With all the time wasted getting the crap beat out of me, I'd have to hustle to meet the ghoul at the drainage pipe. I told Blout to drop me off at Riggs while he went on to meet Mo'Lock and tell him to wait until I arrived. Blout wasn't thrilled with the plan.

"No way," he said. "I'm not going near that freak without you. I'll check the box. You take the car to the pipe."

I tried chiding him. "Are you scared?"

He pulled the wheel extra hard on a left turn, slamming my head against the window frame. "I wouldn't call it scared, punching bag. More like creeped out."

"Splitting hairs." I gingerly touched the swell of bruises on the side of my face. "Besides, you might not like what you find in the box." I tried to sound ominous, but I came off more like Bob Barker. My mouth was too swollen.

Blout gave out a quick breathy laugh. "I'll take my chances. And to be on the safe side, I won't look inside until I meet you back at the drainage pipe."

"They are not going to let you walk out of the bank with the whole safe deposit box." I started laughing, knowing full-well what was coming next.

He turned to me. A big toothy grin was spread across his face. "Wanna bet?"

Blout screeched up to the curb in front of the bank. He got out with the car running, keys dangling in the ignition. I scooted across the seat and pulled the door shut. Instead of charging into the bank as I'd hoped, Blout stood there shuffling his feet. It didn't take a brain surgeon to see he was nervous with me behind the wheel of his butt-ugly car.

"Are you okay? For driving, I mean. What did they give you back at the hospital?"

I let my head bob out of control. "I'm phhhhine! Don't worry about a phhhhing!" I fell against the wheel, sounding the horn for a good thirty seconds. Fun, but we were losing time. "Seriously. We've got work to do. I'm fine and I'm late."

I floored it, leaving Blout breathing exhaust. When I glanced back, he was flipping me off, both hands raised above the smoke. I laughed, but the seriousness of the situation began to sink in. I was through joking for the moment.

I glanced down at the dashboard and saw one of those cheap plastic stick-on digital clocks just above the ashtray. If the clock was right, I was over half an hour late. Mo'Lock would wait, that much I could rely on. He had the patience of a dead man.

I drove carefully, taking the back streets past Dupont Circle straight up Connecticut Avenue until I was near Embassy Row. Once I was clear of the major urban areas I pulled over and parked in front of a liquor store. Not only was I shaky, but a headache had begun creeping up on me, moving around like a probing flashlight beam. In the liquor store, I purchased two pints of rotgut—one for me and one for Blout.

In the car I popped a couple of pills from the hospital and washed them down with the booze. It occurred to me it might not be safe to mix the two, but I figured the results would become apparent soon enough.

It took about ten minutes to arrive at the old reservoir off Wisconsin Avenue. From the street it looked like a small lake, but when you got close you could see a cement bottom and surrounding fence. Problem was, it took eight minutes for the mystery of mixing drugs and alcohol to be solved. It wasn't good. I was dizzy, my head was reeling, and I couldn't feel my teeth.

I steered the car around the chain-link fence and cruised along the elevated access road, raising roostertails worthy of a *Dukes of Hazzard* episode. The drainage pipe was far from the main road and more or less hidden from public view. In my drugged haze, I'd let the car drift to where the shoulder dropped away from the road surface. I took a sharp right to bring the car back parallel with the pipe while jamming on the brakes, but it was too little too late.

The big car skidded over the edge sideways, jumped, and began to turn over. It rolled with me trapped inside being flipped and flopped around like socks in the dryer. With a sickening crunch all motion ceased as I arrived at the drainage pipe. The car came to a halt on its roof a few yards short of the pipe's entrance. Totaled, crushed like an accordion. Blout was going to kill me!

I was pinned, but could hear voices outside. It was Mo'Lock for sure and, from the sound of it, he'd found some backup. And there

I was, the big leader, trapped in a borrowed car that I had driven into a ditch. What an entrance.

I was relieved to see that neither of the bottles had gotten smashed in the crash. The talisman, however, hadn't been so lucky. My pants had a dark sticky wet spot seeping through the pocket.

I kicked at one of the back doors while Mo'Lock pulled from the outside. Finally I was able to crawl free into the hazy daylight.

Mo'Lock's big pale face was right there. "Is this Mr. Blout's car?"

"It was."

"He's going to kill you."

I ignored the comment as I dusted myself off, noticing the volunteer army Mo'Lock had assembled; the Frankenteens Scott and Miriam and a large ghoul I'd never met. The unknown ghoul was huge, with wide shoulders, big hands, and a head that looked like a cement block with slits for eyes and a dark flattop.

Mo'Lock did the introductions. "Cal, this is Hank Gundy. He's offered his services. I'm afraid all my brothers and sisters refused."

I shook the behemoth's hand. "You're not a ghoul?"

Gundy shook his head. "Not ghoul," he said. "Hank a creep."

I shot Mo'Lock a quizzical look.

He waved me off. "I'll explain later."

I swear, there are more varieties of monster than there are insects. Even with all my years of dealing with the shit I still don't know them all.

I turned my attention to the teens. "Thanks for coming," I said. "Where's . . . um, Windshield?"

"Randy," they both said.

Miriam smiled. "He got a gig!"

Not really wanting to hear more, I ushered everyone to the tunnel mouth. Mo'Lock had outlined what he knew of the plan—the layout of the tunnels and the static he'd encountered—and I filled them in on the rest. The teens seemed to understand everything, but Gundy kept looking around distracted. It didn't matter. I suspected that if and when there was trouble he'd know what to do.

"I don't know what we're going to find down there. All I do know is that it involves many, many forms of witchcraft and dark arts, so be ready for anything. Most important of all: if anybody's head starts to hurt, drop back."

Mo'Lock edged up close as I finished my instructions. "Do you see them?"

I whispered back out of the corner of my mouth, "Yup, been there for the last ten minutes."

Just inside the tunnel, where light stopped and darkness began, stood a wall of empty-eyed zombies.

"We've got some company." I pointed them out to the rest of our crew.

Scott stepped forward. "Those are the things that attacked you?"

Mo'Lock and I both nodded.

I took out my gun, an unreturned police issue 9mm, and aimed into the crowd at head level. Although I was wasted, my aim was steady as I squeezed off two quick bursts. One of the zombies' heads snapped back violently, and his body quickly fell to the ground like a rag doll. The others went wild, moaning and beating on each other. They wouldn't cross into the light, but wouldn't retreat either. Then the one I shot stood back up with a big chunk of skull missing, only seconds after the gunfire's echo had faded.

I turned to Mo'Lock and Gundy. "This looks like your kinda job."

Mo'Lock led Gundy inside and pointed, making sure the big guy was looking. "See those necklaces they're wearing?"

"Around stinky men's necks?"

"Yes?"

Gundy nodded.

"You and I are going to run in there and grab as many as we can. It kills them. Got that?"

Gundy sharpened at the prospect of violence. "Got it. Hank take necklace. Stinky man die."

"Let's go," said the ghoul.

They charged into the tunnel, leaving me and the Frankenteens behind to watch and pray. It took only seconds for them to hit the zombie wall. From my vantage point, it looked like a riot had erupted: I couldn't even make out the shapes of Mo'Lock and Gundy as the crowd consumed them. Amidst the furor, though, I heard sounds that hinted at some level of success. There was a distinct slopping and sloshing sound of thick liquid being spilled. Those things were going down in gobs of blood.

Problem was, there seemed to be too damn many of them. I got panicky and pulled my gun out again, edging into the tunnel along the wall. I began shooting into the crowd, thinking it served as a distraction if nothing else.

From inside the tunnel, we heard Mo'Lock shout, "We could use some help in here!"

I was glad to oblige, but Miriam and Scott didn't share my eagerness. They were scared stiff. I ran into the tunnel without them, itching for some payback. I planned to blast first, then tear away their talismans before they could recover. I started shooting as I ran, but my heel hit a thick dark puddle and sent me sliding top speed into the thick of the fray. Through it all, I'd never stopped firing.

I clamored to my feet, but they were on me instantly. I remembered their dry, crusty touch from the stairwell. That time they'd blindsided me. This would be different.

I let them kick and punch at me. I didn't care. All I wanted was a handful of leather, a sliver of glass in my palm. When I had it, I yanked. Time after time, I'd hear a satisfying yelp followed by the sound of hot stew hitting the floor, then I'd grab for more. It was like flushing away the enemy, one of the most satisfying fights I ever had.

I hardly noticed when it was over, with the last dozen or so zombies retreating into the inner depths of the tunnels. Suddenly there was pin-drop silence. I looked around. Mo'Lock was nearby with two fistfuls of necklaces, Gundy was behind us. In one hand he had necklaces, but the other held a leg. I looked down and saw we were up to our ankles in liquified zombie blood. It was fucking disgusting.

We left the tunnel to gather ourselves as Mo'Lock giddily enthused about all the souls that now had a chance to be free.

It took a moment before we noticed Gundy wasn't following. When we turned, the big guy hadn't moved an inch, hovering on the razor's edge of shadow and light.

"Gundy? You okay?" I yelled.

I could see his big face even at a distance. His expression was like a baby about to cry. He dropped the leg and placed a big hand to his head.

"Head hurts," he said.

And that was that. Big Hank Gundy dropped dead where he stood. I didn't need to see his cracked-open skull to know the brains were gone, completely empty save for the thick curl of steam that slowly snaked from the empty skull cavity.

"Fuck," I said.

We'd wait for Blout before we made our next move.

18

I was pissed about Gundy's death, if that's what you can call it—I never did find out exactly what a creep was. I hadn't even known the guy for ten minutes and now he was a stiff.

I told the Frankenteens to get the hell home. I wasn't going to risk the kids, not after all they'd been through. Luckily, it took little convincing. They wanted to leave.

Like that, my pathetic army was cut in half. It was just me and Mo'Lock again. No one spoke, so I took the time to smoke and have a few drinks. I fished the leather case out of my sock, unzipped it and stared at the contents.

"What's that?" Mo'Lock asked. He shambled through the dirt and sat next to me.

I zipped the case and tucked it back in my sock. "Backup plan."

Before he could ask any more questions, we heard a car door slam a short distance away. Blout was walking briskly up the dirt road with the safe deposit box tucked under his arm as the cab returned to the city.

He spotted his car laying upside down at the bottom of the ditch and slowed, shoulders slumping noticeably at the sight. I was afraid he'd drop the box but he clutched it tightly. I watched and waited, half expecting an attack.

"Nice parking space, asshole."

I apologized profusely, but Blout wanted none of it. He was focused on the task at hand, saving all his anger for a fresh new ulcer. For whatever reason, he'd been surprising me lately. Maybe he could sense some bad shit coming. I know I felt it.

The box under his arm was large, much bigger than the proverbial bread box. True to his word, Blout hadn't opened it. He placed it down in the dust outside the tunnel, glanced inside at the aftermath of the fight, and sat down on the ground with a grunt.

"Christ, my head is pounding," he said.

My head was hurting too, but I was still under the protection of a painkiller and alcohol cocktail. I handed Blout the pint I'd picked up for him. He took it and drank the thing down like sugar water. That should do the trick, I thought. If it didn't, I'd get him out of there, like it or not. Even if I had to knock him out, I was not going to have a repeat of Gundy. Not with Blout anyway.

Mo'Lock was shifting on his feet with an expression that I'd never seen before—discomfort. I doubted very seriously that the ghoul was constipated. It had to be his head.

I went to his side. "What's up, Mo'? How're you feeling?"

He looked at me. "I'm not sure . . . it's been so long, but I think I have a headache."

I took the other pint out of my coat pocket. I'd drank some, but most of it was still there. I forced the bottle into his big white hands.

"Take it. Drink," I demanded.

The ghoul looked at the bottle and grimaced. He shook his head.

"It can't hurt you," I said. "Better safe than sorry."

The ghoul was a sucker for clichés. He looked at the bottle like a boxer staring down his opponent. I guess I understood. It had been over a century since he had a drink and his first one was about to be some cheap rotgut.

I glanced over at Blout and saw his face was lazy and calm. His eyes were bloodshot and hooded. He had the look of a man with a poisoned brain—our best defense.

"AAAAAHHHHGGGHHHH!!"

Blout and I jumped, simultaneously pulling out our weapons, but it was just Mo'Lock. He'd swigged the entire bottle in one huge gulp and now stood swaying with wide, crazy eyes. I lowered my gun first and with my free hand slowly guided Blout's down to his side. He wasn't so sure there was no reason to shoot.

Blout and I stood by as the ghoul went through a series of shudders and twitches, until gradually the liquor slipped through his ancient veins and his dark-circled eyes reddened.

I waited a few minutes, then took the bottle from him. "How does it feel?" I asked.

"I feel stupid."

"Perfect."

I rubbed my head and looked from one bleary partner to the other. Blout was trying to find the end of a cigar and having a hard time of it. He'd chugged his entire bottle. Mo'Lock was pressing a finger into his forehead and sticking his tongue out in response to each touch. I sighed. Here we were, the city's heroes. We were doomed.

There was no use wasting any more time. I picked up the safe deposit box and headed into the mouth of the drainage pipe. When I turned, no one else had moved. They were just staring at me blankly.

"Well," I said, "Time to move, you buckin' fastards!"

With that they both shook themselves out of their individual hazes and followed me into the tunnel. Not one of us could walk a straight line.

19

We walked deep into the tunnel, sloshing through the remains of the zombie guards, until the entrance was a pea-sized dot of light behind us. I lit a cigarette and waited for our eyes to adjust to the pitch dark. When Blout's outline became clearer I could see he was agitated and nervous.

"When are you going to open that thing?" he asked, pointing at the box.

I shrugged. "We could do it now if you want. I've got a pretty good idea what's inside."

I felt the key slap against the side of my face and I managed to catch it before it hit the dirt. When I leaned down to feel for the keyhole, I was too ripped and had little luck. My hand clanked the key clumsily against the metal, finding everything except its target.

"You want some light?" Blout switched on his penlight as he knelt down beside me.

"Thanks."

I found the lock and gave it a twist. The box opened with one quick flip, releasing a billowing mushroom of putrescence into the air.

Blout reeled away. "Aw, Jesus!"

I covered my mouth and nose, but the odor was so strong it stung my eyes and forced me to back away from the box. After a second or two the mist cleared and the stench was reduced enough to make it bearable. We knelt and stared down at the throbbing contents of Edgar Cain's safe deposit box. At first glance, it reminded me of those old fifties ads for meat: the colors were too bright and the sheen looked greasy and unreal. But it was real, and it was alive.

A beating human heart.

The disembodied heart rose and fell as if it were still part of a person, still attached to arteries pulsing with blood. Surrounding the heart was a garnish of objects that ranged from feathers to bones. Symbols from a variety of regions and religions were scrawled on paper and wood. It was the same pattern as everything else.

I looked up to Blout. He couldn't take his eyes off the beating heart. Then he caught my stare.

"Is this what you expected?" he stammered.

"I had a hunch it would be something of this sort."

Blout looked back at the heart. "If this is Cain's heart, why don't we just destroy it?"

It was a good question, but not a safe option. Sometimes hearts are not only used to keep something alive, but also to imprison something or keep it in check. We couldn't be sure which kind this was.

"Cain may have put this heart here to protect himself from what was happening," I concluded.

"He didn't do a very good job," Blout said.

Mo'Lock raised a finger. "It could also work to our benefit to have the heart alive, if it is the heart of the killer. It would give us leverage. A hostage, if you will."

So it was agreed—the heart would keep beating for now. I locked up the box and we all headed deeper into the tunnel.

We walked on, deeper and deeper, and I cursed myself for not buying more liquor. I had no idea how long the effects of the alcohol would protect us, and finding out might mean dying. I thought about the leather case in my sock, but shoved the thought away. That was the last resort. Anyway, I still had seven painkillers. If the pain got bad enough I'd convince Blout or the ghoul to take one, like it or not.

I laughed darkly to myself, thinking that only I could stumble onto a case where excessive drug and alcohol use was the best way to stay alive. But here I was with a straight-arrow cop and a hundred-year-old ghoul, drunk in the sewers beneath the nation's capital.

Finally, after what seemed like hours, we came to the intersection Mo'Lock had described last week. I saw the crudely cut hole, definitely not the work of a pro. The edges were rough and jagged and we had to be careful stepping through.

Like the hole itself, the tunnel on the other side was rough hewn. The walls were rock-encrusted, the floors and ceiling uneven and craggy. Support beams appeared to be stolen phone poles and billboard posts, giving it the look of a derelict coal mine. It was very small and confined, and the threat of claustrophobia dug at me like a creeping itch.

As we walked along, the floor gradually began to decline, until the angle was so severe walking became difficult. We all leaned backward, trying very hard not to fall on our butts and wind up sliding out of control.

"Can we take a break?"

It was Blout, sweaty and out of breath. I was sweating too, my shirt soaked through. "Sure, but let's make it quick."

I wanted to ditch my coat, but needed the things in its pockets: mace, a lock blade, blackjack, a small backup pistol, and several clips for the 9mm. If I tried to load all that into my pants I'd look like I shit myself.

"How's everybody's head?" I said as I slid down the wall, gripping protruding rocks until I was sitting.

"I'm okay," Blout said.

The ghoul nodded.

I told them I had the Percocet if they needed it, but both waved me off. I felt like a goddamn pusher.

After a minute's rest, Blout signaled he was ready to continue. As soon as I planted my foot for my first step, I fell and immediately began sliding. I held the box with one arm and with the other I grabbed wildly for anything that would stop my skid. Anything turned out to be Blout's pant cuff, and then we were both tumbling out of control down the slope.

The next moment there was nothing beneath us except absolutely black air. As we hurtled downward, all I could do was hold on to the box and brace for impact.

20

The fall was short but painful. I landed with the box under my ribs and heard a loud crunch. Pain shot through my midsection like an electrical charge. I let out a scream that would have shamed Fay Wray. Broken rib for sure, plus I'd aggravated a couple dozen Stockton-inflicted wounds.

The next second I heard Blout hit the ground beside me with a short hard thud. At least his fat ass didn't land on me.

We both stayed on our backs, moaning. Blout was the first to try to get up.

"Are you okay?" he asked as he stood, dusting himself off.

I stared up at the ceiling of the tunnel. "Just leave me here. I'll be fine in a day or two."

Blout thought I was kidding. He grabbed my arm and pulled me until I was sitting up. At that point we realized we were now in a huge tunnel, at least twice the width and height of the city's drainage pipe. Then we saw the box. When I fell on it, I'd crushed one side. The hinges had snapped and spilled the beating heart onto the floor. Blout shined the penlight beam on the throbbing muscle. It was filthy with dirt, but still beating.

"Oops."

I gathered it up, wiping it clean with my shirt. Blout watched me tend to the moist hunk of meat with a look of total disgust.

"Maybe after we're done here, you can name it and keep it as a pet," he said and turned away.

I picked a few granules of dirt from one of the sealed arteries, then tucked it back into the battered box.

Finally Mo'Lock appeared, landing feet first and seeming damn pleased about it. He had been there before, but I distinctly recalled that the first time he explored the tunnel he'd arrived on his ass, so his smugness rolled right off me.

"Which way did your buddies go?" I asked.

The ghoul looked slowly in both directions, then back again, and once more to be sure. "Whitney Green is east . . . that way," he said pointing. "They went west."

"Then west it is." I started to walk, but stopped when I saw Blout holding his head. "What's wrong?"

"It's nothing . . . just NHHHGHGH!"

The big man buckled and fell. Mo'Lock grabbed him by the shoulders, catching him before he hit the dirt. I could see the dark glimmer of blood running from both of the cop's nostrils.

I fumbled in my pockets for a pill. Blout was grimacing and shuddering. He was gritting his teeth so hard I could see the pressure was producing blood. It was seeping through the tiny seams between teeth and gum, filling the nooks and crannies with crimson red. Getting him to swallow a pill was going to be tough. I grabbed his face at the jaw and pinched hard, trying to get his teeth to part. It worked on the third squeeze and I jammed the pill in.

It was too late, though. Blout's eyes shot open. They were huge, blazing red with anger. It wasn't Blout—something had him. His body was suddenly animated beyond human capability. His arms flailed as though his limbs had no joints restricting their movement.

Without looking at him, Blout grabbed Mo'Lock by the throat and swung him off the ground, using the ghoul as a weapon against me. He slammed into me, sending the two of us flying hard against the wall.

Mo'Lock and I sprung to our feet and readied for the next attack, but none came. Blout was hanging there in the air, floating before us from invisible puppet strings. I saw blood droplets making mud beneath his feet. Whatever had him planned on killing him. Blood ran from every orifice; the tear ducts in his eyes, his mouth and nose, even from beneath his fingernails.

I stared, not knowing what to do. Something was inside him, manipulating his every move; pushing, pressing, possibly grinding his insides to a pulp. The heart jumped wildly in the box I cradled.

I whispered. "What has him, Mo'?"

"I don't know. I feel Blout and another presence."

Blout's bleeding eyes slammed shut tightly, then abruptly shot open again. His lips parted, allowing foamy blood and a long, lung-clearing hiss to roll out. Although his limbs continued to flail, they were non-threatening movements, like a cut-out paper doll blowing in the wind.

I pulled out the 9mm and aimed at the floating cop, with no intention of shooting—yet. Possessed or not, I wouldn't let my friend die without exhausting every last option. I had to wait and let the scene play out.

The noise from Blout's throat changed from its monotone hiss. It began to fluctuate and rise until peaking in a shrill shriek that echoed throughout the tunnel. Mo'Lock winced and covered his ears. Suddenly the noise cut off sharply and fell back to its steady, low hiss. Then, it spoke:

"Get away from this place."

It was a thick, sludgy voice, more like the ghoul's than Blout's. It sounded forced from the gut and passed Blout's unwilling, unmoving lips. Only the jaw moved, seeming out of sync with the vocals. The sight reminded me of a strange ventriloquist act.

"Leave here at once and you will be spared!"

I laughed, couldn't help it. As scary as the situation was, the "Great and Powerful Oz" dialogue threw me. Maybe it was the break in the tension, but in that moment I concocted a plan.

The levitating body lurched. "Get out while you still can!"

I flipped the lid off the safe deposit box and scooped out the heart. I let the box drop to the ground, spilling the garnish of charms, stones, and herbs. I held the heart tightly in my folded left arm and with my right pressed the 9mm into it. If this thing wanted cornball, I'd give it cornball.

"Let the cop go, or I'll let the heart have it!"

Nothing.

Mo'Lock was staring at me, eyes wide. "Cal, are you sure this is—" he whispered.

"Shut up," I hissed. "It might work."

I stepped forward and pressed the gun harder into the side of the heart and repeated my threat. This time I added a five-second time limit and began the countdown.

Still nothing. I hesitated.

"Four . . . Three . . . Two . . ."

Finally, just when I thought my bluff had been called, Blout dropped limp to the ground. He began coughing and gagging, trying to catch his breath. His wide back heaved and arched as he fought to regain control of his body. He was free, but I knew what we'd seen might only be a small taste of the power of our foe.

21

Blout was groggy and agitated, but very much alive. Although the bleeding had been horrible to see, he hadn't lost much blood in the end. It was just enough to achieve the desired effect—scaring the crap out of all of us.

"GHAA! What the hell was that?" Blout sputtered, trying to clear his throat. "I couldn't move, couldn't hear a thing . . . I was floating in tar."

I tried to help him to his feet, but Blout shook his head. He was still too weak. We all took a seat in the dirt again and ate more painkillers. All except Mo'Lock, who waved me off again.

"You sure?" I said, downing another myself. "How's your head?"

The ghoul nodded confidently. "I'm fine. There's nothing there, I'm sure."

Blout was looking more alert despite the pill. Slowly he came back to his old self. He snapped at me for staring and got annoyed with the blood caked around the various openings of his face. When he got around to re-lighting the cigar he'd dropped I knew he was close to a hundred percent.

I grabbed the box and stood, using my free hand to wipe off the dirt that stuck to my pants. It was much more moist than it had been before, less crumbly and more like dough. Definitely doughy. Mo'Lock noticed the same, and was examining one particular wad of the stuff.

"You think we're near water?"

Mo'Lock shook his head slightly. "I don't think this is dirt. Feels like very rich soil."

"Great, we'll start an herb garden."

"I'm no expert, but I thought soil was usually found close to the surface, the top layer."

"Well, add it to the list of weird shit. If there's room."

I started walking on but stopped as Blout grunted and fell behind me. He was injured pretty bad. I began doubting whether he'd be able to continue.

Not that I was much better. With the repeated beating my body was taking, I was asking too much of the painkiller. It couldn't block out pain from injuries and protect me from invading psychic forces forever. Again I thought about the packet in my sock, but fought it off. Not yet, not yet.

We moved along the tunnel, shambling and weaving. The dirt beneath our feet gave in to our every step, adding an unfortunate suction effect that made walking harder. My legs began to ache.

I could make out the rough tunnel walls but not much else—it was just a long dark corridor leading God knew where. I was a little disappointed to see there were no cryptic inscriptions on the walls, no dramatic warnings or symbols to ward off enemies. Then we came to a turn where I could detect a slight glow of light around the corner.

Blout was beside me. "What the fuck?"

I walked toward the glow, the others following. Blout had his revolver drawn.

The light was dim and yellow, most definitely not natural. It had the erratic blink of a bulb casting twitching shadows in all directions. We slowed as we neared the corner, taking each sticky step carefully. Just before we reached the source of the light, I stepped on something that crinkled.

I grabbed the object from beneath my foot. "You were right, Mo'."

Mo'Lock leaned over my shoulder as I presented an empty plastic bag. The logo was a smirking cartoon cow, with "Good Cow Top Soil" printed underneath. The ghoul grinned at me. I threw the bag to the ground and moved around the corner.

There were lights lining the hall, scores of naked bulbs hanging from thick bundles of power cords, but they weren't there to illuminate the path. They were grow lights. Countless plants completely covered the tunnel walls, crammed into every inch of space.

The variety of plants was unbelievable, but all were herbs and roots common to all forms of magic and voodoo. Some, like basil and coriander, were common cooking herbs that also had uses in the dark arts. Others were nastier: hemlock, a deadly poison, and a large cluster of the rare aconite plant, also poisonous.

I pointed at the cluster. "Greek legend says that plant came from the mouth of Cerberus . . ."

". . . the dog that guarded the lower world," Mo'Lock nodded and felt the leaf of the plant next to its hood-shaped flower. "Another misplaced myth, a random use of legend and witchcraft."

I slapped his shoulder. "Now you're getting it."

"Not me," Blout spat. "Care to fill me in?"

I held my finger to my mouth. Blout was yelling, and I thought we'd better keep it down. We were close.

"It's been like this throughout the case, Blout. The voodoo charm with the Egyptian symbol, the writings in Cain's books crossing Greek legend with witchcraft, and now this. This plant's Greek origin fits the needs of the perp—to guard this tunnel—but . . ."

Mo'Lock broke in, ". . . in reality the plant is used for treating gout and rheumatism."

Blout shook his head violently. "I'm completely lost. Is our perp using stuff wrong because he thinks it's something that it isn't?"

"Maybe, maybe not. It all depends on what you believe."

Blout still didn't understand.

I tried my best to explain, "Some things exist whether we believe in them or not. Like the moon, or the sound of a tree falling in the woods, right?"

Blout blinked once and stared at me.

Mo'Lock took a turn. "But what if something that doesn't exist can be created simply because someone believes in it strongly enough?"

Blout looked from me to Mo'Lock.

"You see what we're getting at?"

"No," Blout said, "I must admit I don't."

Mo'Lock clapped his hands. "It's simple. The power of belief can create things which might not exist, granting them power and making them real."

Blout glared at the ghoul for a long time. "Let me tell you what I believe, freak job. I believe this is getting too damn weird, and after what happened to me back there, we need some backup. That would be the smart play."

I said, "If you're getting scared, you're welcome to hang back and wait."

"Don't pull that kiddy crap with me!" Blout growled. "And I'm not scared."

Blout stomped forward. As we continued on our way our surroundings began to change. The tunnel narrowed and the plants thinned to one every several feet.

As Blout rounded a bend, I heard him retch violently and hurried to catch up. Our path was blocked. A pair of disembodied heads sat impaled on a two-pronged spike protruding from the soft ground. Based on the torn flesh and dangling veins at the neck, they had been violently ripped from their bodies. I didn't need Mo'Lock to tell me that these were his missing buddies, but he did just the same.

"It's them, Cal. It's them."

I began to raise my arm to the ghoul's shoulder but stopped when the heads simultaneously snapped open their eyes.

"Mo'Lock, is that you?" the left head said. Its voice was hollow, accompanied by a deep sucking sound that whistled through the open end of its neck.

We all took a step back. Blout was making the sign of the cross.

Mo'Lock recovered from the initial shock and quickly stepped toward the heads. "Tyus," Mo'Lock said addressing the left head, "what happened?"

Tyus blinked once and tried to wet his lips. It was futile. "We failed. Attacked by a mob of zombie hooligans. Please forgive us."

Mo'Lock placed his hand to his chest and for a moment I thought he would weep. "No. Forgive me. I should not have sent you. Where are your bodies? What did they do with them?"

The head on the right spoke. "They burned them before our eyes and set our heads here with a warning." The ghoul head turned his eyes to me. "The warning was for you, Cal McDonald. Stay away, or certain death awaits."

I shrugged and spat. "Whatever. Who gave you that message? Cain himself?"

Tyus spoke again. "It was just a voice."

"In our heads."

I looked at Mo'Lock. "Do you want to go back and get them to safety? Your call."

The heads spoke together. "We'll be fine. Go and stop this thing. This place stinks of death."

The right head made an effort to look past the ghoul and me. "I think your human friend could use some help."

Mo'Lock and I turned to find Blout out cold, spread-eagle on his back. God, how I envied him. He'd get to sleep through it all.

The ghoul and I kept going, leaving Blout with the heads and the message that we'd pressed on. I sensed we were close as the heart beat hard inside the box. Whatever Cain had begun or become, it was soon time for a showdown. I was eager to get it over with. My only regret was that I'd miss the look on Blout's face when the heads gave him our message.

22

The long corridor became thinner and thinner as Mo'Lock and I advanced. The lights were spotty and dim, only a few every other yard or so to accommodate a plant here, a root there. Still, there was enough light to see that the end was a long way off. At least I could see no immediate threats. The only sounds were our own footfalls grinding in the soft, muddy dirt and the occasional drag and kick when one of us lost our footing.

The peace and quiet bothered me more than the action. It gave me time to feel my hurting body, each and every cut, scrape, and bruise. I was a mass of pain and needed the distraction of motion. Without it, the pain was too much. I couldn't focus. It was then, I think, that my mind was first tugged away . . .

All at once, my head began to feel strange. It hit like a breeze, then a wave, building to the force of a wrecking ball. Not pain, not really, more like a creeping paralysis—like a stiff, aching joint. I had to stop. I was confused, unsure where I was.

"Cal, are you all right?" a voice said to my side.

I couldn't see anything. Was I home. Too late?

The voice repeated the question.

I covered my face in my hands. "Yeah, I'm fine Dad . . ."

"What?" Mo'Lock asked.

I felt his hand on my shoulder. "I said I'm . . ."

I blinked, shaking my confusion away as I dug in my pocket for a pill. The bitter crunch was a needed slap in the face. My vision cleared and I saw the ghoul standing there with a look of unmistakable worry.

"Stop that," I said, standing fully erect. "Fucking ghoul."

I walked away stamping my feet and used my tongue to pick at the jagged chunks of pill stuck in my teeth. Behind me Mo'Lock had a hand to his temple and a strained expression on his stiff white face.

"What's up?" I asked, but didn't slow my stride.

The ghoul kept walking, brow raised. "I just had the oddest sensation," he said. "It was as though my brain itched."

"I'm tellin' you, take a fucking pill."

"No. The alcohol is still doing the job. I feel sufficiently bleary."

"Mo'Lock—"

"Cal. No. I can do this, and you've got a job to do."

He wasn't going to budge. It was that uncanny ability to stay focused. He didn't want me to worry or get distracted. No matter how badly I treated him, I was always his number one priority. I thought about it all the time. He could have any life he wanted, even travel the world if he so desired, yet here he was slopping through a subterranean voodoo pit with me—with not so much as a complaint.

"Cal. Up ahead."

Ten feet in front of us, a zombie stood frozen, legs bent and poised to attack, its empty eye sockets dripping oily maggots. One hand was braced on the craggy earth, the other fanned out with palm toward us.

"Shit. Only one?" I laughed.

I handed Mo'Lock the heart and started in, but the thing wasn't looking for a fight. I'd called its bluff. When I got within striking distance, it spun away and ran off into the darkness.

When I turned back to Mo'Lock to gloat, my stomach sank.

Hanging between me and the ghoul was the body of a man, swinging by his broken neck. I backed away, forcing myself to look up at the twisted face. Fuck if I hadn't seen it before. It was my father as I'd found him years before; blue-faced, bloated tongue sticking out grotesquely between tight lips.

I spun away, letting a cry escape, but a new obstacle blocked my way. I covered my eyes, but this only left my other senses open to attack.

"Calvin? Is that you?" The voice was soft and tiny. I remembered it instantly despite the years. Then I smelled baby powder and knew she was there.

I spread the fingers covering my eyes and saw her standing there as beautiful as the last day I saw her—my sister Stephie. Seven years old and so pretty, the image of my mother.

"Stephie! Yes honey, it's me . . . Cal." I heard my voice cracking. I was losing control. It's not her, I told myself. I clamped my eyes tightly shut and tried to speak, but before I could, Stephie's face changed from the sweet child I'd known to one filled with burning rage.

"Why weren't you in the car, Cal?" she spat. Crevices began to appear across her forehead, blood filling the hairline cracks. "You were supposed to be in the car. Me and Mom waited, but you never came."

I shook my head hard and beat myself with my fist. The image before me flickered. "Get out of my head!" I screamed and struck myself again.

Stephie was falling apart. Blood ran from her face as it was raked to the bone by an invisible shattered windshield. She cried my name and called out to our father hanging from the rope. I slammed my head again and screamed, pulling my hair.

"Get out!"

As quickly as they'd come, the images disappeared.

"Fuck!" I slammed my fist into the tunnel wall. I was mad and needed a release. I thought I'd break my hand for sure, but the wall turned out not to be stone and rock at all. The soft red clay fell in a spray of chunks when my fist hit it.

"What now? Mo'Lock!"

"I beg your pardon, sir?"

The voice was the ghoul's, but distinctly different. The hoarse grumble was gone, the imaginary echo no longer there. It was a clear, proper voice. I took a closer look at him. He stood complete and upright, the rigid stance of a gentleman of long ago.

"What is this place? A mine shaft? Where are Caroline and the children?"

I stuttered. I didn't know what to say. It wasn't my ghoul that stood in the tunnel with me. It wasn't anybody I'd ever known.

"Oh, do speak up man! Where are my wife and children?"

"What year is it . . . sir?" I asked trying to sound polite.

The man was indignant. "Are you daft? It's December 15th, 1919," he spat, looking around the tunnel. "Now answer my question. Where are my wife an . . ."

He cut himself off and banged his head with his big bony hands. "NGGGH! Leave me . . . get out of my mind!"

It was Mo'Lock's voice, but it didn't last seven words.

The gentleman came back, but the pompousness was gone. This time his face was dreamy, unaware of his surroundings. His eyes were welling with tears.

"Caroline dear, I promise you the automobile is perfectly safe, perfectly safe."

I stepped toward the weeping ghoul. "Mo'Lock, are you . . ."

The gentleman became unsettled as I approached. "My . . . my name is Michael Locke. Can't you see that I've killed my family?"

That was all I could take. I hauled off and let the ghoul have it right in the side of the head. He reeled backward and I saw his face change. We stood there silent as Mo'Lock wiped the tears away from his face, studying them before wiping his hands on his pants.

"Thank you, Cal."

I looked at him a long moment. "Looks like you and I share something."

The ghoul nodded. "We always have."

Now I really wanted to kill whatever was at the end of the tunnel. I wanted it to suffer, suffer like it made us suffer. I knew the pain Mo'Lock carried was as great as my own and that was fuel, baby— fuel that would bring this evil down hard.

Just then I noticed the place on the wall where a chunk of clay had fallen after I'd hit it. The naked patch was about the size of a jar lid, a glistening moist whiteness beneath the surface of the clay. It reminded me of the flesh of a floater, a drowning victim that has been in the water for days.

I gave the patch a prod with my index finger. It was cold, soft, and clammy and caved at my touch. A shudder ran through my body, echoed by a soft roll that seemed to travel through the ground beneath our feet. I realized then why it reminded me of the flesh of a drowned person. It was human skin.

And unlike a floater, it was alive.

23

I kicked the dirt at my feet and revealed another fleshy white patch. We were so busy trying to get to the end of the tunnel that it never dawned on us that the thing we sought was the tunnel itself. At some point we had entered it and never knew.

It was time to make a move before whatever Cain had become tried to get in our heads again. The surrounding blubbery wall gave me an idea. It was time to get drastic. I shot a look at Mo'Lock.

"Let's fuck this thing up."

I tried not to think about the clammy flesh surrounding us. The idea that we might be inside some gigantic monstrosity was too disgusting to consider. I pushed the thought out of my mind by retrieving the pouch from my sock. I pulled out the needle, spoon, syringe, and last, but hardly least, the packet of chunky white power.

I created a little torch out of some debris, stuck it into the dirt, and lit it. Then I put the chunk into the spoon and spit on it several times. The drugs and saliva cooked over the candle flame until they melted. I filled the needle, pushing the plunger to clear out the air bubbles. A major overdose was on the way.

Mo'Lock knelt down beside me. "Cal, are you sure you want to do this? Aren't the pills working?"

I grinned and gave the needle a little squirt. "Who said it was for me? Let me have the heart. I'm gonna try a little voodoo magic myself . . . with a twist of smack."

I pinned the heart to the dirt with my left hand. The muscle began beating harder, fighting me. The walls and floor began to shudder and rumble. The thing was getting jumpy.

I wasted no more time. I raised the needle in my right hand and jabbed it into the center of the heart, emptying all but a single hit of heroin into the pulsing muscle. Instantly the heart fluttered and beat hard, then settled down to a slow, steady pace.

A low moan echoed through the tunnel like a powerful generator grinding to a slow halt. The sound came from all sides, even from inside my head for a flash.

I took what was left of the smack, enough to overdose an elephant, and stabbed the fleshy patch on the wall. I didn't know how big the thing was, so I couldn't guess how long the drugs would last, but I definitely wanted to err on the side of safety. The bellowing moan sounded again, louder this time. When the floor rumbled violently, I left the needle dangling from the wall, grabbed the heart and Mo'Lock, and ran for the end of the tunnel.

At the tunnel's mouth, zombies blocked the path. Their empty eye sockets panned back and forth, waiting for us to come at them.

The ghoul and I slowed, but we didn't stop. When the zombies saw that we weren't going to turn back, they scattered, clearing a path for us. They were all bluff and wouldn't risk a fight, since we were aware of their vulnerability.

We entered a massive room the size of an aircraft hangar, but more square than rectangle. The walls were parts of many things; red clay, hard rock, and stone. Protruding everywhere, ceiling to floor, was bone-white skin, throbbing and moist. We moved into the center of the room, surrounded by fires tended by zombies. They kept their distance, cowering and shielding the talismans around their necks with bony hands.

Behind me, Mo'Lock was staring in awe at the fleshy room. There was a tangible energy in here I was sure he felt. It made every tiny hair on my body stand on end.

Familiar symbols covered every exposed surface, while altars occupied the lower halves of three walls. One I recognized as a classic voodoo altar, covered with dried blood and melted candles, copper pots overflowing with chicken feet. Another appeared more satanic, with a Hand of Glory—the severed hand of a suicide victim—placed in front of a goat's head. The third was a clean white table combining the symbols of the Jewish, Christian, Hindu, and Muslim religions.

But the fourth wall was where I found what we'd been chasing all along, the source of perhaps a thousand deaths. A thing that had once been a nothing, a nobody. A little man who decided to take whatever he needed to invent his own world. He created a reality by pickpocketing the beliefs of the world and using them to recreate himself as a monster that fed on brains, the very source of the soul. By doing so, he'd made his own world.

It was an unbelievable testament to the power of belief and the ugliness of egotism and hatred. Why is it when humans tap into tremendous power, the first instinct for most is to take, to destroy? Before me was just another example of someone who could have been special, the greatest intellect on earth, but instead used his power to shed blood and sow terror.

I stared at the face in the wall—the face was the wall. It was gnarled by rock and stone, stretched by its own voracious appetite. It looked stupefied by the heroin flowing through its massive system.

It was a face I knew and suspected, but one I still couldn't quite believe I was seeing again.

This was the reason I did what I did. This was a monster.

"Hello, Cain. It's been a long time."

24

Staring at the abomination, my mind raced back to the aftermath of our last confrontation. I'd stood watching them hose off the street, the gooey pink gripping the asphalt, desperately fighting to hold its ground. But the hoses won in the end, and bit by splattered slimy bit, the last remains of Edgar Cain were washed into the sewers.

Unfortunately, Cain had a backup plan. His heart lived on in the deposit box, and as long as the heart lived, so did he. After that, he had all the time in the world to perfect the powers of his abnormal brain, using his own strange blend of religion and magic. Finally he could populate his lonely existence, and eventually reanimate his own splattered, defeated form.

I scanned the room and saw pink-white flesh protruding everywhere from clay and rock. How deep was this fucking head embedded in the earth? How many lives stolen in their sleep? And that terrible force . . .

I had to remind myself that if I killed Cain once, I could do it again. This time, there would be no coming back.

"I wouldn't phink pho loud if I were yoo, detective."

The face was speaking. And it sounded as though the drugs were working. He was trashed.

"Okay, then I'll say it out loud. You're going down, Cain," I said. "You've done enough killing for one lifetime."

Cain's eyes blinked sluggishly. "I'ph kilt no one. I absorbed the lonely . . . the ill . . . the hopeleph." He blinked again and smacked his lips trying to shake the effects of the drugs.

Mo'Lock stepped up beside my right shoulder. "Actually, Mr. Cain, you did far worse than killing them. You stole their souls, their essence. You took what little chance many of these people had for eternal peace."

The face guffawed. "Nonsense! You know nophing!"

I stepped toward Cain's face. "It's over. Face it, you're done."

My confidence infuriated the giant head even more, but he was too wasted to fully react. "W . . . why you . . . Do you know what you are dealing with?! I am the second giant! I could bend and break you with a single thought! I am the single biggest intellect in all the world!"

It was time to act. I held the throbbing heart out so that the face could see it clearly. "Recognize this?"

Cain's eyes widened. "How did you f . . . find it?"

I stepped back. "Brown corduroy bell-bottoms. The key in the wallet. I just followed the corduroy road."

Cain wasn't as upset as I would have thought, but there was still serious worry in his eyes. Then he squeezed his lids tightly shut, and for a moment a dull image flickered in my mind. Stephie again, bloody and begging for help. This time, the image quickly faded.

Cain coughed, blinked, and clamped his eyes shut again.

This time there was a suggestion, a lame imitation of my inner voice telling me to shoot myself. I shook my head and flipped it off like a bronco throwing a quadriplegic.

I tapped my right foot and bobbled the heart hand to hand. "Are you finished?"

I threw the organ to the floor. It flopped once, rolled, and came to rest underneath Cain's chin. Now it was my turn to do the glaring. I stared it right in the eyes and waited for its worry to turn to fear. To speed up the process, I took out both of my pistols, the six-shot in my left and the 9mm in my right.

Cain snorted. "I'ph grown beyond my heart. Go ahead."

"We'll see."

Cain's eyes met mine. Now tears welled in the stretched corners. "Please . . . don't . . ."

I sneered. "Kiss my ass."

I went into my best Two Gun Kid imitation, firing both guns from the hip and making that beating heart dance.

Cain screamed with the sound of a thousand voices.

The heart blew apart into a splattered mess of tissue and goo, a hundred bloody chunks. I kept firing until there were a thousand, reloaded and shot until I had to reload again. The heart was a grease mark when I finished. A crimson smear.

While I reloaded, I noticed Mo'Lock going berserk.

He had smashed one altar and was on to the next, using a steel candle stand as a weapon. Hit by crushing hit, he was destroying everything in sight.

". . . Please, stop . . . please!" Cain pleaded to deaf ears.

He screamed and begged and howled for help that would never come. Or so I thought.

Because right then, I heard three clicking sounds behind me. Mo'Lock and I turned in unison, raising our hands as we swiveled. It was a reflex. You always reach for the sky when you have guns pointed at you.

At the mouth of the chamber stood Randy, Scott, and Miriam— the Frankenteens. Each held an M16, and they all wore a look of condescending "I-screwed-you" pleasure that made my stomach twist in a knot so hard it actually hurt.

"Motherfuckers."

Cain giggled at our backs. Randy raised his weapon and stepped forward.

"You're the motherfucker, McDonald," he spat. "You're the one who took everything away from us!"

I glanced at the ghoul, utterly shocked at the sight of him. His eyes were wide, blazing. I'd seen him angry before, but this? This was different. It sent a chill down my spine.

I kept my hands raised. "I tried to help you kids. How was I supposed to know you were as messed up as Lazar." I pointed a thumb back toward Cain. "And I don't even want to know how you got hooked up with this loser!"

Randy twitched angrily and squeezed off a shot at my feet. Cain squealed. Randy shot again and this time he hit me right in the same goddamn spot he'd shot me the first time! I reeled back and screamed. It hurt like a bitch.

Scott and Miriam looked nervous.

"Mr. Cain contacted us," Scott said. "In our heads."

Miriam smacked Scott in the chest. "Shut up!"

Randy moved forward again.

"The next one goes through your head, McDonald!" He yelled and raised the M-16 as promised.

I didn't even see Mo'Lock take the gun out of the kid's hands. It was that fast. Then the ghoul stood over Randy, his face twisted in such a grotesque sculpture of rage that I hardly recognized him.

"You lied to me."

That was all he said before proceeding to dismember Randy limb from limb. He ripped the kid's arms from their sockets effortlessly. Skin tore with a rubbery snap and bones popped with a sickening crunch. In a matter of seconds, Randy was returned to the pile of miscellaneous organs and limbs he'd been in Dr. Polynice's Lab.

Then Mo'Lock turned to the other two.

They shot at him as he marched. He took the bullets right in the chest but kept on advancing steadily. After they'd been disarmed he tore them apart as he had their leader, without making a single sound. It was the most terrifying thing I'd ever witnessed in my life, and I've seen quite a lot, thank you. I was never happier to count Mo'Lock as a friend. Plus, I learned an invaluable lesson—never lie to a ghoul.

When he was finished, arms and legs were scattered all over the chamber floor. I could see Mo'Lock took no pleasure in what he'd done. Regardless, I gave him a nod. He paused and returned the gesture.

I looked up to Cain triumphantly. "Got anything else?"

Cain smirked, and the chamber began to rock.

Mo'Lock and I stood in place, dumbfounded. We were out of options. The heart was obliterated, but Edgar Cain still lived. He'd actually become powerful enough to do without his heart. Cain's eyes glowed with renewed malevolence as his wide lips parted and he spoke the words that were running through my mind.

"You are so screwed."

The walls shook, throbbing as the heart once had. Clay and stone loosened and crumbled, crashing down around our heads.

I rolled away from the falling debris, reloading the 9mm and revolver as I moved. I tossed a gun to Mo'Lock who just stared at it.

"What am I supposed to do with this?" A gigantic wedge of damp red clay landed at his side. He didn't even flinch.

"Just shoot!"

Cain's eyes spun in his head. "No!"

I raised my gun into the air and fired once. Above us the fleshy surface burst open as the slug impacted, and gooey pink matter spat out in violent, gushing bursts. I looked at Mo'Lock and he gave me an affirmative nod. We'd get out of this mess yet.

"Looks like this baby's about to blow," I said. "What say we help it along?"

Cain began screaming again, trying anything to distract me. When I felt him pulling at my brain, I shook my head, leveled the 9mm at his distended face, and fired twice. The skin parted slightly where the bullet struck, but there was no blood.

Nothing.

But deep inside the head, the pressure was building, pushing at the small hole until it split and ripped lengthwise. Before I could react, a geyser of snotty pink goo shot across my face.

I dove, rolled to one knee, and picked up one of the Frankenteens' M16s, unleashing a blaze of automatic fire into the right wall. Behind me, the ghoul was shooting in dangerously random directions. Each shot brought forth a gusher of crude pink brain matter. The fleshy walls rumbled and shook, percolating like bags of boiling tar. And then the smell wafted into my nostrils. I gagged, my stomach lurching. The stench was worse than death, hot and thick, and impossible to ignore.

Cain was finally silent.

His forehead spit pink and gray, his eyes teared and saliva-soaked lips blubbered uncontrollably. I almost felt sorry for him. Almost, but not quite.

Mo'Lock and I met in the center of the room, dodging falling slabs of clay and rock. A growing roar rumbled ominously inside. On the ceiling and walls, tiny geysers of matter tore at the small holes, enlarging them.

I looked down at my feet and saw we were already ankle deep in fetid soup. Edgar Cain's eyes were closed, but tears ran freely through closed lids.

"Cain," I said. My tone was soft, almost a whisper.

The face opened its eyes.

I leveled the M16, point blank, between his eyes. "In your next life, get out of the house more often."

I emptied the clip into his face, killing him once and for all. Unfortunately I also opened the brain matter floodgates. The gunk had now risen to our knees, and all around us the flesh walls were stretched to breaking. The evil was finally dead, but so were Mo'Lock and me if we didn't make tracks quickly.

Mo'Lock looked at me. "Got a plan?"

I nodded. "Run."

Running knee-deep in the thick, ever-increasing brain matter proved easier said than done. I could hardly move, let alone raise my legs above the slop. At least Mo'Lock had a height advantage. He used it to jump free of the current and gain about a half yard each time. I had to push my way through, which, considering the shape I was in, was no simple task.

By the time he reached the tunnel, I was still several yards behind. The head pudding was now waist high and the walls and ceiling threatened to burst. If it cut loose before I got to Mo'Lock, I'd had it for sure.

Lucky for me, the ghoul's loyalty was stronger than his own sense of self-preservation. When he saw I was having a hard time, he cut through the flowing gunk with relative ease, grabbed my wrist, and headed back to the exit. The fact that he was dragging an extra hundred and ninety pounds with him had little effect on the ghoul.

Just as we reached the exit, the far wall split with a thunderous tear. A tidal wave of brain rushed into the room. Steam rolled off the bubbling surface, producing a new eye-searing wave of stench. It was like a slaughterhouse in August filled with rotten eggs, bad cottage cheese and just a hint of old foot. Mo'Lock gagged. I tried to draw air through my mouth, but it was little help.

At the exit, the streaming brains were causing a nasty undercurrent. One moment Mo'Lock and I were gripping the walls of the tunnel, the next we were swept away, riding the wild pink gunk. Behind us, I heard another flesh wall swell and burst, and the speed of the rapids pulled us along even faster. I tried to grab hold of the walls, but it was hopeless. We were moving too fast and it took all my energy to keep my head above the torrent. I figured the tunnel would fill and either rake our heads along the ceiling or simply drown us. Either way, it was looking mighty grim.

The surface in front of me bubbled, foamed, and broke. Stinking pink muck spattered, blinding me momentarily. When I managed to clear my vision, Mo'Lock was right in front of me, his sight seemingly unaffected by the fumes. He must have swum backward to find me. He threw his long arm around my neck, pulled me close, and helped me stay above the current.

"Hang on!" the ghoul yelled.

"I'm trying!" I screamed back. "But I think I left my Palm Pilot back there!"

"Shut up and save your breath, Cal!"

We were traveling through the tunnel at three times the rate we had walked in. It was difficult to tell where we were, save for the fact there was now little more than a foot and a half of air separating us from the jagged ceiling. The thick current tugged and pulled at our legs, slamming us side to side against the tunnel walls. Mo'Lock did his best to hold onto me, but the constant pounding made the task next to impossible.

Twice he lost me, only to grab me again. The second time, I went under and got a mouthful of grotesque, gelatinous head pudding. I choked and almost swallowed. I thought I'd drown in the crap for sure, but somehow I forced the slime from my mouth, shut my eyes tight, and held my breath. I thought I'd try to ride it out, hold on until the tunnel ended at Whitney Green. Maybe there the pink sludge would spill into the burnt foundation of the building and I would find air.

Then I felt a hand grabbing at my head, followed by a painful yank that removed several clumps of hair. I gasped and gulped greedily—fresh air. Mo'Lock had pulled me to the surface. I spat and choked, trying to clear my eyes and ears.

"Cal!" The voice screamed.

It was Blout just ahead of us, sounding closer by the second.

I screamed. "Blout! Over here!"

"Up ahead, Cal! My hand! My hand! Can you see it?!"

I tried to focus through one eye. Ahead was the point where we fell into the tunnel. I could just make out a dark object swinging back and forth from the ceiling.

"See it?" Mo'Lock yelled at my ear.

"I think so." I blinked my eyes hard. The slime was stubborn and sticky. Finally I was able to make out the fuzzy outline of Blout's hand hanging down just yards from me and closing fast. "I see it!"

There was another surge of brains. We were thrown against the left wall of the tunnel and a second swell almost scraped our heads against the ceiling. Mo'Lock pulled me closer, then moved his hand to the back of my shirt and held on like a mother cat holds a kitten's scruff. I could see Blout's hand dangling from an unseen ledge.

Mo'Lock strained to hold me further above the pink and gray rapids. "Grab hold, Cal! Grab hold of his hand!"

Blout was screaming as well. He couldn't see us, so he had no idea I was about to hit. I hoped the sudden jolt didn't drag him over the edge.

"I'm here!" I warned. I saw his fingers flex and spread wide, ready to grab hold.

Another second, another swell of brain and our hands met. Blout had me. But Mo'Lock was slipping. I reached with my free hand, grabbed for his suit coat and got it, but the rapids threw and twisted him and the collar tore.

"Mo'Lock!" I cried out, dangling in the air.

Blout pulled me out of the torrent. As I hit dry ground I got a glimpse of Mo'Lock being taken away by the rapids. He flailed his arms and yelled something I couldn't make out. Then he was gone.

26

I was on solid ground. I rose to my knees and pounded my fist on the dirt. "Damn!"

Blout was right there beside me. "Christ, are you all right?"

I felt his hand on my shoulder, and swung my head around to face the big man. I was pumped. I must have looked like a rabid dog, but this thing wasn't over. I had to stay pumped or I'd drop like a rag doll.

Blout's slacks were wet from the knees down. He'd gotten himself out before the tunnel filled. "How'd you get up here?"

He shook his head. "I didn't. I found a manhole back a ways. I climbed out there, doubled back, and came here," he said, impressed with himself. "What the hell happened down there?"

"You don't want to know, trust me," I said. "But Cain's dead."

Blout jumped. "You sure this time?"

I nodded and started walking away. "It ain't over yet. We've got to get to Whitney Green." I stopped, and turned. "Did you get the heads?"

Blout shuddered visibly, but nodded. "I left them at the entrance."

"Thanks. You're a pal."

Outside the tunnel I picked up the heads. Blout had wrapped them in his jacket, and they were pleased to hear the danger had passed. I told them what had happened and they were as anxious as I was to rescue Mo'Lock.

"Mo'Lock's as tough as they come," said the head called Tyus. "I'm sure he's fine."

I wasn't so sure, but agreed anyway.

Blout stood by, watching me converse with the two disembodied heads with an air of absolute disgust. Then he went to his car to radio for backup. I heard him mention Whitney Green. I didn't like it. I had to get there before any cops did.

I ran to the road. Cars were whizzing by in pre–rush hour panic. I tucked the bundled heads under my left arm, and with my right waved to passing taxis. Blout was yelling as a cab screeched to a halt. I ignored him. I opened the back door of the cab and tossed in the bundle as Blout ran toward me.

I waved him off. "Wait for the backup. Meet me at the Green."

The driver was a ghoul as I'd hoped, so I explained the situation to him. He knew Mo'Lock and understood the immediacy of the dilemma. He burned rubber and we headed toward Whitney Green at seventy miles an hour. I introduced the heads as I unwrapped them, but the driver already knew 'em. Cozy community.

Ten minutes later we came to a screeching halt just outside the entrance of Whitney Green. I shot out of the cab without paying, leaving the severed heads behind. The driver agreed to take care of them. I didn't know exactly what that meant, but then again I didn't care.

"Just save Mo'Lock," he told me. "That would be payment enough."

I sprinted to the edge of the burnt pit that was once Cain's home. Now it was a huge hole, bubbling and foaming with slimy, surging brain matter. It spread out before me like a lake of frothy, stinking pulp. I scanned the surface for any sign of movement among the floating debris. There was nothing.

A horrible sinking feeling began to well in my gut. I felt panicky. Where the fuck was Mo'Lock?!

I could hear sirens wailing in the distance and closing fast. When the cops saw this, they'd do their best to cover it up, meaning I sure as shit didn't want to be there. I got panicky. Pacing the edge of the hole, I cupped my hands and began to yell.

"MOOOO'LOCK!" I hollered and repeated even louder, "MOOO'LOCK!"

From the shadows somewhere behind me, a figure shifted. "I'm not deaf, you know. I'm right here."

I spun on my heels. Mo'Lock stepped from the shadows, dripping pink slime.

I ran over to him, grabbed him by the shoulders, and shook him. "You crazy fucking ghoul! You scared the crap out of me!"

Mo'Lock smiled.

"Don't get the wrong idea, gruesome." I could feel the adrenaline fading quickly and all the pain beginning to return. "I just need someone to get me to the hospital."

27

I dreamt about terrible pain shooting through my ass, and being chased by rolling dumpsters overflowing with decapitated heads. After that, I woke in a hospital room bandaged from head to toe. The blinds were closed and the room was dark. I could see my arm was in a support, dangling above my bandaged torso. Beside me I heard a beeping apparatus that I suspected did little more than raise the per day rate.

My head was wrapped in bandages and gauze so thick that I could hardly lift it to see whether I was alone. I used every ounce of strength to raise my head off the pillow and was rewarded with the sight of a lumpy figure slumped in a chair next to the window. It was Blout, fast asleep.

With a great deal of effort I got my hand on the bedpan so comfortably rammed under my ass. I dragged it out to the edge of the bed where I let it fall to the ground. There was a huge clanging noise. Blout shot to his feet, reaching frantically for his holster. I had just enough energy to chuckle. Then I passed out again. This time I dreamt of nothing, and that was fine by me.

I woke later and found Blout still in the room with me. He was asleep again, but now light seeped in at the corners of the closed shades. I dragged my head to the edge of the mattress and saw a mountain of crumbled fast-food bags and crushed coffee cups on the floor.

Christ. How long had I been out?

"Who do you have to fuck to get a drink around here?"

Blout stirred. When he stood I could see that he had a large, square bandage on the left side of his forehead. A spotty blotch of dried brown blood showed through. His hands were wrapped with bandages, but in a way that gave most of his fingers freedom to move.

"You ain't fucking me no more this week. I've had enough."

His face was stone. I waited for the explosion. Instead I got a big toothy grin.

"Welcome back, asshead." He slapped my leg. It hurt. "You had us scared for a while there. You know they had to pump your damn stomach?"

Then the big guy reached into his overcoat and pulled a small stuffed rabbit that had a "Get Well Soon" sign. "Here, I bought you this fuckin' bunny."

The bunny landed next to me, rolled, and fell on its cute little face. I tried to sit up, but quit after a brief and futile attempt. "How long was I out?"

"I think it's a record for you. Almost four days. Today is the fourth day, but it's early."

"Damn." I was impressed. "Everything turn out okay?"

"Yeah, it seems there was some kind of weird spill at the burned-out Whitney Green apartments. I called out the Hazmat crew and they gathered what they could, destroyed what they gathered, and burned what was left in the pit." Blout had a big grin plastered across his face.

I snickered and felt my ribs throb. "What about the media?"

Blout laughed again. "You kidding? Chemical spills are the one thing that keeps their asses out of our business. Nobody knows nothing about nothing."

"But you're keeping the file open?"

"Damn right. I'm not about to report the case closed. I am not going to put myself in a situation where I have to explain what happened down there." He was shaking his head.

I grinned and pulled my arm out of the sling, trying again to sit up. This time Blout helped me and I made it. "What's the matter, Blout? Afraid nobody will believe you?"

"Exactly. I'll leave that crap to you."

I nodded. We both ran out of witty banter, and fell quiet. It was a little uncomfortable.

"It's over, isn't it, Cal?" Blout said, low and quiet.

I nodded. "Definitely."

"You're sure this time?"

I glared. "Absolutely."

Blout stuck his big hand out in front of my face. "That was real good work you did. Thank you."

I took his hand and shook it. There would have been another awkward silence, but the door was pushed opened by a scurrying male nurse, followed by the doctor. A heartbeat later, Mo'Lock lumbered in wearing a spiffy new suit.

Blout shot a look at the ghoul, then quickly back to me. "I've got to get going," he said and shook my hand again. "I'll check back before they let you go."

I thought Blout would go to great lengths to avoid Mo'Lock, but as he passed by the ghoul he gave him a slap on the shoulder.

Mo'Lock waited patiently while the doctor and nurse checked me out. When they had gone, he made sure the door was shut. He turned and tossed me a little stuffed rabbit much like the one Blout had given me.

"All my friends are comedians," I said.

Mo'Lock smiled. "Pull its head off."

"What?"

"Pull the head off."

I gave the bunny head a twist and pull. It came off with a pop, exposing the neck of a half pint of good stinky hooch. I grinned and looked up at the ghoul. "God bless you."

"I figured you'd have a bad case of the DTs when you woke up."

"Naw, they've got me pretty pumped full of juice. I don't feel a thing."

The ghoul stepped around to the foot of the bed and lifted my chart off the hook, scanning it with big, dead eyes. After a second, he let out a long whistle. "Four hundred stitches. That a record?"

"Yeah, I'm breaking them left and right. Where's my goddamn trophy? So what's been going on while I was in la-la land?"

The ghoul touched his hand to his chin. "Surprisingly quiet, really. The lawyer for the man who was suing you left a message with a new court date. I wrote it down."

"Great. Enjoying my apartment?"

"Yes, thank you. Landlord stopped by. He said he wants you to pay for the front door. He left a bill. The insurance co—"

I waved him off. "Okay, okay. What about work? I need some cash—a lot of cash—and I need it yesterday."

Mo'Lock stood at the foot of the bed staring at me for a moment, as if he was deciding whether or not he should tell me anything that might get me excited. Then he took out a small spiral memo book, flipped it open, and began to read.

"We got a call this morning from—"

"We?"

"You got a call from a woman named Veronica Vanderbilt."

"As in the 'we-got-more-money-than-anyone-in-the-world' Vanderbilts?"

"The one and only." The ghoul went on. "She sounded very scared and would like you to come to the house as soon as possible."

I was feeling better by the second. "What's the skinny?"

"She has a teenage son who is acting very strange. Sleeps all day and stays out all night."

I shrugged. "Sounds like a teenager to me."

"This morning she said she found something in the boy's closet that alarmed her. She didn't want to call the police. She was too embarrassed, so she called you."

"What was in the closet?" I rolled my eyes, pretending I didn't see the answer coming up Main Street.

Together we said, "A coffin."

I nodded. "What'd you say my . . . our rate was?"

Mo'Lock grinned. "A grand a day plus expenses."

"Sounds good. Now help me out of this fucking bed." I tipped the headless bunny into my mouth and emptied it, then got shakily to my feet. There was no time to waste. We had a new case.

GUNS, DRUGS, AND MONSTERS

Something was going on that last day of March, but I was too fucking out of it to realize. The city was getting on my ass. Everything about it—the people, the weather, even the monsters—was working over my nerves. I didn't know it, but I was itching for change. I was about to get a big dose of it, but I didn't know that either.

Twice, I noticed a black sedan outside my apartment. I figured it was the Feds looking in on me, as they would on occasion. But, this was post 9-11 and the Feds had better things to do with their time than put a tail on their favorite crackpot spook hunter.

In hindsight, I knew I was being followed. But that's what hindsight's all about, right? Trying not to look as retarded as you actually were by saying you knew something weird was going on?

The day started with my newspaper being stolen. In fact, all of the newspapers in my building had been taken. Then, while I was on the can spinning a three-coil monster of my own, the power went out. I had to finish my masterpiece, shower, and dress without light.

My head pounded. I was still more drunk than hung over. I'd lost a bundle to a bunch of ghouls down at the Black Cat Club. They always cleaned me out because I drank and they didn't. They'd bide their time until I was sloshed and then start hammering at me with outrageous bets they knew I couldn't turn down. Fuckers.

I decided to retrace my steps and head back to the Black Cat for a little breakfast drink. It was a crappy D.C. day. Rainy, soggy, and warm. Nothing kills a buzz as fast as a faceful of humidity. Outside was the black sedan, but I didn't pay any attention—even when it pulled away.

I got distracted by Brent, the postman/ghoul, on his daily rounds. He was a nice guy, well over a century old and as creepy as they come. He never crammed my mail into its narrow slot either. He'd always go the extra mile and climb the stairs to place it on my step.

"How's it going?"

Brent stopped and nodded as he shuffled bundles of mail. "Good, good," he said. "Looks like I don't have anything for you today."

"Probably just be bills anyway, right?" I gave him a little punch in the arm. In typical undead style he looked at his arm, then at me, before he smiled. "Yes, sure. I suppose so."

Most ghouls have the sense of humor of a dead slug. They aren't big on jokes, kidding, irony, puns, or teasing. They did like riddles, but who likes riddles over the age of fucking five?

"You seen Mo'Lock?"

Brent shook his head. "Haven't seen him for a few days."

I looked around, giving the area the once-over. "Neither have I. That freak-ass ghoul's always wandering off on me," I said, then looked at Brent. "No offense."

"None taken." He walked off to finish his rounds.

I shagged ass in the other direction and hiked the nine or ten blocks to the Black Cat. The club looked like an old warehouse: a nondescript brick front with an unlit neon sign bearing its name. As I pulled open the door, I heard the blare of police cars in the distance, that sudden burst of noise that meant somebody, somewhere, was in trouble. I was just glad it wasn't me.

Inside, the club was dark. The bar was open, but the chairs were still up on the tables and the room smelled of dirty mop water. At the bar was Dante, a short, aging punk rocker with jet-black spiked hair. He was a fixture in D.C.; the kind of guy who would support the local music scene and run for city council at the same time. I liked to hang out in his place because I felt comfortable around the so-called "freaks." Everyone from goths to vegans hung out at the place. The last thing they cared about was some scarred-up old bastard knocking back shots at the end of the bar.

Dante looked up as I approached, but the usual friendly greeting didn't come. Instead, he just looked at me and gave me a somber nod. Something was bugging him. I assumed I'd done something the night before and had conveniently blacked out. I've been known to start a fight or two when I get loaded.

I slid up to the bar and tapped the rail for a beer and whiskey. Dante looked around and pulled a glass from beneath the bar pre-filled with frothy brew.

I tried to smile. "Expecting me, huh?"

Dante looked nervous, like he wanted to say something to me, but wouldn't. Or couldn't.

I sniffed the glass and swigged the whole thing down in one long gulp, killing my headache and bringing a warm calm over my body. By then, Dante had pushed a napkin in front of me with writing on it, but it was too late.

The napkin read, "DON'T DRINK THE BEER."

I looked at him. He stared. Suddenly, I knew I was in trouble. I could see Dante wanted to say something, but something was holding him back. I stood up and started to leave. As I grabbed for the door, whatever was in the beer began to crawl up the back of my brain and take effect. My head started spinning and my jaw went numb. I turned back toward the bar and saw a tall man step out from behind Dante, shoving him aside.

I stepped into the gloomy daylight as my arms started going numb and my eyes began to vibrate in their sockets like hot ball bearings. I stumbled forward, heading for home. One block. Two, three, four. Every step felt like I was dragging a wet sack of mud. I didn't have to look over my shoulder to know the tall man was behind me, patiently following me back to my apartment.

By the time I reached my place, I could hardly see at all. The world was a black tunnel closing in on me, and my unrelenting pursuer was right on my heels. I turned and got a good look at the man swimming in the murk. He was black, over six foot five, and wearing a tan suit with a tropical handkerchief in the pocket. I knew him, but couldn't place the name. I could barely place my own.

I stumbled up the stairs, fumbled with my keys, and crashed inside. When I spun to slam the door, the tall man was right there, smiling and backing me inside my apartment with a gun. I tried to stare at his face, but the muzzle of the gun was in the way. All I could see were his eyes, deep-set and bloodshot red.

The tall man kicked the door closed, smiled, and smacked me across the chops with the gun. I fell backward and hit my head. Everything went black.

When I came to, I was tied to a chair. That I expected. What shocked me was that the chair was on top of my desk and the desk was pushed against the wall so that my back was against the office window! The shock of the revelation cleared my head like a cranial enema. I noticed the tall man standing nearby, waiting for me to eyeball him. Without the toxic muck on the brain I ID'd him on the spot.

His name was Dr. Polynice. He was a twisted fucker who chopped up kids, then reassembled the parts for reanimation.

Once these zombie kids were brought back to life they were sold to sleazebag perverts all over the world. I put Polynice and his partners out of business a long time ago. He should have been rotting in jail.

"When did you get out?"

Polynice swayed on his feet. "Yesterday."

I nodded. "That would explain my missing paper."

"The escape made the front page. Guards died. It was very messy."

Polynice spoke with the slightest hint of a French accent. He'd grown up in Haiti, where he'd learned and mastered voodoo. Afterward, medical schools in the States gave him the knowledge he needed to combine his arcane skills with modern medical science. He was one well-trained, learned, and sick motherfucker.

My gun was on the couch next to my knife, mace, and brass knuckles. He'd cleaned me out. Then I noticed the bag on the floor. It was a doctor's bag. One of those big black leather numbers, and I didn't have to see inside to know it was filled with all sorts of shiny, sharp nastiness. But Polynice opened it anyway, letting the light shimmer on the scalpels, surgical saws, knives, and syringes inside.

"You're not still pissed about that whole prison-for-life thing, are you?" I asked.

Polynice smiled pleasantly, saying nothing. He began to slowly retrieve one sharp instrument at a time, placing them on the desk in front of me like a waiter setting an elegant table setting. He set each instrument close, just out of my reach. It didn't matter. He had me tied so tight I could hardly breathe. All I could move were my toes, my head, and the very tips of my fingers.

"You destroyed my life's work. You disgraced me, my family, and my profession," Polynice said in his island lilt.

"Profession?! Since when is being a psychotic pederast butcher a profession?!"

Dr. Polynice paused and looked me in the eyes. At his height, even though I was on top of the desk, we were practically at the same level.

"Do not confuse me with my clients."

By now he had six tools laid out. Any one of them could skin the flesh off my bones. "Oh, please! You killed those kids. You chopped them up and reassembled them, knowing full-well what some sick fuck intended to do with them!"

I saw the doctor shudder. He didn't like what I had to say. I saw an opening and jumped in.

"Come on, Doc, admit it. You were a little into it."

Polynice looked up from his instruments. "I brought dead tissue back to life. Mine was the power of the creator."

"But you killed 'em, Doc!" I laughed. "Come on, seriously, you made one of those little cuties for some personal fun time, didn't you?"

"I DID NOT!" Polynice slammed his fist on the desk, shaking. "I would . . . n . . . never do that to another . . ."

"Had a hard time in the clinker, Doc? Somebody bigger than you bend you over the bunk?"

Polynice looked at me. Tears were welling in his rabid eyes. His entire body was trembling.

"You put me there."

I glared back. "Fuck you. I'd do it again, and I will."

Polynice grabbed a scalpel and came at me. I'd already decided if I was going to die it wasn't going to be at the hands of this sick bastard. I pushed from the only place I had any leverage—my toes—and rocked backward as hard as I could. As Polynice slashed at me, I fell back and went through the glass and out the apartment window.

I fell hard and fast, hitting the soggy pavement two stories below with a resounding crash and a shower of glass. The chair shattered, a couple of bones broke, and I lost some skin, but I was alive. I shook the ropes and shattered wood off and ran back in the building at full speed.

At the top of the stairs a panicked and horrified Dr. Polynice froze in his tracks. The look in his eyes was pure horror. Nothing like out-crazying the crazy. He didn't know what to do when he saw me with blood pouring down my face, flaps of skin hanging off my shoulder, and a big shit-eating grin plastered across my mug. He had three ways to go; up to the other floors, back into my apartment, or right at me. No matter what, he was mine.

Polynice chose "apartment," dashing suddenly out of my line of sight. I was on him in a split second and almost ran throat-first into his scalpel. Sliding underneath the doctor's clumsy attack, I rolled to my feet next to the couch where all my toys waited. I thought about grabbing the brass knuckles, but snapped up the gun instead. I had it on him before he could take a second slash.

Polynice dropped the scalpel and raised his hands. "You've got me. I surrender."

I shot him in the kneecap, and when he hit the floor I put another slug through his shoulder.

Dick.

The cops were pretty decent about this arrest. They usually gave me a hard time, being an ex-cop and all, but the whole state had been looking for Polynice since he'd escaped. He had killed four guards and a nurse just to get his vengeance on me. What an idiot. For a doctor, someone who was supposed to save lives, Polynice had destroyed quite a few.

Plus, the bastard bled all over my apartment. There were holes in the hardwood floor from the shots I'd fired. The window was shattered. Rain was blowing in and the whole place had a thick layer of gunpowder and body odor floating right at nose level like milky fog.

Just then my landlord, Judy something-or-other, decided to stop by for an impromptu inspection of the building with some people who were along to assess for refinancing or some such shit. Judy was a dried up, little old lady—a strip of overcooked bacon in a jogging suit.

In the past, I'd managed to keep her at bay. I had "avoiding the landlord" and "pretending not to be home" down to an art. But when the cops dragged Polynice right by her, bleeding and squealing like a stuck pig, she would not be denied. The jig was up.

I smiled, but she didn't notice. She stepped through the open door and slowly scanned the blood, smoke, and broken glass. Her face slowly turned red, starting at her shriveled neck and climbing right to the top of her small, bulb-shaped head like mercury up a thermometer. I dropped the smile. What was the use? She had me, dead to rights. It didn't help that I was three months behind on rent.

Even the cops still hanging out in the apartment sensed the tension. They packed up their shit and edged toward the door as the landlord slithered toward me.

"Strike three hundred, McDonald," she said. "I want you out of here by the end of the week."

"You can't do that."

"Try me."

She started counting on her fingers. "Unpaid rent. Running a business from your home without proper zoning or license, constant damage . . . and GUNFIRE!"

I glared down at her, but she stood firm.

"You're throwing me out?"

She nodded.

I spoke low. "I can get you the rent."

Now she smiled. A tight, wrinkled little smile. "You've been here for years and I've looked the other way. I'm tired of the noise.

I'm tired of the police, the damage, the constant complaints. Did I mention the gunfire? I'm tired of having a non-paying tenant who gets shot at twice a week."

A couple of cops giggled like schoolgirls in the doorway until I leveled them with an evil glare.

I couldn't believe she would throw me out. I had zero in the bank. Make that zero with dust on it. I'd narrowly escaped being slashed to death by a Jamaican voodoo doctor. But this? This I found very upsetting.

I lowered my voice to a whisper. It was time to beg.

"I promise you, things will change."

"They certainly will." She wouldn't drop the smile. It remained plastered on her leathery face all the way out the door.

I just stood there, dumbfounded. The last two remaining cops were still in the hallway staring at me. I walked over and slammed the door in their smug faces. On the wall near the door, a *Speculator Magazine* clipping, brown and aged, hung from a tack. The headline read, "Cal McDonald, Monster Hunter." The picture of me was blurred and grainy. It was the only article *Speculator* had published about me that didn't attempt to make me out to be a total ass.

I ripped the clipping off the wall, balled it up, and threw it down. It rolled about a foot before it slowed and stuck in a small smear of blood.

I looked around the apartment, at the yellowed walls and scratched wood floors. I scanned the sunken brown couch with the exposed stuffing and springs. The only thing worth a dime in the whole place was my desk, my files, and the collection of weapons I had stashed under the bed in the other room. I bet if someone took the time they could find enough powder to get high for a year, but basically that was it. That was my life; some wood, some papers, and a sack full of sharp things.

While I stood staring at my mess of a life, someone started tapping lightly on the door. It was an annoying little tap, but I knew who it was. I pulled open the door and Brent, the postman, stood there with a large square box. His face showed worry, but it always did.

"Guess I was wrong," he said. "You got this."

I took the box from him.

I stared at the short ghoul and turned my head. "Mind if I ask you a question?"

Brent sighed. "No, I suppose not."

"What did you do when you were, you know, alive?"

The ghoul looked puzzled by the question. "What do you mean, what did I do?"

"You know. What job? Were you an adventurer in the 1600s or some crap like that?"

"I was a postal worker."

He didn't even blink. If I'd offended him, he wasn't showing it. Then he timidly nodded and walked away. Fucking ghouls. They were harmless, loyal, and about as kind as a monster could be, but they were so fucking weird sometimes.

"Thanks, Brent!" I called after him and kicked the door closed before he responded.

Usually, nothing brightens the day like an unexpected package, but this one crawled up my ass and gave me the creeps right off the bat. It had an odd weight, heavy and shifting ever so slightly. It had a California postmark. The name and address on the label were mine, but there was no return address. It was trouble. I could feel it.

I used a penknife to slice the tape. The cardboard flaps popped open, eager to show me the gruesome sight inside.

It was a human head, severed clean just above the Adam's apple.

Weirder still, I knew whose head it was.

It was an old friend of mine, Sam "Hecky" Burnett. He was a private detective, and a hunter of the strange, bizarre, and outright freakish—just like me. The only difference between us was that he looked for the shit.

I've always tried to avoid the craziness and live a normal life, but not Sam. Not that insane old bastard. He savored the hunt. He loved tracking monsters like some folks love music or sports. He was obsessed, a fanatic. He had an encyclopedic knowledge of the supernatural, a mind like a thousand forbidden libraries, and I can say without reservation that he was one of the toughest sons-a-bitches I ever met.

Now he was just a head.

The look on his face was peaceful, like he'd fallen asleep and someone had made off with his body without waking him.

I hesitated, and then gave the forehead a poke. Nothing.

When I lifted the head from the box and moved it to my desk, the first thing I noticed was that the wound was almost completely bloodless. The slice was as clean as any I'd ever seen. In fact, the slice was so clean, it looked like it had been cut by a laser. It was so evenly severed, so straight, that I was able to stand the head on my desk by the stump of its neck without any other support.

Sam's head was covered with old scars from past battles. One ear was gone. The other was hardly a flap and a hole. His nose was bent and lumpy, and the rest of his face was a crisscross maze of healed hacks, scratches, and scrapes. Poor, ugly old bastard. What a way to go.

I sat in my chair and stared at the face of my probable future; the monster hunter, finally beaten. Finally outsmarted. Somebody, more likely something, had done this to him. Now it had been sent to me, I assumed, as some kind of twisted warning. Fuck them. It would take more then a head to frighten me. I wasn't scared in the least.

Not until the eyes fluttered. Not until the head moved.

I jumped back. Sam Burnett's severed head spoke.

"Cal?!"

The fucking head was alive! I jerked backward so hard that the legs of my chair dug grooves into the floor.

"Is that you, Cal?"

My chair tipped, toppled and I fell. I smacked my head against the hard plaster of the floor. I opted to stay there until it spoke again.

"Cal? Where'd you go, fer Christ's sake?!"

Slowly I peeked over the edge of the desk. Sure enough, Sam's head was sitting there, eyes wide open and alert.

I muttered, I stumbled, and finally spat out a somewhat coherent sentence.

"Hey, Sam. How you been?"

"I've been better, you big fuckin' pussy! Get off the floor and talk to me. We got troubles."

Despite the fact that I had a talking head on my desk, it was the "we" that bothered me the most. As I sat, I noticed Sam was smiling.

"You shoulda seen the look on your face. You were about as scared as I've ever seen anybody! Big bad detective, my ass! You're still a punk."

I felt my face flush. The head was right. I was lucky I hadn't pissed myself. "You wanna tell me what happened?" I said, hoping for a diversion from my embarrassment.

No such luck.

"Yer eyes popped out of yer head like two Ping-Pong balls," the head laughed. "What's the matter? Ain't you ever seen a decapitated head before?"

I glared at it. One more word and I was gonna punt him out the window. "You finished?"

"Haw!" Sam wanted to keep going. "Okay, Miss McDonald, I'm done. Big pussy."

I let the last jab slide. Despite the levity, something big and strange was up and I wanted to get to the bottom of it.

"Okay, fine," I said, "Now tell me what happened. Who did this to you?"

Sam's face went hard. "Damn kid."

"What?!"

"You heard me. I got bamboozled by a damn kid. An evil little son-of-a-bitch named Billy. Fifteen years old and smart enough to out-curse Aleister Crowley."

"A kid?!"

"Yeah."

"Fifteen?"

"You heard me, fuck-face."

Now, it was my turn to laugh, and I did. I let out a howl that made Sam more pissed than I'd ever seen him. But he was old enough and smart enough to know he had it coming. He just took it and waited for me to finish.

"So this kid," I said, "this Billy. What's his deal, and how the fuck did he do this to you?"

Sam rolled his eyes. "I was getting to that, so if yer ready to shut yer fuckin pie hole, I'll continue."

Then Sam looked around the apartment as if he'd just noticed the glass and blood.

"What the fuck happened here?"

"Remember Dr. Polynice?"

"The guy with the thing for kids?"

"No. The one who helped that guy."

Sam thought about it a second. "The voodoo guy. I thought you put him away."

"I did . . . again."

Sam batted his eyes. I could tell he would have nodded if he had a neck—then went on. "Anyway . . ."

I took out my flask and swigged a hit as Sam talked. As I listened, I dug in my desk for any kind of pill. Anything to take the edge off.

He told me about a lead he had on some cult operating out of the Valley in Los Angeles. Some place called Sherman Oaks.

"You've been in L.A.?" I interrupted.

Sam looked annoyed. "Yeah. I like the heat, and work is pretty steady."

"So you got mailed from the other side of the country?"

"Yeah." He rolled his eyes

"How was the flight?"

Sam glared at me. "You want to hear this or you want to trade travel stories?"

I shrugged. No sense of humor. I found a yellowish capsule under some old cigarette packs in the side drawer. I wasn't sure what it was, but I hoped it was in the barbiturate family. This was no time for speeding.

The head noticed when I slipped the pill into my mouth. "I thought you quit doing all that shit!"

I swallowed. "The key word is all," I said. "I quit the hard stuff."

"Stuff'll kill you."

"I thought you had a story to tell."

Sam grunted and went on.

He told me about the Sherman Oaks cult. It was a devil cult with an odd calling card that caught the attention of local authorities. Evidently some pets—cats, dogs, a rabbit, and a ferret—had gone missing. One by one, the pets were discovered dead, flayed, and skinned like trout. Each pet was found at a different site in the woods surrounding the town, and at each site satanic symbols were found. Nothing too obscure or arcane, pretty much what you'd find on any respectable Metal album. Pentagrams and goatheads, that kind of shit.

The locals were freaked, but things got worse. Much worse. Kids started disappearing, babies and toddlers. That's when Sam was called in by a cop named Ted Dawson of the Sherman Oaks Sheriff's Department.

Sam got to checking around, and he found that it was more than just your run-of-the-mill, satanic-ritual-for-kicks case. There was some bad mojo going down. Strange things were suddenly happening around Sherman Oaks, California. Bad things. First, a teacher at the local middle school melted like butter in a microwave at a school assembly, and then some winged creatures were spotted plucking bodies from graves.

Sam was stumped until he tracked down a small crowd of teenage boys. All three—Carl Potter, Brian Hogue, and Billy Fuller—were your typical pimple-ravaged rejects. When Sam checked records at the local library, he discovered the three boys had checked out every single book on witchcraft and black magic, along with a half dozen volumes on alchemy and serial killers. Sam knew he had his suspects and he was ready to move in on them.

But something happened before Sam could lower the boom: Brian Hogue got hit by a hipster's pick-up truck outside a Bob's Big Boy in North Hollywood. The driver said the kid wandered into the road like a zombie and just stood there waiting to get hit. The truck dragged him face down on the pavement for half a block. He died on the scene.

Next, Carl met with a mysterious demise when he drank a gallon and a half of liquid drain cleaner as Sam walked up the steps to his house. Carl's parents said that they tried to pry the jug from their son's hands, but it was like he was possessed. By the time he'd emptied the jug, the drain cleaner had passed through the poor punk, turning his guts into liquid that poured onto the floor via his asshole. He died on the way to the hospital.

"So it was the kid Billy?" I asked, "He was the ringleader. He was on to you and he killed the other two to sever his ties."

"Yeah, he was on to me, Einstein."

"How did he know you were onto him?"

Sam looked good and annoyed now. "I underestimated him. He heard I was asking around. I still thought I could walk up to the punk's house and haul his ass down to juvie."

But Billy was waiting for Sam when he arrived at the Fullers' ranch-style nightmare house. Sam walked right into a trap.

"When I looked down, I was standing in the middle of a magic circle he'd made out of the ground bones of the dead," Sam's head said, flushing with anger. "I was trapped, I couldn't move. Then the little brat shifted the dimensions between my head and my body. He separated me in two. Each part still alive without the other."

I shook my head.

"That is some fucked up shit," I laughed.

I knew the concept. Each second of time that passes is a separate moment in which everything exists. To put it in simple terms; if five seconds pass for a cow, then there are five different cows that can be tapped by dipping into the pool of time. What Billy had done was take Sam's head and place it in a slightly different time than his body, tearing them apart, but not killing them.

Smart kid. Evil as all hell, but smart.

"So, where's your body?" I asked.

"Somewhere in Southern California would be my guess."

I shook my head. "So how'd you . . . your head get all the way here?"

"The fucking punk dumped me off at Dawson's place. After old Teddy came to, I talked him into taking me to you."

I glanced at the box on the floor, at the postmark. Sam knew what I was going to ask before I asked it.

"Teddy chickened out. He mailed me."

I started laughing again.

"That's right, laugh it up!"

"I'm sorry," I choked, "I really am, but you gotta see the humor in it all."

Sam stared me down. "All I see is a bunch of dead kids and a crazed teen geek wielding power that can kill a bunch more. You gotta stop this Billy and get my fucking body back!"

Sam paused for a second, then screamed, "That's all I see . . . you fuck!"

He always made me feel all warm inside.

With all the over-the-top shit I've seen in my day, I'm still not one for signs, but even I had to step back and look at this fucked up situation. I wake up, narrowly escape being killed, get evicted, and get a package with Sam's head and a desperate plea to go to California. The way I figured it, I'd been in the D.C. area my whole life. It was time for a change of scenery.

I decided to go to California without much hesitation. If you knew me at all, you'd know this was crazy. The closest thing to impulsive I ever did was snort two lines of speed instead of one. I generally liked the cozy insanity of the nation's capital, but lately I'd been feeling an itch for change. Things had grown stagnant lately. Same old cases, same old creeps, same old monsters.

Of course, I'd been off the hard stuff for almost a year. I suppose that had something to do with the itch. I'd go to California, stretch my legs, and see what there was to see.

But first I had some details to take care of, and my ghoul of a partner, Mo'Lock, was nowhere to be found. We had no formal agreement, but I'd come to rely on the fact that he'd pop by and help me out on cases on an almost daily basis. I'd known him for years, and undead or not, I considered him my friend. It wasn't like him to disappear for more than a week at a time. It had been three since I'd last seen him.

I made a few calls around town, with Sam grumbling at me from the desk the whole time.

"Screw your girlfriend," he snapped. "Let's get this show on the road!"

The head was right. I had more pressing business than finding Mo'Lock. I had to deal with packing up and blowing town. I also had to figure out how the hell I would get Sam's head back to California. I'd most likely be flying, and there was no way on God's Green Earth that I'd be able to smuggle a human head past baggage check. No way around it: I had to mail Sam's head back to his house and meet him on the other end.

"Like hell you are!"

Sam wasn't too pleased with the idea.

"You have any better ideas?"

Sam almost tipped himself over. "Yeah, we rent a private plane and . . ."

"You gonna pay for it? I've got a pocket full of lint and half a Vicodin to my name."

"So how you gonna pay for your plane ticket, smart-ass?"

Sam was starting to get on my nerves. "That's one reason I need to track down Mo'Lock. He can loan me the cash."

Sam rolled his eyes and grunted, "I shoulda called in some real law enforcement."

That did it. "You already did, and he mailed you to me."

I lifted Sam's head and dropped him back in his box. He yelled and even tried to bite me. I packed him in tightly, with packing paper in his eyes and mouth, then sealed up the box.

"See you in Los Angeles."

I resealed the package and scrawled "return to sender" across the label with a thick black marker, since Dawson had put Sam's home address as the shipper. Sam kept yelling and whining like a sixty-year-old baby, so I gave the box a couple good hard shakes, then set it down while I surveyed my apartment.

My initial assessment stood firm; I didn't own shit. I packed some clothes, some books, and some papers. That was it. I made out a couple of labels with Sam's address on them and taped one to the box of weapons and the others to boxes full of shit I couldn't carry. If I had the time and money, I'd send for them. If not, I supposed I could live without most of it.

Mostly, I wished I could take the books. I had three shelves lined with volumes about everything from vampires to political conspiracy. They were the only thing besides drugs and alcohol I paid for.

Who knew, maybe I'd make it back before leatherface Judy threw it all out onto the street. I doubted it, though.

In only a matter of hours everything had changed. I looked around the office and thought about all the shit that had crawled through it and all the things that I'd fought and overcome. All of it started at that old desk. I ran my hand along the uneven surface and remembered the day Mo'Lock and I had stolen it from the office of a lawyer who represented a local fraud psychic who was selling curse cures.

His name was Doug Fleck—a big, fat, lying piece of shit. He actually had the balls to come around and look for the desk. I beat him half to death with a table leg.

Good times.

I got a little lump in the throat.

It was time to move on. I grabbed the bag I'd packed and kicked the package with Sam's head into the hall. I took one last look around. I'd miss it, but I knew I could do better. I flicked the lights off, and turned to go. That was the last time I saw my office-slash-apartment in Washington, D.C.

It didn't take me long to track down Brent for the third time in a day. He was at the end of his rounds, which put him only a few blocks away. His truck was parked beneath a tree to block the drizzle as he sorted outgoing mail into small bins. He knew why I was there.

"I still haven't seen Mo'Lock."

"I want to send this back." I handed him the resealed package with Sam's head.

"You don't want it?" Brent looked side to side, then leaned in close. "There's a fella's head inside, ya know."

I nodded and smiled. "I know. I just need it to go back. I'm going to fly out and meet it on the other side."

I watched the ghoul's face as he worked out what I said. Suddenly, there was clarity. His eyes widened, his head bobbed, he gave me a wink.

"I'll make sure it gets back for you, Cal," he said. "Don't you worry."

A yellow taxi pulled up and the driver, another neighborhood ghoul, leaned out the window and softly honked the horn.

Brent and I spoke in unison. "Hey, Simon."

"You seen Mo'Lock?" I asked.

The cab driver shook his head. "Not since last week. You got something you need done?"

I rocked on my feet. I thought I'd sneak away clean.

"Well," I said, "it look's like I'm leaving town."

Brent looked shocked. "For how long?!"

"For good, maybe. It's time for a change."

"Is it us?" Brent asked sincerely.

I shook my head, "Of course not. It's just . . . I dunno. It just feels like the right time to make a move."

Simon and Brent exchanged a look of disbelief. They were shocked, but they thought I might be fucking with them.

Simon got out of his taxi and joined Brent and me at the curb behind the open mail truck. "You're joking."

"No," I shook my head, "I'm not. I have some business in Los Angeles, so I thought I'd scope the city out while I was there."

"Los Angeles, huh?" Simon rolled his grayish tongue in his mouth. "Bunch of freaks out there from what I hear. And I mean that in the worst possible way."

"And it's sunny all the time," Brent added.

I held my hand out and caught some drizzle in my palm. "It's gotta be better then this."

Simon extended his hand.

"You'll be missed, Cal McDonald. The city won't be the same without you."

Brent got a little choked up when he shook my hand. I gave him a slap on the back and he pushed me away. Funny little guy.

There was a long silence. Then Simon said what we were all thinking.

"What about Mo'Lock?"

I shrugged. "He's MIA. I gotta go. It's urgent." I nodded at the taxi. "You wanna give me a lift to the airport?"

Simon took my bag without saying a word and loaded it into the trunk. I said goodbye to Brent and asked him to tell Mo'Lock I'd left. Brent promised to spread the word around the ghoul populace that I'd be out of town for awhile. I didn't want some freaks crawling into town thinking the place was unprotected.

Simon drove me to the airport. He took the scenic route, twisting up and down every fucking street in the city. On the way we went past the police precinct where I'd worked briefly as a cop. I got thrown out, but that's another story. Suffice to say the massive intake of drugs and police work don't always mix.

It occurred to me that I'd forgotten to tell my old pal Blout I was leaving, but I hadn't heard a word from him since the Edgar Cain case. I figured he need to distance himself from me for the sake of his job. He was up for Captain. He didn't need me fucking things up for him. Another normy out of my life. And people wonder why I surround myself with freaks?

The farewell tour continued, passing the Black Cat Club, the scene of many a drunken brawl, and around Dupont Circle. Dupont was known for its gay community, but it also had considerable vampire traffic. I'd nailed a few bloodsuckers to the walls of the tunnels beneath the Circle over the years.

Simon wove through downtown and down by the Mall where I got a final glimpse at the Capitol Building, the Smithsonian, and the Washington Monument in the distance. It was a funny thing. I'd lived in D.C. my entire life, and I never once went up in that fucking thing. I'd shot a creature who called himself the Master Eye off the top with a rifle once, though. He fell and exploded like a massive water balloon.

As we moved away from the Mall, I spotted the Lincoln Memorial beyond the reflecting pool and smiled. Far beneath the memorial is a cavernous pit where the city's ghouls gather. To this day, I think I'm the only human that was ever invited to attend.

I caught Simon glancing at me in the mirror and dropped the stupid grin. I figured it was as good as any time to ask him what I needed to ask.

"You got any cash I can borrow?"

Simon's sunken eyes flashed in the rearview. "How much you need?"

"What's a plane ticket to L.A. cost?" I said. Most ghouls worked almost around the clock, but they didn't have much use for the cash they made.

"Yeah," he said after a short pause, "no problem."

The rain had slowed to an annoying hot mist by the time the taxi dropped me off at the airport. It was crowded. A swell of people clogged the doors and the walkways trying to stay dry. I thanked Simon and walked away without ceremony. He watched me until a cop tapped his hood and told him to move it along.

Inside I bought my ticket and waited to board the plane.

For the first time, my thoughts went to what lay ahead of me. In D.C., I'd come to understand the workings of the strange world in which I lived. Don't get me wrong, there were always surprises. Outbreaks of the undead or new forms of bloodthirsty creatures wandered into my path, but they knew I knew my way around, and that's what made me strong. Heading out to the other coast meant a whole new set of rules. God knew what the fuck lurked out there.

I've always attracted the darker side of life. Ghouls, ghosts, zombies, werewolves, mummies, vampires, and all sorts of nasty, unnatural creatures. I have two rules that I live by. The first is that I don't go after them if they don't come after me. Number two is to break the first rule if someone's got enough cash to make it worthwhile.

And this thing with Sam? That had me worried. What kind of kid could conjure up that kind of power? We're talking about something Aleister Crowley tried to do and failed. Splitting a human body into two different times was no easy feat. I'd seen it done before, but none of the victims had ever survived. Sam probably knew that too. The old bastard must've been scared shitless.

I thought about Sam as we boarded. There was the distinct possibility that I would never find his body and reunite it with his head. Who knew what the kid had planned, or what would happen to Sam's head if the body was hurt or destroyed?

The whole thing freaked me out, and I knew why. It was purely selfish.

Sam was me. He was an older version of myself, a glimpse into my future. Was this how I'd wind up? Slowly being whittled down to a scar-covered nub until I was eventually outmaneuvered by some psychotic freak? Fuck. I wanted to think I was more than that. I wanted to believe that I'd eventually move away from this monster hunting crap and do something else. But I'd thought about it for years—shit, my whole life—and it never happened. Every time I attempted to turn my back on the strange, it came looking for me.

As the plane took off smoothly, I watched my lifelong home fade below me through the small, circular window until it disappeared behind the clouds. Just like that, I was gone. I settled into my seat and stared out the window steadily for the next few hours. Mostly I saw clouds, but occasionally we dropped altitude enough for me to get a glimpse of the ground below.

As we passed over Kansas or one of those little farmy states I spotted a small object moving in and out of the clouds beside the plane. Whatever it was, it was small and fast as all hell. It easily kept pace with us, swooping in and out, up and down, as if fighting the tremendous air disturbance the wake of the plane caused. Finally it swung close to the wing and I got a good look at the object. It wasn't an object at all. It was humanoid, a small, naked creature with a rough tan hide and leathery wings that moved like a hummingbird.

I'd never seen one up close and personal, but I was pretty sure it was a gremlin, the annoying troublemakers of the monster world. And, just my luck, I had one tracking my plane. I looked around the cabin and, by the calm demeanor of the passengers, I guessed I was the only one who saw the creature. I determined there was a specific pattern to the gremlin's swooping flight pattern. It was staying out of sight, but at the same time, slowly moving closer and closer to the wing.

We've all heard the stories. The little creatures are reported to feed on metal and are attracted to the huge man-made flying machines. Gremlins became famous in the 1940s during the war as a friendly symbol of Air Force sabotage.

But behind every legend there's a little shred of truth, and this little bastard was intent on destroying the wing of a plane with over two hundred people inside. I had to do something without upsetting the passengers. Screaming "there's a man on the wing!" these days could land you in federal prison for twenty years.

The creature had been gliding closer and closer, and finally it started taking quick swipes at the underside of the far tip of the right wing. The sharp talons on its large webbed hands tore the metal like paper with each swipe.

I looked over and saw an old woman sitting across the aisle from me. I had two businessmen types in the seats next to me, but they were fast asleep against one another thanks to multiple rounds of Bloody Marys.

"Excuse me, old lady?" I said.

She looked at me with pure disgust.

"Do you have a hand mirror? I have something in my eye."

She looked at me for a long time. I blinked my right eye repeatedly for sympathy. Finally she dug inside her enormously overstuffed purse and took out a small round mirror smeared with lipstick and chocolate and handed it to me across the two sleeping suits.

"Keep it," she said and crammed her purse under her seat.

I felt like telling her I was trying to save her cranky-ass life, but what was the use? She'd just think I was nuts and demand the mirror back. Old bitch.

When I looked back out the window, not more than sixty seconds since I last looked, the gremlin was latched on to the wing like a starving leech. It was gnawing at the tip with long, sharp needle-teeth. Now that it was stationary, I could see it was no bigger than a medium-sized dog. Its body was shaped like a small, naked man with dried leather wings. The wings reminded me of thin slices of beef jerky.

The little fucker was going to town, chewing and biting and tearing. Each swipe of his talons brought sparks, shredded steel, and sometimes wires.

I took the hand mirror and aimed it out the window toward the wing. The sun was behind the creature, so I tilted my hand up until the mirror caught the light. I reflected the beam back down toward the thing on the wing. The air was a little rough, so I had a hard time catching the little fucker with the beam, but I finally managed to level it right at his face. At first, it just lit up the gremlin's wide, ugly face. Fucker didn't even seem to notice until I shined the light into its eyes.

The gremlin looked up in a shot and squinted. Its eyes were perfectly round saucers of black, like headlights filled with darkness. I held the mirror as level as I could, keeping the beam aimed straight at its eyes. The stubby creature started to get agitated quickly and stopped gnawing on the wing. It swatted at the light with its claws, trying to knock it away. It got flustered and confused when I moved the light to its chest. It tried to brush it away and actually cut itself with its own claws.

It was a far better reaction than I'd anticipated, so I aimed the ray of light right at the gremlin's exposed genitals. The creature clung to the wing with one paw as it watched the light crawl down its body. When the beam stopped on its crotch, the creature swiped hard with its own talons and mutilated itself.

There was a stunned moment where the creature stared down at his shredded genitals with utter disbelief, then it lost its grip on the plane's wing and fluttered away like a trash bag in the breeze.

The flight was fairly uneventful after the gremlin incident. The suits next to me woke up over Arizona and started drinking again. The old woman read and reread the in-flight magazine so many times I wanted to slap it out of her hands, but that was about as exciting as it got.

As we descended into Los Angeles, I looked out the window and saw the desert and mountains turn to endless acres of homes with tiny, bright blue circles beside them. For a moment, I couldn't figure out what the circles were. Then I realized they were backyard swimming pools. I'd never seen so many pools in my entire life. They were everywhere.

That was the first tip that I was heading into some strange and unusual territory. Arriving at LAX was the second. The place was like nothing I'd ever seen and was crawling with ghouls, freaks, and unnatural beings of every variety known to, well, me.

I made my way out of the gate and spotted a couple of ghouls working a shoeshine stand. I gave them a nod. They just stared blankly and turned away. Nearby, a group of what looked like Armenian undead looked me up and down as I passed. To tell the truth, I didn't know exactly what they were. I could see they were dead, but the sun was out, so they weren't vampires. One thing was for sure: they reeked of evil.

I kept moving through the airport and everywhere I looked something stranger waited. It wasn't always something unnatural, at least not in the classic sense. I saw women with their skin pulled so taut on their faces that I could clearly see their skulls beneath the tight flesh and caked makeup. I saw men with suntans so deep that their flesh resembled old beef jerky. I witnessed some of the most bizarre fashion I'd ever seen, and I don't mean punk-rock weird. That I like. I mean huge gold sunglasses and white bell-bottoms with feathers and rhinestones on a sixty-pound woman who looked like she hadn't eaten since 1998.

Los Angeles would take some getting used to.

Everyone else veered toward baggage claim, but I'd reduced my life to one bag, so I made straight for the taxi stand downstairs. On the way, I had to walk through an army of pamphlet peddlers and beggars, all of them human. On my right a Scientologist flunky shoved a book at me. I slapped it away. On my left a Hari Krishna asked me how I was doing and tried to block my path. I plowed over him like a bulldozer.

Outside, the biggest shock of all waited. I stepped out of the air-conditioned building through the automatic doors and into the heat . . . and it was nice. It was hot, but the air was dry. It was nothing like back in D.C. where the humidity climbed to a suffocating 98 percent. Of course, D.C. was built on top of a swamp. This was desert weather. I couldn't believe it. I stood outside in the bright sun and enjoyed it. Now that was strange.

The cab driver wasn't a ghoul. He was an old black man who never so much as glanced at me through the rear-view mirror. I gave him the address for Sam's place and he took off like a bat out of hell. I expected to get a nice tour of the streets of Los Angeles, but instead the driver introduced me to the high-speed world of California freeways. I hadn't seen driving like that since I ran the speed course at the police academy. We were doing at least ninety-five and weaving in and out of lanes so fast I was thrown from one side of the back seat to the other like a rag doll.

About forty minutes and a hundred bruises later, the driver spun off the freeway and onto some actual city streets. It was here I caught the driver looking at me, and he spoke at last.

"First time in L.A.?"

I was crawling off the floor of the cab. "Yeah."

"Well, a fella that's never been to L.A. needs to see some sights," he said with a strange drawl. "How about I show you a movie star's house?"

I shrugged. "Sure. Sounds good." I was in no rush.

The driver careened wide around corners and over hills, until the scenery around us changed from distinctly urban to something like residential. The streets were unnaturally clean and the houses were huge, but what really struck me as odd were the palm trees lining the streets. You never saw anything like them back east, unless you went to Florida. But who the hell went to Florida?

He finally came to a stop at a corner where he pointed at a modest, but by no means small, Spanish-style house.

"See that?"

I nodded.

"That's the home of Mr. Don Rickles."

I stared. "Wow."

And that was the end of the celebrity homes tour.

The rest of the ride was a blur. The cab drove me down Sunset, which was all expensive shops and stores before turning into a solid mass of flashy signs and restaurants. From there he drove down an alley-like back road that wound like a snake, climbing steeply uphill before peaking and spilling us down on the other side. I knew enough about L.A. to realize we'd left the city proper and were headed into the dreaded San Fernando Valley.

The trees were more normal on this side of the hill, but the number of butt-ugly strip malls doubled, and the whole area was flat as a board. There were hills through the haze in the distance, but it was mostly endless suburbs as far as the eye could see. Talk about fucking scary.

Almost as soon as we drove over the hill, the cab made a couple of quick turns into a strange little residential area with single-story, squat-looking homes that resembled adobe forts, except these little forts had bars on the windows and graffiti tags all over the walls. I couldn't make out any of the graffiti. To me, it just looked like a bunch of spray-painted circles and squiggles.

The street looked rough, a compact ghetto made just for me. Kids were standing on the sidewalks in clusters, watching closely as the cab pulled up. I could feel their eyes on me, checking me out. I saw one kid point and another whisper to his partner as he checked his waistband for his gat.

They looked like they were going to start something until the cab stopped in front of Sam's address. Then they all turned their backs.

I laughed. Sam must have scared the crap out of them.

I paid the driver and thanked him for the tour. He sped out of there without saying a word. I hoisted my bag and walked toward the door, ignoring the eyes that watched my every step.

The yard was fenced in by a low, rusted chain-link fence. There wasn't a lawn to speak of, just a lot of dirt that looked like it had been dug up recently. The dirt was unsettled all the way around both sides of the house, like someone had started planting some shit then gave up.

The rest of the house was no prize. The white stucco walls were yellowed and stained, the gutters were broken, and the red clay shingles on the roof were cracked and split. The porch had once been a screened-in area, but someone had torn out the wire mesh and removed the door. Now all that remained was a green wooden frame around the outside of the deck. The place was a complete shit-hole.

At the door, I found the key Sam had hidden. Next to the mail slot was little piece of paper about the size of a fortune cookie strip that read "Burnett Investigations." Classy.

I unlocked the door and went inside.

It was pretty much what I expected, an old man's version of my place in D.C. It was part home, part office. There was a desk and a couch, some file cabinets, all kinds of clippings and weird pictures taped and tacked indiscriminately all over the walls.

It was a lot messier than my place. Actually, it was fucking disgusting. There were old food containers on the floor with both large and small black pellets along the walls. It looked like a wide variety of rodents used the place as a toilet. I cleared the couch of crap and threw my bag down.

The front step and mail box held no delivery slip—there was nothing but a pile of junk mail. I'd beaten Sam's head across the country, and without the head there wasn't a hell of a lot I could do, so I raided the liquor cabinet. It was the one thing that looked to be well stocked. I helped myself to some whiskey and beers and turned on the TV. Just when I had a decent buzz going, I heard footsteps outside the door. I reached for my gun, and realized it wasn't there. Then there was a knock.

The knock sounded timid, but I wasn't taking any chances. I found a Colt .45 in Sam's desk, checked to make sure it was loaded, and approached the door.

"Who's there?

From the other side of the door I heard, "Jerry."

"Who the fuck is Jerry?"

"You don't know me."

Fuck.

I tucked the gun away and yanked the door open. Jerry stood on the porch looking nervous. He was a kid, I'd say around eighteen or nineteen. He was shaking, with sweat running down his face. With some people you can see who they really are when they're afraid. This kid's eyes read innocent. I decided to give him a chance.

I gestured him inside, checked the street, and then shut the door.

The kid bobbled around the room before sitting on the couch. "I'm Jerry—Jerry Gallagher."

I gestured for him to go on. "And?"

"I've never done this. I'm not a narc or nothing, and I'm not even sure if anything is happening, Mr. Burnett."

I fought the urge to laugh. The kid thought I was Sam. He was here looking for help. I thought about saying something, but decided I was bored and went along with it. Shit, I had to wait for the head anyway. Might as well kill some time. What's the worst that could happen?

"Well, why don't you tell me what you think might be going on," I said, trying to guide him along.

The kid took a breath. "It's my roommates. I live in this loft downtown, you know, near Staples Center?"

I shook my head. What the hell was a staple center?

"Well, I've only been there a month or so, but I've been getting weird feelings about these two guys. There's five of us all together."

I nodded repeatedly, praying he'd get to the point. I found a pill in my pocket, probably speed. I hoped it would balance me out. The whiskey mixed with the time difference was making me woozy. My buzz was officially killed.

"Anyway, John and Sean live downstairs in the basement. At least that's what we call it, 'cuz it's below street level and doesn't have any windows. The rest of us live upstairs, and at first we thought maybe they were fags or something—which I wouldn't really care about. But now, I think something else is going on." The kid stopped and looked at me stupidly.

Suddenly I wanted to rip him off the couch and strangle him. He talked so much and so fast my head started to ache. But I egged him on anyway.

"And just what makes you think something else is going on between this Sean and John?"

Jerry sucked air to fuel up for his next rant. "Well, I hear noises down there late at night. Weird noises. At first I thought it was, you know, fag stuff. But then the other day they left the basement unlocked. They're usually real careful about keeping it locked. Anyway, I went down there with my other roommate, Myra—she's scared too—and we found this freezer. We opened it up and . . ."

The kid produced a small baggie, fogged with steam. "We found this inside. I kept it in the freezer upstairs 'til I decided to come here."

I took the baggie from Jerry and sat at Sam's desk. The bag was still cold. It was the "zip-lock" kind and it opened easily. The contents thumped onto the desktop—a human hand. A small, frozen, dismembered baby's hand, clenched in a tiny fist.

"Think you got something here," I said, poking the hand with my pen. "Are you the only one who saw this or who knows you have it?"

"No, Myra knows, but she's the one who talked me into coming to see you, Mr. Burnett."

I thought about coming clean with the kid, but blew it off. What did it matter to him what freak hunter he was dealing with?

I slid the frozen hand back into the baggie and looked over at the kid. I spoke nice and slow so I wouldn't slur and he'd understand the plan.

"I want you to take this back. Do you think you can get it back into the freezer without tipping off John and Sean?"

"I think so. Myra swiped a key off one of their desks. I don't think they noticed."

"Good, then put it back and announce that a friend from out of town is visiting. I'll be there around six."

Jerry looked me up and down. "You're kinda old."

I glared. "Then tell them I'm your retarded cousin from Alabama. I don't care, just make it sound good. I need to get in the house."

I escorted him out, getting the address and making doubly sure he understood the plan. I think he got it, but I was still nervous because he was. Nervous people screw up cases more than just about anything else.

He turned back to me. "Oh—uh—about money. How much is this going . . ."

"I knew the second you came in this was a freebie, kid. Pay me in beer." I shut the door in his face.

Back at Sam's desk I dialed info and got some numbers for local hospitals. I had them patch me through to the maternity ward. After four duds, I got some guy at a downtown hospital who could barely speak English.

"This is Dr. Jacobs, up in records," I said in a high whine. "Can you give me the numbers on the missing infants again? I can't find mine anywhere."

There was a pause, and I thought I was busted. "Ah, jes, jes, doker. This the same as jesterday. Jus' two. One Tuesday, an' one Thursday."

Bingo.

I slammed the receiver down. The hand looked newborn. It was too small to be much more than a week old. So, it seemed I had kidnappers on my hands, maybe Satan worshippers, or even cannibals. That would explain the freezer. That, or they were keeping it frozen to dispose of later. Whatever it was, these were sick fucks, and I had me a new case to kill the time until Sam's head showed up in the mail.

First thing I learned about L.A. is no car, no life. After Jerry left I had a few more drinks, then stood outside the house waiting for a taxi that never came. I stood there until it got dark. A small crowd of kids with bald heads and wife-beater tees were watching me from a house down the street. After I'd stood there for awhile, two of the teens strolled down and crossed the street to where I stood.

They were both Hispanic, and covered with tattoos. The older of the two had a teardrop tat beneath his left eye. They stood there staring at me for almost a minute before I turned and gave them a nod.

"You Sam's kid or something, dude?" Teardrop said.

"Just a friend."

"You waiting for something?" the other asked. "Looks like you're waiting for something."

"Trying to catch a cab."

The two guys busted up. They started laughing, falling all over each other like I'd just told them the funniest damn joke they'd ever heard. I stuck my hands in my pockets and nodded while I waited for the comedy show to stop.

Teardrop slapped my shoulder. "Where you from?"

"D.C.," I said.

"Oh, well, out here they ain't got cabs that drive around 'less you in Hollywood or some shit like that. Here you have a car, or steal a car if you have to. I'm tellin' you right now, ain't no cab coming on this street."

I looked at Teardrop and his buddy. "Rough neighborhood?"

They started to laugh again. "Don't look at us, man! Cabs don't come down this street 'cuz of your buddy, Sam. Shit, ice cream trucks don't even come here no more. That's one fucked up dude you got for a friend. I mean, we're cool with his ass and all, but he sure does have some weird-ass shit comin' around."

"My name's Cal," I said and stuck out my hand.

We shook. Teardrop's hand was bone cold.

"Welcome to the neighborhood. You staying around awhile?"

I shrugged and stared into Teardrop's eyes. "Maybe."

Teardrop touched the Sacred Heart tattoo on his chest with one hand and gestured to his buddy with the other. "My name's Benito and this here is Junior."

Benito concluded with a wide smile and I saw the fangs. He meant for me to see them. The boys were vampires, but I'd seen them in the sunlight, so something wasn't right.

"Good to meet you."

We all stood there in silence for a while. We were all smiles, but we were checking each other out, trying to figure whether we had a problem. Usually when I stood this close to a vampire I was either killing them or thinking about killing them. These guys didn't give me the slightest bad vibe. I decided to open the dialogue.

"You know another thing that's different here from D.C.?" I said.

Junior responded. "No, what's that?"

"In D.C., vampires can't walk around in the sun."

Benito looked at Junior and nodded, then they both looked at me.

"We ain't full-blown," Benito whispered. "That's why Sam don't stick a stake in our heart and shit. We can live off raw meat and, you know, the occasional snack."

"But we don't never hurt nobody, 'less they ask for it," Junior added.

I waited a few seconds then smiled.

"Then it looks like we're okay."

Benito gestured toward me. "So, you need wheels? You got some money?"

"A little."

"My cousin owns a rental place. You go there and he'll hook you up. Just tell him Benito Cruz sent you."

Benito called his cousin and told him to expect a big ugly white dude, then gave me walking directions to the lot. I thanked the semi-vampires and walked off. It was the first time in my life I'd turned my back on a vampire, but true to their word, they didn't attack. Nice neighborhood.

Benito's cousin's lot was a little dump of a place off Ventura Boulevard, but he had a nice selection of cars. I laid down a decent chunk of the cash Simon had loaned me and got set up with a jet-black '63 Pontiac Catalina. The car roared like a fucking lion. I probably should have went with a cheap Honda Civic or something, but the Catalina just cried out to me. Besides, I'd look like a jackass in the Civic. I put down as much cash as I could, but because I was "friends" with Benito, the cousin would let me pay off the balance later.

I rumbled from Ventura to the freeway and headed toward downtown Los Angeles. It was way past the time I said I'd meet Jerry, but I figured he'd wait.

I arrived at the warehouse loft a little before eight. The street was deserted. Strictly urban. I saw a couple crackheads milling around an alley, but that was it. I guessed downtown L.A. wasn't the happening spot for hipsters or the undead.

The pill I popped had hit a little harder than I'd expected, so I was pretty jumpy. I parked my new ride outside the drab building. It was flat gray with clouded, dirty windows and a door that looked like a loading dock. I hit the intercom beside the double steel doors.

No sooner had the bell rung than a voice started yelling from somewhere inside. It was a female voice, high pitched and panicked. She screamed that she'd be there in a second. My guess was that it was Myra.

Bingo. She answered the door wrapped in a towel, and her hair was dripping wet. She had a tattoo of flaming dice on her right shoulder and a tribal design around her wrist. Her hair was black and cut with shorter-than-Betty Page short bangs. I guess I was wrong about the hipsters.

"Oh, I thought it was Joey. Sorry, you must be Jerry's friend. Uh, you want to come in?"

"Yeah, that was the idea."

She pulled the door open a little more, told me to make myself at home, then scrambled up a cold flight of cement stairs. As I entered the warehouse, I noticed the stairs didn't go down any further. If there was a way into the basement that Jerry mentioned, I couldn't see it.

I followed Myra up the stairs. She was small and thin and looked like a spider monkey as she took the steps two at a time. Her towel had come open in the back. I looked away.

At the top of the stairs a door led into the loft. It was a wide open space with all sorts of mismatched furniture scattered around. There was artwork plastered on the walls and even a motorcycle being worked on in the far corner. There were beer cans by the case stacked neatly in the corner near a hand-written recycling sign. The walls were covered with haphazardly hung concert posters by artists like Coop and Shag. It looked like Jerry and his pals were full-blown, Creeper-wearing hipsters.

Above a sunken foam couch was a poster of John Travolta with his eyes gouged out, his teeth blackened, and horns drawn onto his forehead. I threw my bag aside and sat on the couch. In an area I couldn't see, I could hear Myra running back and forth, muttering loudly to herself about her hair. I wandered around the loft and glanced out the windows at the back of the building. Instead of the expected alley there was a small yard with grass and a fenced-in garden. I had to give the kids credit, it was quite a swinging pad.

As I lit a cigarette and settled back, I began to wonder where my little pal Jerry was. He knew I was coming. The little prick had better not have flaked on me. I'd strangle him for sure.

From the couch, sagging to the point where I nearly sat on the floor, I could see the door to an old-fashioned, steel-caged service elevator. That was your basement access right there.

After a couple of minutes, Myra appeared again. She was just sort of standing there, smiling, and staring at me as though she were sizing me up.

"You don't look like a detective," she said, walking toward me.

Fucking great. Jerry told her. Stupid kids can never keep their mouths shut. "Well, that's the point of being undercover. Any idea where our boy Jerry is now?"

She sighed. "No, I haven't seen him since he got back from your office." Then she looked me over in an odd sort of way, with her head tilted to one side. "How old are you?"

"How old do I look?" I shot back.

"Anywhere from twenty-five to forty-five," she smiled. "I can't decide."

I felt myself begin to flush red. "Somewhere in the middle."

Myra smiled pleasantly and adjusted her bangs without ever once taking her dark, intense eyes off me. Just when I thought she'd embarrassed me enough, she took another step. "You seeing anybody?" She gestured at my ringless hand. "You're not married."

I stared at her blankly, stunned, like she'd just asked me where the sky was located. What a stupid question.

Despite thinking much more, all I said was, "No."

Myra looked puzzled. "Why'd you say it like that? When was the last time you dated someone?"

That tore it. I leaned forward. "Hey, who's doing the investigating here?"

But she was unshakable. "It's been a long time, hasn't it?"

I usually have two responses to being cornered. One leaves somebody bloody on the floor. The other results in a lot of running. Because Myra was so attractive and straightforward, I chose neither and just answered the question.

"I don't date," I said. "People I like tend to wind up hurt . . . or worse."

Myra looked at me for a long time, but she wasn't judging me. She was trying to figure me out. Then she stopped and glanced toward the door. She looked back at me and nodded. Somebody was coming up the stairs.

After a moment, two guys appeared at the top of the stairway. John and Sean, I guessed. One was tall, with red hair and an expression somewhere between grim and nasty. He wore a silk skull and crossbones shirt with jeans rolled in fifties cuffs. The other guy was a bit shorter, but pleasant looking, with blond, slicked-back hair. They looked to be in their mid-twenties and both had big green army duffels slung over their shoulders.

Red walked right through the room without even so much as glancing our way and went straight to the service elevator. After noisily opening the cage, he waited impatiently as the blond stopped in front of us and placed the duffle down on the floor. I could see by the way the muscles in his forearms strained and relaxed that the load wasn't light.

"Man, that laundromat is a fucking pain," he said, and extended his hand to me. "Hi, I'm John. You must be Jerry's friend?"

We shook hands as I nodded and fake smiled. I lit a cigarette and watched him as he leaned over and picked up the bag. His legs tightened. His calves flexed. That was some heavy laundry. After flashing another grin, he met Red (who I assumed was Sean) in the elevator.

Myra was staring at me. "You want to go get some beer?" she asked.

"Yeah," I said.

I needed to talk to her. I got a distinct freak vibe off of both John and Sean, and I'd seen bags with that kind of weight before. The bags were either filled with bricks wrapped in cloth or chopped-up body parts, and the baby fist seemed to support the second possibility. Nothing weighs down like human tissue.

I didn't say anything to Myra, but I had the horrible feeling Jerry was in those duffels.

We left the loft and walked along the deserted streets. It was dark and about as empty as any urban downtown that I'd ever seen. Some cities are like that, even parts of D.C. There are city blocks that are only populated during the work week. At night and on weekends, they become ghost towns.

"The walk was a good idea," I said as we strolled.

"It wasn't all a lie. We do need beer." Myra watched the ground as she walked, as though she were searching for something.

The speed had washed away the effects of the drinks I'd had earlier. I was getting shaky and it was getting difficult for me to sift through the facts in my head. I wanted another hit, or maybe something else to soothe me. It was strange; being in a new town had a sobering effect. It seemed harder to maintain a decent buzz.

"So, what do you know about those two?" I asked Myra as we waited for the signal at an intersection. There wasn't a car in sight and I felt like an ass waiting to cross.

"Not a lot. We all moved in separately. I don't really know them all that well."

"Did Sean and John know each other before they moved in?" The walk sign lit and we began to cross.

"I don't think so."

"How long have they lived there?"

"I'd guess about four, five months."

"And how long have they been hanging around together?"

"Maybe about the last two months." Myra smiled, as if catching the drift of my questions. "It happened all of a sudden, like overnight."

"Anything else you can think of—odd things, I mean?"

Myra stopped and turned to me. She had a sheepish but earnest look on her face, as if what she wanted to tell me was a bit awkward.

"Well . . . someone's been shitting in the backyard. I think it's John or Sean."

"Weird."

We continued walking to the store. My head was swimming with duffle bags, baby hands and yard-shit. I needed a drink, or a smoke. Night had fallen and there was a murky pink haze in the air.

As we walked, we passed an alley. Standing in the shadows was a tall, thin, ghostly pale man. His eyes were wide and vacant, but they followed our every move.

As we passed he whispered, "Ready for the shit to fly, Cal?" His voice was raspy and dry.

He knew me. Word traveled fast among the dead.

"Not just yet, thank you," I tossed back as we passed. I heard him snicker. He liked my joke.

As we were about to turn the corner, the guy yelled after me as if he forgot something, "Somebody came around looking for you!"

I stopped and turned. "Yeah? Who?"

The dead man shrugged.

I flipped him off and kept walking.

Myra was staring again. "What was that?"

I smiled. "A ghoul. Pretty harmless, really. They lurk around, acting creepy."

Myra nodded. She was part of the same generation as me. Raised on TV and movies about vampire lovers, joke-cracking psychos, and little girls possessed by the devil. There was a calm acceptance that isn't found in older folks. "What was that he said?"

"Some ghouls get their jollies taunting the living with stories about a 'day of the monsters.' They aren't usually superstitious, but they all seem to believe one's coming. There will be nothing but darkness and all the monsters of the world will roam free. Blah, blah, blah. Bunch of bullshit, gives them something to occupy their dried-up brains."

We finally got to a store where the beer was cheap enough to satisfy Myra, so I waited outside while she went in and bought it. I asked her to grab me some smokes and a new lighter. Mine was dead. She was in and out in no time with a case of good, cheap cerveza, the kind that didn't give you a hangover, just kept you farting for a week. Fine by me. I offered to carry the case, but she refused.

As we strolled back to the loft, a police car cruised by us slowly. I didn't want to, but I looked over anyway. The cops inside the squad car were clean, slick, and blond. They checked us out and then moved on. I must've tensed up. Myra noticed.

"You're not a cop, are you?" Myra asked, with suspicion in her voice.

"I was, for about a year. I'm a private investigator now."

"What happened?" she walked beside me with a spring in her step, looking me right in my eyes.

"Drug test. I failed with flying colors."

Myra smiled. My slipshod career as a law enforcement officer seemed to have scored me some points. I decided to give it a test run.

"Do you think there's any way you could get John and Sean out of the house? I want to get a look at that basement."

"God, I don't know. Maybe John, but Sean won't even talk to me."

"Forget it. How about just offering them some beer? Maybe distract them and give me a chance to check them out closer."

"Sure, John's a classic freeloader. He'll stampede for free alcohol."

Back at the loft, we put the beer in the refrigerator and settled into the living area. Myra showed me some of her artwork. It was good. The subject matter—hotrods and chicks—was a bit tired, but she had talent.

I could hear one of the two suspects coughing in another area of the warehouse. Choking on a baby, I thought, then dismissed the idea. No use jumping to conclusions until I knew exactly what I was dealing with.

On Myra's request, we settled in on the couch and commenced drinking and smoking. I drank down two cans of beer in the time she polished off one. It was the speed. My tolerance was up. My teeth tingled.

After a while, I heard the coughing again and this time it was close by. I looked up to see John standing at the entrance to the kitchen area.

"Mind if I grab a beer?" he asked, smiling.

"Help yourself," Myra and I said together.

I turned and winked at her. She giggled and put her hand on my knee.

In the kitchen I heard the fridge open and close, then John coughed, hocked, and spit. Lovely.

By the time he came into the room, I needed another beer. He settled into the chair beside the couch as I moved past, into the kitchen. He watched me, smiling like it was the only expression he could muster.

In the kitchen, I grabbed the rest of the six we had started and threw its plastic holder into the trash. That's when I saw where John had spit. And, more importantly, what he'd spit. Spattered against an old carton of milk was a sizeable wad of grayish phlegm.

That wasn't strange in itself, but what was mixed in with the slime was: thick black hair, and lots of it.

It seemed John had a hairball.

With suspicions flying like machine gun shells, I walked back to the main room where John and Myra were discussing the rent, something about who owed what. John had produced some Jim Beam (a welcome sight) and offered the bottle to me before my ass had even hit the couch. I took a huge swig that made both of them whistle. I was a little embarrassed, but the whiskey washed it away in seconds.

"So, did Jerry ever show his sorry ass?" John asked, taking a timid swig.

Myra cracked her second beer. "Not unless he came in while we were out."

John shook his head, looking right at me without losing that smile for a single second. "Shitty thing to do. I mean, inviting you, then disappearing."

His grin widened as he finished speaking. There was a black hair stuck in his teeth.

I decided to play it. His cocky attitude was pissing me off.

"You've got something in your teeth," I said.

He didn't react at all. He just plucked the hair from his teeth and flicked it away. "You visiting long?"

Before I could answer, a crash and a quick yell came from downstairs. John and I both jumped to our feet simultaneously. I don't think he knew he was doing it, but he had his hand against my chest to prevent me from moving. When he did realize, he removed his hand. The smile returned instantly.

"Sean is such a klutz. I better go see what he broke."

He moved fast to the service elevator, and then he was gone, into the basement. I needed to get down there. I knew I'd find all the proof I needed to figure out exactly what the hell they were up to and nail these fuckers.

I turned and looked at Myra.

"I think it might be a good idea for you to get out of here," I warned.

She shook her head. "I'm staying right here."

"I thought you had a date."

"I lost interest." She smirked just enough to turn my beaten old face red, then came up to me and put her hand on my cheek.

She started to lean toward me, eyes beginning to close slightly. All of a sudden there was a buzz in the air. She had been flirting with me the whole time and I hadn't even noticed. Now, as she moved toward me, all I could do was stand there like a lug and stare. But before we could connect, the elevator started coming back up. I was shaking, and it had nothing to do with danger.

Peril I could take. Women made me shiver.

Myra and I stepped apart as the elevator opened and John came out. He had a scratch on his cheek. It was light, but I could see four jagged red lines and the glistening of wet blood. John had been clawed by something. I tensed up, knowing things were about to get bad.

John didn't walk over to us; keeping his distance instead. He just stood there with the fake smile all but gone. He had a dreamy, disoriented look about him, like he was drugged or suddenly overcome with fever. He mumbled something about beer and suddenly walked into the kitchen. I gave Myra the silent "scram" signal, but she wasn't having any of it. She had no idea what we were dealing with. To tell the truth, neither did I, but I had my guesses. None of them were good.

"Myra, could you give me a hand?"

It was John calling from the kitchen. His voice was different. In fact it seemed to change as he spoke. It went from normal to a low grumble in mid-sentence.

I shook my head at Myra, but she shook hers right back. "It's okay," and she left the room before I could stop her.

I don't know what was wrong with me. Maybe the new surroundings threw me off my game. I couldn't get my bearings on the situation. I felt trapped and exposed. I was acting like a guest in someone's house even though there was danger in the air. I had to force myself into action.

I checked my gun, making sure it was loaded, then tucked it back into my belt as I moved quickly toward the kitchen. The hairs on my arm stood on end.

I halted just outside, jumping across the entryway to get a quick assessment of the situation inside. As I moved past the door, the service elevator behind me went down to the basement on its own. In the kitchen, I saw blood, a huge swelling pool on the floor.

I feared Myra was already dead.

John thought he was fast, but I heard the noises he made—claws clicking on the ground, clothes tearing beneath a growing body. I knew what I was dealing with. John and Sean were motherfucking, baby-eating, friend-murdering, ass-licking, piece-of-shit werewolves!

I ducked back toward the couch and tried to look normal. John came through the door, but he was covered in shadow. I couldn't get a clean look. He was human, but his clothes were ripped. I didn't want him to suspect that I knew so I let out a momentous belch and picked up the bottle of Beam. It seemed to work. He came striding into the room smiling.

Then his clothes began shredding from his body. His hands and feet were already claws and paws.

There was nothing I could do but sit there, holding the bottle dumbly, watching him transform in front of me. He seemed to be in pain, but at the same time getting some kind of orgasmic pleasure out of it. His body twisted, expanded, and contorted as hair sprang from every inch of his now-naked body. His snout pushed out and his ears grew upward into points. His eyes turned into wide, green-flecked circle and, I swear to God, he still had that fucking annoying, fake smile. That's what made me mad and propelled me into action.

I threw the bottle of whiskey into his face.

It shattered against his snout, whiskey spraying his face and eyes. He let out a deafening howl of agony. I knew Sean would arrive any second, so I leapt at the flailing beast, jumping over the table with my new lighter in hand, and tackled him. We both went down with a brutal crash. His claws raked my back, my skin split, and I felt the warmth of fresh blood wetting my sweatshirt. Panicked, I jammed the lighter against his head and flicked it. His head burst into flames, like grandma's wig in the fireplace.

He screamed and threw me hard backward into the wall. I felt a rib bend and snap, and the weight of my gun falling onto me as I flipped backward.

Behind me, Sean was coming up the elevator. Above the howls of the flailing, burning werewolf I could hear him barking impatiently inside the cage. I leapt to my feet and tried to stop the elevator, but it was useless. The controls were somewhere else. All I could do was look down through the mesh and watch as a second, larger werewolf came up to the floor.

I ran, jumping over the flaming monster, and grabbed a chair. Before Sean could open the elevator gate, I jammed the chair legs into the mesh on both sides of the gate. He crashed against the meshed steel from the other side and howled. His weight bent the steel door, popping ancient rivets from their sockets and splintering flecks of paint. He was fucking huge. The chair would hold him inside the cage for a minute, tops. I had to get the hell out of there.

Suddenly, John grabbed me from behind and raked his claws across my cheek. I reeled around. He was still on fire, swinging blind. His eyes were seared shut, welded by melted flesh and fur. He howled. I made my move and shoved the gun into his mouth, pulling the trigger again and again until I heard only empty clicks. John was on the floor twitching and bleeding. The back of his wolf-like head was gone.

Everything was moving fast. My back was to the elevator door. Sean was beating it down, pounding the thick mesh apart one powerful blow at a time. I scanned the room for anything to use as a weapon, but I was panicked and bleeding badly. I didn't need anything in particular, no silver bullets or wolf's-head cane. All those myths were total bullshit. I just needed something sharp, flammable, or blunt to bash its skull in.

I ran into the kitchen and my worst fears were confirmed. Myra was dead, sprawled on the floor. Her throat had been viciously removed, her face frozen in her last second of life. Her eyes were wide, mouth agape. She saw her killer before he scratched out her windpipe.

I hardly had time to react as Sean's clawed, red-haired fist came smashing through the steel mesh of the antique elevator. My gun was empty. I was out of options, so I ran for the stairs and out into the streets. Cowardly maybe, but until I had a plan or some kind of weapon, it was my only choice.

It didn't buy me much time, though. Sean was big, fast, and angry, and he was on my ass in no time flat. All werewolves are so fucking angry. That's why I hate dealing with them. Of all creatures, they're the most unreasonable. There's just no talking to them.

I knew I didn't have time to get into my car, and I wasn't about to let that big red freak have at my slick paint job, so I bolted down the desolate street toward what I now recognized as the Staples Center. Maybe if we hit a populated area he'd give up and turn around. I paused and looked behind me. At the end of the street, right next to the Catalina, a huge red wolf stood on hind legs. I also noticed a piece of paper on my windshield. If I got a ticket I'd really be pissed.

Sean came straight at me. I had about a hundred yards on him, but he was fast as shit. When he dropped on all fours he could probably outrace a car. I didn't wait to find out if my guess was right. I bolted toward the intersection where Myra and I had stood only an hour earlier. Traffic had picked up considerably. Maybe I could get him hit by a car.

I kept right on running. Suddenly, people were everywhere. A stadium event must have let out, changing the ghost town into a mob scene. Traffic was heavy, but I didn't slow down—not even slightly. I ran right into the intersection with Sean nailed to my butt. Unfortunately, the plan (if you could call it that) didn't go quite as well as I'd hoped.

I got mowed down as soon as I hit the street, rolling over a car's hood and flying through the air like a scarecrow shot out of a cannon. Horns and brakes blared, but above it all, I heard the howling cry of the werewolf as he leapt after my rag doll body. There was chaos, people screaming and yelling out in confused terror. I lifted my head and there he was, the biggest fucking werewolf I'd ever seen. He was poised over me, arm raised, about to slash me open.

There was nothing I could do. I was dead meat.

Then another car ran me over, hitting Sean too. I guess you could call it one of those good/bad things. I felt the tires roll over my legs. It was fast, but it still hurt like a bitch. I heard Sean howl as the car dragged him into the intersection. Another car came screaming out of nowhere, smashing him between it and the first car.

As I crawled to my feet, the huge, red-haired werewolf ripped the hood off the first car with a single stroke and threw it into the windshield like a massive, deadly Frisbee. The hood shattered the glass, decapitating the two people inside. It all happened so fast I hardly had a chance to react. Bedlam and blood engulfed the street.

To make matters worse, Sean-wolf was still alive and madder than hell. He turned away from the smoldering wreckage and glared right at me. His stare bore into me, human eyes bizarrely pierced through the animal features. He wanted to be sure I saw what he did next. He effortlessly lifted and threw aside the offending car with its headless passengers. I watched dumbly as the car tumbled over the curb to the sidewalk like a crushed beer can.

I weighed my options again, and once more decided to run like hell. I was surprised I could even move. I was covered with blood, my back stung, my chest ached with every stride, and I could hear Sean closing in behind me. His breathing was a loud, angry rasp.

Up ahead a few yards, I spied the alleyway where the ghoul had been standing earlier. He was still there, this time gesturing for me to come. At first I thought he was fucking with me, but then he spoke.

"This way, Cal," he rasped. "This way."

I ran into the alley, moving so fast that I hardly saw the ghoul's creepy grin as I passed. "Thanks," I panted. "What's your name?"

"Emek."

"I owe you."

The end of the alley divided into three directions, so I stopped running and turned. What I saw was unbelievable. Emek was on top of the werewolf's head, with his arms and legs wrapped all the way around the spinning beast's face. But that wasn't the best part. My new pal Emek was laughing, flailing one arm high like he was busting a bronco.

It lasted all of thirty seconds.

The werewolf ripped the ghoul off his head and slammed him to the pavement. Then, with a series of lightning-fast swipes, he ripped Emek's torso to ribbons. Throughout the thrashing, the ghoul kept laughing.

I managed a smile, and then ran to the right. What I knew, and what the Sean-wolf clearly didn't, was that you can't kill a ghoul. At least not that way. They're undead, for Christ's sake! Maybe Emek had bought me a little time. I ran and ran. The pain in my legs was terrible and I was praying I hadn't broken them. Either way, I'd need a hospital if I got out of this.

Any hopes of escape were quickly dashed as I rounded the next turn. I learned the hard way that some L.A. alleys are dead-ends. Not only was Sean mere feet behind me and closing, but I was running straight toward a tall wooden-plank fence that was way too high to jump or climb. Sean's claws scraped my shoulder, and I felt his breath at the back of my neck.

This was it, I thought. This is how I'd die.

I had one chance, and I took it. I jumped, throwing myself into the fence as high and close to the center of the timbers as I could. I hit the fence sideways in a ball and felt the wood splinter on impact. The broken boards flipped backward, pointing behind me as I'd hoped, and exploded into a mass of pointed shards.

Rolling, I heard the sounds I'd prayed for: a hard impact followed by the gurgling of the Sean-wolf impaled on the broken fence.

I hit the ground and leapt to my feet, but immediately fell again. I couldn't get up. I was a mess, but at least I was alive. Sometimes the best plans come out of sheer panic.

Not five feet from me was Sean, human again, impaled on a dozen broken planks of wood. He was still alive, just barely. He craned his head up toward me as I used a trash can to help me to my feet. Blood was pouring from his mouth and one eye was gone. The socket bled freely.

His one eye looked pathetic and sad, as though he wanted to say something to me. Whether it was "fuck you" or "thank you," I couldn't tell. Frankly, I didn't care.

"Tough luck, dog-boy," I said, hobbling away as the cops showed up on the scene.

The hospital was nice about the whole thing. Hospitals generally like me. I give them lots of business and tell them stories they don't believe. They patched me up, pumped me full of dope, and handed me to the cops. The LAPD were a different matter, but for the same reasons; they don't like my stories or my business. They grilled me for hours and hours even though I was in a deep morphine haze. I told them the story—the truth—over and over. Of course, they didn't believe a word, but finally one of the little geniuses sent a car over to the loft.

They found what I'd described—as well as the body of Jerry Gallagher in the freezer—with pieces of several others. They found John's body outside the kitchen door and enough evidence to link John and Sean to a long series of murders dating back a couple of months. Evidently, there had been a sudden spike of missing persons in the downtown area and from nearby hospitals. The thefts were Sean and John's attempt to lay low. Eventually, though, their bloodlust got the better of them and they started attacking people on the street.

There was only one part of my story that didn't check out. The cops found blood in the kitchen, but they didn't say anything about Myra's body.

No Myra.

I could only guess what had happened to her. Probably nothing good. Whatever the case, she was out of my hands now. Probably long gone. In a way, if she did turn into one of those things, I was happy for her. At least she was alive. I liked her. I'd hate for her to have died that way.

The LAPD were kind enough to let me go at four AM with their usual warning to get a real job. They warned that if I wanted to operate in Los Angeles I'd better get the proper license. Fuck them. Where the hell do you get a license for what I do anyway? Idiots.

I drove back to Sam's place feeling every slice and break on my body. Total: two hundred plus stitches, a broken rib, twisted ankle, and bruises the size of footballs everywhere. Overall, I'd say I was damn lucky to be alive. And my pay for all this was one big-ass zero.

I was glad to be back at Sam's. It was cozy, in a pathetic, disgusting sort of way. There was beer in the fridge, whiskey on the desk, and an answering machine full of angry bill collectors that I didn't have to worry about because, for once, they weren't after me. I shed my clothes, shredded and crunchy with dried blood, and took a long shower.

When I came out, she was waiting for me in the living room.

Myra squatted, snarling at me in her wolf form. She must have followed me. She was small and still feminine, but mean looking, with glaring red eyes that didn't blink. Her claws extended and retracted over and over.

I tried to talk to her, to calm her down and tell her we didn't have to do it this way, but she was gone. Her eyes showed no sign of recognition.

I backed away slowly, but with every step I took she advanced two. She was so close that I could feel her hot breath on me.

"Myra," I whispered, "Walk away. Don't do this."

The she-wolf just growled.

I was fucked for the second time in a night. I kept backing away, but she kept coming. Soon, my back was against a wall with nothing in reach.

I slugged her as hard and fast as I could. She wasn't expecting that, and she reeled backward, losing her balance. I did it again.

This time I caught her right in the snout, and she yelped and swiped at my chest, catching a bit of skin. Before she recovered I grabbed the desk chair and smashed it across her head.

She was down, and hurting, so I hit her again, then again, until all I was holding were two splintered chair legs.

I paused, for too long. She was up and coming at me with murder in her animal eyes. I grabbed the whiskey bottle off Sam's desk and smacked it across her face. It shattered, spraying her with burning liquid. It was the second werewolf in one night that I'd downed with whiskey, but shit, you've gotta stick with what works.

Myra was blinded, taking swipes at me and wailing like a wounded dog. I had precious little energy left, and had to think fast. I was staying just out of her reach. She was temporarily blinded, but her vision was clearing fast. Soon she'd have me. I began to make noises as I moved. She followed, flailing at the air without result. Finally, I had her in place. I took one of the shattered chair legs and rammed it through her heart.

She stumbled backward, blood spouting like a fountain from the hole in her chest. By the time she hit the floor she was dead, and human.

I was too tired to think. Simultaneously, I dialed for the police and dug for another hit of speed, since it looked like I was going to be spending what was left of the night chatting with the LAPD boys yet again. But as the phone rang, something began to happen. Myra's body smoked and sizzled like hot bacon on the floor.

"LAPD. What's your emergency?"

I hung up and watched as Myra's body sizzled down to a bubbling mass, then to ash. Within a minute she was gone. Sometimes that happens. I don't know why.

Three days passed without Sam's head arriving in the mail. I spent the entire time in a drunken, alcohol-and-painkillers-induced stupor. I felt like shit. My wounds ached and had me worried. Any number of things can happen when a lycanthrope gets their paws on you. Usually you die. Sometimes you turn into one of them, sometimes you go crazy from a weird fever with rabies-like symptoms. I'd caught the wounds pretty early and had the nurse at the hospital pump me with antibiotics. I just had to keep an eye on the bites and scratches and hope I didn't suddenly develop a craving for Alpo.

I kept thinking about Myra leaning in to kiss me, then a couple hours later lurching forward to kill me. How fucked up was that? It seemed I'd traveled across the country to live the same screwed-up life I always had. I guess I was a fool to think it would be any different, but deep inside, I'd hoped for more.

And though I tried not to think about it too much, the absence of Sam's head had me more than a little tweaked. I had the address of the kid who separated Sam from his body, but I didn't want to risk anything without having the head, too. The downside was that the kid had more time to do whatever the fuck he wanted with the body.

I'd woken up around three that afternoon with a massive headache. I wanted nothing less than absolute quiet as I attempted to pull my head up from the couch. I had to be slow and careful getting up, lest I make noise and send my brain into a spiral of pain. I eased my stiff and sore body over the edge of the couch until my feet were near the floor. I didn't dare open my eyes. My eggshell skull barely contained my rattled brain.

Had I thought about it, I would have remembered the floor was covered with cans and bottles. My feet hitting the ground sounded like a garbage truck dumping its load. I screamed, eyes shooting open. I was dead center in a room of pain.

"Fuck! Fuck! Fuck! Fuck! Fuck!"

Somehow I made it to the bathroom, where I swallowed any pills that gave promise of relief, and then sat on the toilet until it was dark again. I drank the remains of a beer I found on the floor next to the shower and after a while I started to feel better.

I threw up. Felt even better.

I walked into the kitchen and grabbed what was left in the Mr. Coffee and drank it straight from the pot, realizing too late that I hadn't made coffee since I'd arrived. With my last gulp, I felt something solid slide down my throat.

I needed some time to recover. It had only been a few days since the werewolf debacle and I was still suffering badly. Half of my stitches had gotten infected. The wounds throbbed constantly, no matter what I put on them or how they were dressed.

Some downtime was just what the doctor ordered. But my life just never seems to work that way. Things were about to get back to the bizarre.

Outside the house, someone was leaning on their car horn. I tried to ignore it. I laid back down and covered my head with a pillow, but nothing would make that fucking sound stop. Finally, I grabbed the .45 and marched out the front door, ready to shoot the person in the car right through the fucking eye.

But it wasn't a person, and it wasn't a car. It was a U-Haul truck with a ghoul driver. I knew him. It was Mo'Lock.

A wide smile spread across my face. I couldn't help it. I put the gun away and walked toward the curb as he climbed out of the truck's cab.

"What the hell are you doing, you crazy fucking ghoul?!"

Mo'Lock grabbed me by my shoulders. The corners of his mouth curled ever so slightly, which for the undead was a sign of almost total joy.

"I got your message," Mo'Lock said. "From Simon. I packed your stuff and drove out here as fast as I could."

I ignored him and pointed at the U-Haul. "That's my stuff?"

"Everything you left behind."

"Where the hell were you? I looked everywhere for you before I left," I said, the slightest hint of aggravation in my voice.

The ghoul looked sheepish. "New Jersey."

"New Jersey?!" I hit myself in the head. "What the fuck is in New Jersey?!"

The ghoul walked away without answering and opened the back of the truck. The back was loaded with all of my crap, every last little scrap of paper I'd left behind. He'd even packed the rotten food from the kitchen and the trash from my office wastebasket. Stupid ghoul.

We got the truck unpacked pretty quickly. It soon became clear just how alike Sam and I were: the house now had two desks, two pairs of filing cabinets, two couches, and so on. We had double loser supplies.

As we emptied the last load, I looked up the street and saw Benito and his pals. They waved at me. I waved back. Then I spotted a large figure walking up the sidewalk toward the house. It was Emek, the ghoul who'd helped me out with the wolf-boy.

Mo'Lock looked at the approaching ghoul. "Who's that?"

"Emek. He's cool."

"He's undead."

I winked at Mo'Lock. "Jealous?"

Emek walked up to us, stopped, and stood silent before us, a living corpse. His posture gave the appearance of a loosely dangling marionette. He was shorter than Mo'Lock by a foot and had light, close-cut hair. There was a lonely quality about him that surprised me. Ghouls back east are pretty social. They don't have much to do with the living, but they interact with each other quite a bit.

Emek looked nervous. You don't see this much with the dead. When you do, it usually means trouble.

I introduced him to Mo'Lock and they exchanged undead pleasantries in a babbling mish-mash of English spoken at a superhuman rate. I figured they were comparing notes on undead life on the east versus the west.

Emek's nervousness set me on edge. But he'd saved my sorry ass, so I'd hear him out, if the two ghouls ever decided to shut up. I broke up the chat and invited them both into the house. As we walked to the front door, both ghouls looked at the grassless yard with the huge grooves gouged into the yard.

"Nice lawn," Mo'Lock said. I told him to fuck off and pushed him into the house. It was good to see the stupid fucking ghoul.

"So what's up?" I asked Emek. "Speak to me."

I was sitting on Sam's couch. Mo'Lock stood near the window, eyeing the new ghoul with a suspicion I'd never seen in him before. His entire stance was rigid and stand-offish, so Emek lingered awkwardly near the door. Ghouls always preferred to stand. Again, I don't know why. They're a mysterious bunch.

Emek's eyes were wide, like those fucking awful paintings my grandmother had an overzealous affinity for: those doe-eyed punks with flowers and puppies. His teeth were tight together, pale lips parted as though he was freezing to death.

Finally, he spoke. "Cal McDonald," he said, "I've come to warn you."

I glanced over at Mo'Lock and bit my nails.

"Warn me?" I lit a cigarette and tossed the match.

"There's a guy in town. He heard you were here and what you've done," Emek stammered. "Now he's looking for you."

The new ghoul was really agitated. His palpable fear freaked me out more than the warning.

I let his words sink in, flicked my ashes on the floor, took a nip of whiskey, and looked from one ghoul to the other.

"And?" I said in a bored voice.

Mo'Lock moved around to the side of the couch. "How does anyone know that Cal is in Los Angeles?"

Emek looked at Mo'Lock. "Word is out. Everybody knows."

I leaned back in the couch. "I'm a fucking celebrity."

"Not exactly," Emek said, looking around the room. The whites of his eyes almost eclipsed the tiny black specks of his pupils. If he had irises, I couldn't see them. Those pin-prick pupils dug right into me, and my cigarette dropped from my lips. Something in his tone got my heart going. There was weirdness in the air. I couldn't put my finger on it, but something was definitely wrong.

I picked up my smoke. When I sat back up, he was looking at me with the same stare. He hadn't flinched.

"You don't get it," Emek said. "This guy's very bad news. He's been running the L.A. underworld for a long time."

"He some kind of magic type?" I was in no mood. The pain in my wounds was really coming on strong. I had a scrape on my shoulder that stung like a bitch.

The ghoul leaned forward. "No. He's a vampire. The biggest, meanest, and oldest one ever. No one's even seen him for over fifteen years. He doesn't need to hunt anymore. He's got things that do that for him. The only time he surfaces is when he's got some score to settle. It seems he's picked you. If I was you, I'd be worried."

"I am," I yawned. "I'm very, very worried. What's this big shit's name?"

"David."

"The vampire's name is Dave?"

"Well . . . um . . . yeah."

I glared at the ghoul. "That's not the most fear-inspiring name I've ever heard. Yours scares me more."

Even Mo'Lock let out a little breathy laugh. I shot Mo' a look and wink.

Emek suddenly slapped his hand on the coffee table, agitated. "I didn't name him! The point is, this guy's after you. Word has it he's holed up at the old Houdini house in Coldwater Canyon."

"What's he gonna do, saw me in half?"

"You do what you want. We're even now." He turned and stomped toward the door. "Good luck."

I stood up. "Whoa, whoa, whoa. Hold up there, Emek."

The ghoul stopped at the door, upset. He thought I wasn't taking him seriously and thereby disrespecting him. I put my hand on his shoulders.

"Look, I wasn't taking any shots at you," I told him. "I've dealt with a lot of these freaks before, so I make fun. That's all."

Emek nodded. "Let me ask you this, Cal. When was the last time you dealt with werewolves and vampires in the same week?"

I looked at Mo'Lock and we both shrugged. The new ghoul had me there. That was pretty weird. I deal with a lot of shit compared to the normal world, but authentic cases of the supernatural are pretty few and far between, even for me.

"Look," I said, "I'll check this Dave shmuck out and see what his beef is, okay?"

Emek pointed at his sunken eyes. "Look at everything differently. Something is in the air."

"Uh, okay."

With that he was gone. Mo'Lock and I stood in the door and watched him walk out of the gate, past the U-Haul, and down the sidewalk.

It wasn't that I didn't take Emek's warning to heart—I did believe him. I just wasn't scared. I was too distracted by the pain of my wounds. I lifted my shirt to look at one of the bigger ones on my chest. It was definitely healing; there was no discoloration. It just throbbed.

Mo'Lock made a disgusted face. "You should have those looked at."

I vowed to go to the doctor if it didn't feel better in a week or two. At the moment, I had to get myself psyched about this Dave fellow. This vampire.

I could sit and wait for him to come after me, or go get him. Both choices seemed a little stupid, for different reasons. Waiting was boring—I'd had my fill of that, wasting time until Sam's head arrived. But going after him meant I was sure to get into a scrap, and I didn't really feel like putting my body through any more punishment just yet. Fortunately, I was now a bit more prepared for vampires since Mo'Lock had been kind enough to lug my shit cross-country.

In one of the boxes, among piles of papers and back issues of *Speculator Magazine*, there was a cigar box filled with my vampire-killing supplies. I sat at Sam's desk and examined the contents.

Inside was your standard Holy Cross and its companion vial of Holy Water, along with two wooden stakes and a Star of David to use against the rare, but deadly, Jewish vampire. The real reason I dug the box out, though, was six custom-made hardwood .38 caliber bullets.

I'd had them made about a year ago, after a couple of strutting jackass vampires were running around the Mall killing off tourists. I killed them with stakes, but what a pain in the ass! Most vampires have a tendency to wake up before the stake's all the way in, which kind of upsets them. They get hopping mad and start fighting back. That's exactly what happened, so I had to forget the stakes and go to Plan B. I burned one and hacked the other with an ax. It was a big fucking mess. By the time I'd downed them, I'd broken both my legs and one of my arms in three places. No fucking way I was going through that again: hence, the wooden bullets.

Just for the record, you don't need wooden bullets to stop a vampire. I've killed some with straight-up lead ammo. Shit, I killed one with a hammer! But it takes almost fifty shots to blow enough holes in them to overwhelm their weird immune system. Wooden bullets don't burn the flesh, so the holes stay open and they bleed out faster.

Mo'Lock watched me while I loaded the bullets into the .38.

"Is that safe?"

"Probably not."

The ghoul moved to the other side of the room and looked out the front window. He narrowed his eyes and scanned the yard and beyond.

"You know this neighborhood is overrun by vampires already?"

"Yeah," I said, "I talked to them. They're cool."

"Cool vampires?"

I shrugged. "What can I say? They came over, introduced themselves. They were nice."

Mo'Lock nodded. He was impressed. "This Los Angeles is an interesting place."

I was packed and ready to go. "I guess," I said as I walked towards the door. "You coming?"

"You want me to come?"

I stared at him for a good thirty seconds, then walked out the door. I wasn't gonna put up with any sensitive, whiny crap. He was trying to make me feel guilty for ditching him in D.C. Against my better instincts, I glanced over my shoulder as I reached the Catalina. Mo'Lock was standing in the window like a rejected puppy. I almost felt bad for him. Fucking ghoul.

I flipped him off with a smile, climbed in my car, and sped away. I had me a vampire to shoot.

It was a nice night for a drive, considering I was on my way to kill a bloodsucker. I tried to take my time, but the Houdini house was near Sam's. A quick drive over a steep, winding hill put me at the house twenty minutes after I'd left. I'd swallowed a handful of painkillers so my head was a bit light. My teeth were numb and loose, and all my wounds throbbed. I'm not one to complain, but those things were itching like they were trying to win a fucking contest.

I scanned the Houdini house. Like many houses in L.A., it was huge and crammed into the side of a hill. The driveway looked more like an obstacle course than a place to leave a car. I parked at the bottom and walked up as I cased the joint. Based on the map, I was less than a half a mile from Sunset Boulevard, but I might as well have been in the backwoods of West Virginia. There was no traffic, and besides the Houdini house all I could see were trees.

I snooped around the side of the huge Spanish-style house, looking for a way in. All of the windows were boarded up, even on the upper floors. Classic vampire scenario. Finally, as I moved around toward the back of the house, I found a window that hadn't been boarded shut. It was pitch black inside, but I hoisted myself onto the sill and slid into the house anyway.

The place was a wreck and stunk of piss and vomit. I stood there a second, waiting for my eyes to adjust, when something very odd happened. I heard a small noise. Nothing bad, just a creak. My heart jumped ever so slightly—nothing weird about that. But all my wounds started pulsating, as if reacting to the fear. That shit was a little too weird, even for me.

My eyes adjusted enough so that I could make my way around. The room I was standing in must have been some kind of game room. The walls were lined with dusty, padded benches, slashed and spilling their stuffing. In the center of the room was the remains of a red velvet-topped pool table. From the looks of it now, it was used primarily as a toilet. There were turds all over the torn velvet top and even a small pile in one of the corner pockets.

I've seen a lot of weird things in my life, but the idea of a vampire climbing up on a table to take a dump was beyond my comprehension. Wouldn't it just be easier to use the floor? But, I had to admit, the turd in the corner pocket was pretty funny. Vampires like to come off like they're better than anyone else, but they crap just like you and me if they eat. With all this fecal matter, I guess ol' Dave liked to chew his victims as well as suck them.

I moved into the next room and down a long corridor toward the front of the house. As I neared the end of the hall, I stopped. There was a door just ahead of me with light, dim and flickering, seeping beneath it. Bingo. The light was from a small fire, probably a candle. Big-shot Dave was probably having his morning tea at his grand piano by candlelight. Vampires are such hoity-toity jerk-offs. They all think they're some kind of aristocrats or some shit. I was looking forward to shooting him.

I decided against luring him out. Just lunging into the room shooting seemed like much more fun. I took out my .38 with the hardwood slugs and carefully grabbed the knob. I listened for a second. All was quiet. At my feet, the candlelight flickered, licking at the tips of my shoes.

Using my uninjured shoulder, I pushed the door open and stepped quickly inside. Everything slowed as adrenaline flooded my system and I scanned the room for my target. He was there, on the other side of the small dusty room, lank and deathly pale. He was shorter than I imagined, but it had to be him.

He was more than a bit surprised to see me. His black-circled eyes were wide as dinner plates, thin brows arched cartoon-like to his greasy hairline. His skin was a smooth, eggshell-white. I stepped forward, he stepped backward, and neither of us said a word. That was fine by me. I hate deathbed monologues.

I raised my gun nice and slow until it was leveled at his heart. The vampire tried to keep backing away, but a casket was in the way. I stepped forward and closed the space between us until I was just out of his reach. "Say goodnight, Dave."

The vampire stammered. "I . . . I . . . I'm—" was all I let him get out.

I let loose with the wooden bullets at close range, unloading the gun into his chest. Blamm! Blamm! Blamm! Blamm! Blamm! Blamm! It was beautiful. He was too busy gurgling and flailing as his chest exploded to even attempt an attack. It was bloody, but quick.

And way too easy.

"What he was trying to tell you . . . ," said a voice behind me.

My heart jumped. My wounds throbbed. I swung around, holding my empty, smoking gun. There was a huge shape standing in the doorway.

". . . was that he wasn't David."

Standing at the door, blocking the only way out, was the biggest, ugliest motherfucker I'd ever seen in my life. He was leaning casually against the door frame, baring his fangs, and tapping his long white fingers on his thigh. "You just shot my manservant."

Son-of-a-bitch.

I was so screwed. I'd used up all of my bullets on some poor, bug-eating, vampire manservant, and now I was face-to-face with probably the biggest undead goon I'd ever seen. If I was going to survive, I'd have to use my wits.

"I don't suppose saying sorry would help?"

The vampire shook his head slowly.

I gave the situation considerable thought in the time it took my stomach to sink to my knees, then bum-rushed him. The cocky sumbitch wasn't expecting the attack at all, so I hit him dead in the chest with all my weight. We both flew backward. Our combined weight must have been over four hundred pounds, so we went right through the wall behind him in a cloud of plaster dust and termite-infested wood.

He wasted no time, using a leg thrust against my chest to vault me across the room like a wet rag. The bastard was strong. I slammed into the casket on the other side of the room and fell in a heap. It hurt. Hurt bad.

The casket tumbled over. Soil from inside scattered all over me, the floor, and the bleeding corpse of his servant. By the time I looked up from my blood-mud bath, Dave was standing over me.

My wounds were burning, as if my body was suddenly a massive beating heart on speed. Each infected laceration felt about to rip open at any second.

I scrambled clumsily to my knees and grabbed hold of two slats of broken wood. Dave was behind me, so I didn't try to stand. Instead, I spun around, holding the pieces together to form a cross. The big bloodsucker stopped short, hissed, and reeled away. It worked. He really was old. Only Old World, fallen Christian–type vampires were scared of crosses.

I got to my feet, keeping the slats crossed and out in front of me. I maneuvered around, keeping Dave at a distance. He was hissing at me and baring his fangs, putting on a big old dramatic show. Tiny flecks of foam curdled at the corners of his mouth and from his small upturned nose.

"Okay, here's the deal," I said. "I'd like to leave here in one piece, so I want you to give me a little head start."

He glared at me and hissed. "I'll get you now or I'll get you later. I can wait. I've got all the time in the world."

He put down his arms and closed his mouth.

I slowly backed out of the room the way I had come, keeping my eyes locked on his until I was out. I waited outside the door a second to see if he'd try to follow me. Nothing happened. I think the appeal of getting me later stopped him. Whatever the case, I turned and bolted for the window. I leapt through it, ripping my jacket as I did. I got up fast, trying to ignore the pain, and continued running until I got back to the car.

Before driving off I glanced up at the house. In one of the windows I could see the shape of the vampire watching me, backlit by the flickering light of the candle. Dramatic asshole.

Round one was over.

I drove back over the hill to Sam's house via the back streets of Studio City. When I passed Benito and his crew standing outside one of their houses, I noticed they had a barbecue going. Wives, kids, and family were milling in the yard. As I drove by, Benito gave me a nod and waved his roasting fork toward me. I nodded back and smiled. He had on an apron that read "Make Mine Rare."

I parked at the curb. As soon as the door closed I heard a light, airy, clicking sound. I turned. At first I didn't see anything, and then behind a car at the end of the block I spied a brand-new red VW Beetle. The dealer sticker was still in the back window. The driver's side window was open and someone inside had just lowered something. Since I wasn't shot, my guess was a camera.

I pretended not to see anything and began walking into the house, but at the gate I abruptly turned and ran at the Beetle. The driver jumped, scared, and tried to start the car, but I was at the window before the engine sparked. The driver froze as I grabbed the door. It was a woman. She was young looking, with dirty-blond hair and the largest almond-shaped blue eyes I'd ever seen. She was beautiful.

"What are you doing?" I said a bit too loud. My voice cracked at the end.

I expected denial, mace in the eyes, or at least some indignant anger, but instead she turned red, looked at me, and then stared down at the steering wheel. I'd seen this before, just not toward me. It was the way a fan acted.

"You are Cal McDonald, right?" she asked.

I had rushed the car pissed and ready to kill. Now, suddenly I was flustered. I could feel my own face flushing red. "Yeah. Yes. I am. Who are you?"

She flashed her blue eyes at me and smiled. "Sabrina Lynch. *Speculator Magazine.*"

I stared at her. Sabrina Lynch. The name rattled my brain. She worked for the rag that ran pictures of me naked and covered with pink slime, the magazine that called me D.C.'s crackpot detective, the one that had once accused me of taking money for fake ghost-chasing jobs (true, but beside the point). It was also the magazine which featured my old cop buddy, Jefferson Blout, on the cover after the second Big Head case. Blout was so embarrassed, he hasn't spoken to me since.

I let go of the door and backed away from the car. Suddenly she wasn't looking so cute and that flirtatious look on her face seemed more like a wise-ass smirk.

"Any comment for our readers about why you're in Los Angeles? Can you shed some light on the disappearance of Sam Burnett?"

I didn't say a word. I turned away and walked back to the house. I heard her snap one more picture and then drive away. Bitch.

Back at Sam's, I stood in front of the bathroom mirror with my shirt off and studied my wounds. It was very strange. They had stopped stinging the moment I was safe, almost the exact second I was clear of the vampire, as though they were in sync with my emotions.

I poked at a nasty gash running over my left shoulder and half-way down my back. A werewolf—Sean, I think—had gotten me from behind when I was running. The wound was deep and infected. The slash across my right cheek was almost completely gone. A little pink, but that was it. But back at the Houdini house it had throbbed as vigorously as the fresher wounds.

I wasn't too worried about the vampire attacking anytime soon. I'd only left him an hour ago, and I was sure he thought I was sweating it out. I did take one precaution, though: I was wearing a cross I'd kept in the box with the bullets. I knew I should be a little more concerned about the Dave situation, but the wound weirdness distracted me. Something about it had me really worried.

Then Mo'Lock appeared at the bathroom door.

"You okay?" he grumbled.

"I thought you were pissed at me."

"I was angry. I came all this way and you left me behind. But I was also worried. Did you kill him?"

I turned and rolled my eyes as I pushed past him into the living room where I grabbed the bottle of Beam. "Well, I killed somebody. It wasn't Dave," I said. "But we did meet."

"What happened?"

"We had a little scrap. That's one pissed off vampire." I took a drink. "But I got away."

Mo'Lock shifted on his feet. "What now?"

I swallowed, choking a little. "I haven't the slightest idea. Just wait, I guess."

Mo'Lock started pacing back and forth in front of me. I sipped the whiskey until he started talking. "I went out for a walk while you were gone. This L.A. is an interesting place."

"Yeah?"

Something was on his mind. He wasn't very good at concealing his limited emotional range. A little agitation showed on him like a fresh bruise. I waited for him to cough it up.

"I met some fellow ghouls. They are rather lazy. Evidently it's possible to live here without working. But they told me some things which I found rather disturbing."

I yawned and rolled my hand in the air for him to go on.

"They spoke of a coming darkness. The time of the monsters, you know, the floodgate."

"Oh yeah, that. So what?"

"Well . . . I think it's started. Something or someone has triggered the event. Look around you. Haven't things been stranger than usual since you arrived? You've had steady work!"

"I wouldn't exactly call it work. More like an attack. Is there a point coming soon?"

The ghoul was getting uncharacteristically excited. "I've phoned back east and the same thing is happening there. My brothers and sisters feel it too. Some are so scared they won't even come out of the sewers. They think you're a part of it."

I took a good long drink and then stared at Mo'Lock with the dullest expression I could muster. "Wouldn't I have to know what the fuck you're talking about to be involved?"

Mo'Lock nodded earnestly. He saw that I truly had no idea what he was going on about. I'd heard this kind of talk before and nothing ever came of it.

"It's in the air. I can feel it. Something has been set in motion and it is aimed at you. Something big. Very, very big."

"You're talking shit. You know that, don't you? The only reason I'm getting more business is because I'm new here, not because of the coming of some goddamn monster Armageddon. You watch, as soon as we get Sam's head in the mail things will settle down." I took a few swigs and watched Mo'Lock pace, then added, "And what the fuck do ghouls have to be scared of? You're the damn undead, ain't you?"

"Plenty, if it's the right kind of threat. At the core of our being, we are a thing which exists on a spiritual, mystical plane. If that plane is disturbed, we're all in trouble."

"Even the human race?"

"Especially the human race."

I thought about it. I'd heard the ghoul go on like this before, but this time there seemed to be some extra weight to his argument. I took a couple of short sips and mulled it over as Mo'Lock watched me. I could feel his big eyes on me, so I looked up at him and met his gaze. "Let's say this shit is going on. Is there anything that can be done to stop it?"

He shrugged.

"Then what the fuck are we worrying about it for?"

He shrugged again. "It is a strong feeling, Cal."

"Well, let me know when the feeling gets a little more specific. I've heard all this before and nothing terrible's ever happened."

Mo'Lock looked at me dull-eyed. "Nothing but terrible things happen to you."

I raised the bottle to him. Touché.

Then I noticed a pile of mail on the table. To my surprise and dismay, they had my name on them. I picked up an overdue bill from D.C., a last notice on a couple of credit cards, then I saw the yellow change of address sticker. I threw down the bills.

"Did you put in a change of address for me?"

Mo'Lock nodded. I laughed. That explained how *Speculator* found me so fast. But I wasn't laughing for long. Poking out from the pile was a small pink slip. I put down the bottle and yanked it out. It was a package delivery slip. It said "Delivery Attempted" and "Final Notice."

"What the fuck?!"

"What is it?"

"It says here they tried to deliver a package twice! Now we have to go to the post office and pick it up because it requires a signature."

"You think it's Mr. Burnett's head?"

"D.C. zip code."

Mo'Lock snapped his fingers. "Ah, yes. With everything going on I forgot to mention that Brent said he would send Mr. Burnett's head Priority Mail so it would get here as fast as possible."

I rubbed my eyes. "So the first and second delivery attempts probably happened the first few days I was here."

I stood up and quickly fell back onto the couch. Painkillers and hooch made for a major head rush. The ghoul stepped over and helped me up. We had to get to the post office.

Mo'Lock followed me out of the house. I got the zipper of my jacket stuck on the screen door, yanked, and ripped both my jacket and the door.

"Perhaps I should drive."

"Perhaps you should."

The post office was packed. The line stretched from the desk, where two of a possible five stations were open, all the way past a wall of P.O. boxes to the back entrance. I stood impatiently with Mo'Lock, gripping the pink slip in my hands while I watched customers take their sweet time at the counter.

As we crawled up the line, I glared at several idiots who evidently had never mailed anything before. They stood at the desk with unpacked boxes begging the clerk to guide them through the complicated process of taping a box closed and putting an address label on it.

Finally it was our turn to stand like retards at the counter while everyone stared at us. Luckily, I had the ghoul with me. He tends to draw most of the attention, and one return glance from him causes most people to look away immediately.

I handed the clerk—who was not a ghoul, but sure as shit looked like one—the pink slip. He looked at it lazily, sighed, and lumbered out of our sight. After a long, silent wait, he shuffled back holding only the pink slip.

"Package is on the truck. Should be delivered today."

"But this says final notice," I said.

The clerk just looked at me and shrugged. I began to reach for my blackjack, but Mo'Lock pulled me away from the counter and out of the post office. The clerk didn't even react. He just yelled, "Next!"

Outside I pushed Mo'Lock off me and composed myself. "Now what? I came here to help that old bastard find his body, but I can't do shit without the head."

"Back to the house and wait for the mailman?"

I stomped off, wounds aching and stinging. I was pissed off. All of a sudden, I had three thousand things on my mind. I had Sam's head case to think about. I was in a new city. Plus, I was being stalked by some broad from a magazine that seemed to like making me look bad. That really fucking ticked me off. I mean, you'd think a magazine that wanted to prove the existence of the supernatural would be nice to the one guy who had first-hand experience!

Maybe the ghouls were right. Maybe something was going on. Something bigger than everybody suddenly jumping on my shit.

Then, out of my anger, I had an idea.

First we drove by Sam's house and left a note for the mailman to leave the package, then we headed out to locate the offices of *Speculator Magazine*. If something was up, if there was one shred of truth in what the ghoul claimed, the magazine should have been tracking an increased amount of bizarre activity. Plus, Ms. Lynch had mentioned Sam. Maybe she had something on the prick bastard who snipped his head from his body.

Finding Sabrina Lynch and the magazine office proved to require some real detective work. The address for the mag led Mo'Lock and me to a post office box. It wasn't an official USPS box, just a service that provides you with a street address. We tried, in vain, to get some info out of the proprietor, but she wouldn't cough up. I tried the White Pages, and even called information, but Lynch was unlisted and the magazine phone number was an answering service. Out of sheer desperation, I even put a call in to Sam's sheriff buddy, Dawson, in Sherman Oaks, but there was no answer.

I was getting frustrated, but I refused to give up. I was jittery and needed to keep on the move. I needed the distraction. My entire body stung like a massive paper cut dipped in rubbing alcohol. I kept throwing back painkillers, but all they did was slur my speech and make my gums throb.

It was in moments like these that my old cravings came back. What I needed was a line of smack to drown out all the noise. I could almost feel the calming haze, but I would never go back to that. I had enough problems without becoming a junkie again.

I remembered the dealer sticker in Lynch's window and, through some miracle of brain-cell survival, I recalled the name at the top of the sticker: Miller/Cruz Volkswagen in North Hollywood. Mo'Lock and I headed deep into the San Fernando Valley to find the dealership. As we ventured further, the ghoul started getting jumpy.

"What's up, Mo'?" I asked as I steered along a vast flat row of what looked like warehouses but were, in fact, stores.

"Look around," the ghoul said. "There's sun everywhere. The only place I see shade is beneath parked cars."

I glanced around as I ran a red light. I hadn't even realized the sun had come up. I'd been up for two days straight. What the ghoul said was true. Somehow the sun beat down so straight and so even that there was little or no place to find shade. It didn't help that there were no trees and all of the buildings were plain gray or brown pillboxes.

After passing under a freeway overpass, we came upon block after block of car dealerships, laid out like graveyards filled with rows of bright, shiny tombstones. I drove slowly by each dealership looking for Miller/Cruz. As we drove past, salesmen gathered, eyeballing us like slobbering zombies waiting for a chance to bite the flesh off the bones. Talk about creepy. I'd rather deal with zombies.

The Miller/Cruz lot was the smallest of all. They seemed to only deal Beetles and had only two salesmen working, neither of whom were named Miller or Cruz. Mo'Lock and I stepped into the showroom and were immediately approached by both men. They introduced themselves as Jon and John and commenced the hard sell. I let them go for about two seconds, then held up my hand.

"You keep pretty detailed records of everybody you sell a car to, right?" Jon looked at John and nodded.

I weighed the options: come back later and break in, pay off the two J's for info, or distract them while Mo'Lock snooped. I didn't have patience for any of that, so I pulled out my gun and pressed it to Jon's forehead.

"Red Beetle sold to a woman recently. Blonde. Somewhat professional looking. Ring any bells?"

Jon peed himself and nodded. "We've only sold two reds in the last month. One was a dude."

They coughed up the sales info immediately. Just like that I had Sabrina Lynch's address, phone number, and bank info. No problem except for the stain in Jon's trousers. I felt bad. The strong arm wasn't necessary and more than a little rash, possibly even stupid. If they squealed to the cops I could be traced back through Sabrina Lynch. Luckily, Mo'Lock had some cash on him, so I asked him to give John and Jon five big ones each. That seemed to make everybody happy. Well, except for the ghoul, but fuck him. He'd get over it.

It turned out that the home of Sabrina Lynch and the offices of the internationally distributed *Speculator Magazine* were one and the same, and neither was all that impressive. The place was an apartment, one of those *Melrose Place* deals that looked like a small motel with a pool in the middle. But, unlike the TV show, this one had no gorgeous tenants, just a hunchbacked pool boy trying to scoop a beer bottle out of the water with a plastic bag taped to a broom handle.

I checked the mailboxes, found her name, and headed up to apartment six. As we climbed the noisy metal stairs, I looked at the ghoul. He rolled his eyes. I didn't think Los Angeles was agreeing with him.

"What's the matter?" I asked.

"I can't put my finger on it," he said. "Something is wrong . . . like a cloud following us."

We reached the landing to Lynch's apartment. I stopped and turned to Mo'Lock. "Let me know when you figure it out. In the meantime, shut the fuck up. You're freaking me out."

We proceeded to the door. Inside we could hear all kinds of noise: the TV, a woman's high-pitched voice talking to a pet, a phone ringing. I knocked, and the place went silent. Bang. Just like that. I knocked again. I heard movement, papers ruffling. Panic sounds.

"Just a minute!"

I pounded hard on the door. "IRS! Open up! We've come for the car!"

Silence again, then the door was yanked open, and Sabrina Lynch and I stood face to face. Her hair was pulled back into two small ponytails. She was wearing sweatpants and a T-shirt which bluntly read "FUCK." I tried not to, but I smiled anyway.

Lynch twisted her lip and smirked. "Not funny and rude. Great combo you got going there, McDonald."

I looked past her, into the apartment, and saw piled papers and clippings scattered everywhere, alongside photos and maps with Post-it notes. Where there wasn't furniture, there were stacks of boxes overflowing with back issues of the *Speculator*. The rest of the small apartment was pure function: fax machine, phones, computer, desk chair, couch, and coffee table. The kitchen was a small area against the far wall. There was only one other door; the bathroom, I guessed. No bedroom, which explained the sheet and pillow on the couch.

I had all the time in the world to scan her place from the door, because Lynch had finally noticed the ghoul standing behind me. When I looked back to her, her eyes were filled with an odd blend of wonderment and suspicion. She didn't even know I was looking at her. Mo'Lock had her transfixed and it made the ghoul very uncomfortable. I found that hugely amusing.

Finally she looked toward me with dazed eyes. "Is he . . . ?"

I nodded.

"Wow."

Mo'Lock held out his gigantic, bony hand to her. "I'm Mo'Lock. I work with Cal."

Lynch shook his hand and flinched slightly at his cold touch. She smiled so widely I thought her face would tear, and she started to breathe heavy. She was so excited meeting an actual ghoul that she was hyperventilating. But she quickly regained her composure and went from fan to reporter in the blink of an eye.

"So, you tracked me down," she said. "What do you want?"

"Well, we came for a tour of the *Speculator* offices, but I just got one from the door here." I flashed a big fake grin and continued. "And . . . I wanted to ask you some questions about the Los Angeles scene."

"Like what?"

Mo'Lock leaned in. "May we come inside?"

Lynch jumped and started breathing hard again. I thought she was about to have an anxiety attack. Then, to my surprise, she stepped back and gestured for us to come in.

The wall to the right had a complete publishing schedule for the magazine plastered on it with due dates, ship dates, and a ton of stuff that made no sense to me. I knew there were at least a hundred issues of *Speculator*. It was a slick product. I couldn't believe it was all done from this little rat-hole.

She knew what I was thinking and stepped over to me while Mo'Lock looked around in his odd, slow way.

"I have over a hundred and sixty-five writers and photographers and ten editors scattered all over the world. Most of the work is done over the Internet. There's a large community of investigative reporters interested in the paranormal and only one magazine that will run their stories."

I scanned the schedule. Words popped out; vampire, telepathy, and UFOs were a prominent part of the next issue, followed by an all-Bigfoot/Loch Ness Monster Special. Grainy photos were posted on the wall. Most were the familiar ones everybody has seen; the noodle-like head of Nessy sticking out of the water, Bigfoot striding through a clearing, and a closeup of an oversized plaster foot impression.

Then I spotted a Post-it with "SHERMAN OAKS CULT" scrawled on it. I pointed to it.

"What's this?"

She eyed me suspiciously. "A tip I received. It didn't pan out. Why?"

"Just curious."

"Sherman Oaks was the last place your buddy Sam Burnett was seen alive."

Mo'Lock pulled himself away from a stack of papers and walked over, clearing the apartment in three strides. "How do you know that?"

She looked from Mo'Lock to me and laughed. "Look, you guys want to tell me what you're looking for? I'm not used to people barging in here and asking a bunch of questions!"

"I'm not used to people sneaking pictures of me."

Lynch laughed again and smiled. "Fair enough. I guess I've embarrassed the famous Cal McDonald enough to cut you some slack." Her body language relaxed and I could tell in the beat of a heart that she decided to trust us.

"One thing though," she said, holding up a finger.

"Name it."

"If I help you, I get an interview. No holds barred, tell-all."

"Deal."

I told Sabrina Lynch about how I came to move to L.A., about the head in the box and the kid who separated it from Sam's body. She said she got an anonymous tip about a teen cult in Sherman Oaks, but the lead was thin and she couldn't find anything justifying further investigation. Later she heard about Sam's disappearance. That's when she showed up at his place and saw me.

"I was kind of shocked to see you. I'd run stories and pictures of you so I recognized you immediately as Sam's East Coast counterpart. I had a hunch something was going on."

"That's sort of what we wanted to ask you about. Have you noticed a surge of paranormal criminal activity?"

She titled her head. "How do you mean?"

"A lot of weird shit happening."

The question made her a little agitated, but she was trying her best to conceal it from us. She wrapped herself in her arms and sat down. She looked like a woman that tried to put up a good front, but had just surrendered. She looked scared.

Mo'Lock pushed me toward her. I slapped him away, but gave in and moved around the couch. It took me a minute, but I eventually sat down awkwardly on the edge of the cushion. I looked over at her. Her face was different. Suddenly she was tired, worn out, and vulnerable. Her eyes were round and sad. I hated myself for thinking it, but she really looked beautiful. My heart beat faster and a wound on my lower back throbbed.

"You feel like talking?" I said.

She looked at me and for an instant I thought she was going to cry. "I'm sorry about running the story about you being a fraud. I trusted the contributor. I should have checked the sources."

"Water under the bridge, Lynch. That's not what's upsetting you."

She smiled faintly and let out a long, slow sigh. Then her face took on the strong, sharp-eyed look I'd seen before. "There have been a record number of sightings in the last month," she said. "Almost three times as many as I usually field."

Mo'Lock asked my question for me. "What do you mean by sightings?"

"I get calls all the time. Most of the time they're cranks or crazies. I check most of them out on the off chance I'll get a story out of it, but it's usually a dead end."

"But lately?"

She tipped her head and blinked. "Lately it's been weird. I get a call about a ghost and I find evidence of a ghost. Last week, somebody reported a pride of werewolves killed downtown. I checked it out. Evidence points to werewolves, but they were all dead and I haven't figured out what happened."

I glanced at Mo'Lock.

"It's been this way every day," she went on. "Vampire reports, things flying in the sky over Griffith Park, people walking through walls, the dead coming back and contacting their loved ones . . ."

"Devil cult in Sherman Oaks?"

"Yeah. It's unbelievable. My whole career I've struggled to find enough material for four issues a year. Now, overnight, I'm getting enough leads to fill volumes!"

I shifted on the couch and our knees accidentally touched. "So something is going on. That's obvious. It's got to be either a random natural eruption of the supernatural or something that was caused by someone intentionally."

"As I've said, and it's been echoed by others, there appears to be a shift between the unnatural and natural world," Mo'Lock added. "What this means, I do not know. I can only say that my brethren are frightened, both on the East Coast and here in Los Angeles."

Lynch looked down and that frightened look returned. "Last night something happened that I can't explain," she said. There was an unsettling quiver in her voice. She stood and walked to the single large window in her small apartment.

"Around three o'clock last night I heard a scratching at the door. It was light, and I didn't get up until the sounds changed to a tapping. When I looked through the peephole, there was nothing there. I peeked through the shades . . ."

She looked white as a sheet. I followed her to the windows as she retraced her steps.

"There were two . . . people. Kids, I guess. Teenagers, standing out on the walkway staring at me."

"What'd they look like?"

"Dead. They looked dead. One of them, the tall one, his face was . . . gone; wiped away right down to the skull. The other kid, his skin was blue, and he was wet with black grease from his chest down."

She looked at me as if to see whether I believed her. I did. She was probably talking to the one human being who would. Well, two, if you counted a decapitated head bouncing around the back of a truck in a box.

"Did they say or do anything?"

"No, they just stood there for hours, staring. It was horrible."

Although I had a pretty good idea who the kids were, now wasn't the time to fill her in. Why scare her more? They had to be Brian Hogue and Carl Potter, former playmates of Billy Fuller.

Were the dead kids looking for help from Lynch because of her association with the occult? Or had Billy sent them as a warning to stop snooping around?

I was tempted to pay Billy a visit, but didn't dare as long as Sam's head was AWOL. With the head in postal limbo, the kid had the edge on us. We didn't want him to do something to permanently divide Sam from his torso. I'd have to wait and steer clear of Sherman Oaks for the time being.

I told Lynch not to worry, but to set up a camera to get pictures if the dead kids came back. She said she'd already planned on doing just that. I told her to call me if she was scared. That seemed to strike her as odd for some reason.

"Are you going to protect me?"

I felt myself starting to blush. "All I meant, Lynch, was . . . we're here if you need anything."

She batted her eyes at me. It was an act; I could see that. But it was working. Suddenly, I was having trouble breathing and wanted to get out of there fast.

"Please, call me Sabrina."

I didn't get a chance to reply. She duped me by turning her attention to Mo'Lock and left me standing there with red cheeks and a stupid look on my face.

She shook Mo'Lock's hand. "It was very good to meet you."

"The pleasure was mine, ma'am." The ghoul bowed his head like some pansy from an old movie.

But Sabrina Lynch wasn't finished. She was angling for something. "Do you mind my asking exactly what you are?"

Mo'Lock touched his hand to his chest. "I'm undead. I am what humans call a ghoul."

"But I thought ghouls robbed graves and ate children."

Mo'Lock let out a stale breath. "I gave up eating children decades ago." He said with a twist of undead sarcasm. "However, certain factions of ghoul in the Midwest and Deep South still practice the eating of flesh."

"Would it be possible for me to get a photograph of you?"

Mo'Lock shook his head. "I'd rather not."

Sabrina was just about out of charm.

"Well, you still have the interview with me," I smirked.

Mo'Lock thanked Sabrina Lynch for her hospitality and walked out. I followed, giving her a wink on the way out. When she smiled, I could see it wasn't part of any act.

I followed Mo'Lock down the stairs to the pool where the hunchback had given up trying to snag the bottle. He sat with his feet in the water, eyeing the bobbing bottle like it was the greatest mystery of the twenty-first century.

We'd made it all the way back to the mailboxes when I turned and saw Sabrina outside her apartment, taking pictures of us. Mo'Lock and I flipped her off as we disappeared out of the steel gate. Let's see her print that.

There wasn't a hell of a lot we could do to be proactive and that really had me hot and bothered. I had to wait for Sam's head to be re-redelivered so I could go after devil-kid Billy. I also had to see what this fucking "day of the monsters" shit would turn into, if anything. These types of unnatural events are like a hurricane. All you can do is sandbag the house. It'll happen when it happens and you won't know how bad it is until it's blowing seawater up your nose.

Mo'Lock was trying to convince me to get my injuries checked out, but I wasn't having it. Unless I was laid out on a stretcher, I had no intention of going to a hospital. Besides, I had all the prescriptions I needed. Instead, we wound up cruising up Ventura Boulevard, near Sherman Oaks. I still didn't feel ready to corner Billy, but I thought we might as well stop in and see Sam's sheriff buddy, Ted Dawson.

Dawson's office was in a small municipal building on a side street, about four blocks from a mega-mall named after the area. As soon as we walked up to the main entrance I knew there was trouble. The flag on the roof was at half-mast. Somebody was dead and I had a gut feeling it was Dawson.

Inside, my hunch was confirmed without even talking to anybody. There were flowers all over the lobby and in the middle of the cluster was a photo of Sheriff Ted Dawson. Behind that was a huge sheet of paper signed by co-workers and locals with condolences.

Mo'Lock and I were about to leave—I knew Billy Fuller had something to do with the cop's death, and I didn't need specifics—when a deputy with a black arm band stepped up.

"Can I help you gentlemen with something?"

"Just came to pay our respects, "I said. "Dawson worked with a friend of mine."

The deputy nodded. "Shame, a man dying like that."

"Terrible." Suddenly I was curious and the deputy was in the mood to talk.

"I mean, how could a guy die of a fall in the middle of nowhere?"

"Fall?"

"Yeah, didn't you hear? They found him in the middle of a high school football field in Burbank."

"Burbank? That's pretty far away."

"Yup. He'd died from a fall. Coroner said at least five, maybe as much as eight hundred feet in the air, except there ain't no building that high within a mile of the field! Explain that one." He shook his head, looking despondent and confused at the same time.

"Weird."

"Big weird," he said, then dropped a flower in front of the picture and left.

I nudged the ghoul and we did the same.

We hit the road again. It was getting dark, so I steered us back toward Sam's. With any luck the package would be delivered in the morning. Then we could finally get on the case and nail this kid before he put a hex on the entire San Fernando Valley.

By the time we pulled onto Sam's street, it was pitch dark. Oddly, Benito and his half-baked vampire crew were nowhere to be seen. Since I'd arrived they'd always been on the streets or in one of the yards frying up some meat, playing music, and generally keeping an eye on the neighborhood. But this time, nothing. The ghoul and I were the only living (or non-living) souls in sight.

Then, as we prepared to head to the house, I noticed someone sitting in a car right across the street. I couldn't make out who it was because the entire cab was filled with smoke, like something out of a Cheech and Chong movie. I walked over and gave the window a tap. The window rolled down. Smoke rose from the crack and cleared the air enough so I could see Benito's pal, Junior, working on a joint the size of a polish sausage.

"What's up, Junior? Where's the gang?"

Junior was skinny as a rail and his shaved head and sunken red eyes gave him a mischievous look no matter what he said or did. "They got hungry."

Junior offered me the joint through the window. It had been a long time since I'd had any weed, so I took it and dragged off the stick hard. After about three hits I offered it to the ghoul. He shook his head, so I took two more hits and handed it back.

"Thanks."

"No sweat, monster man."

I smiled and walked away. As soon as the pot hit me I regretted taking it. My heart started pounding, and suddenly Mo'Lock freaked me out. He looked at me like a disappointed parent.

I scanned the dirt yard with its ugly rake marks, and suddenly the gash on my shoulder began to throb like a motherfucker. It hurt before, but this time it was different. It was a long, sustained ache that rose, fell, and was gone.

"What's wrong?"

"I dunno," I said, looking at the dirt and the deep raked grooves. "Something's not right here."

Mo'Lock stood alert and scanned around. He watched me as I stared at the yard and then upward to the sky. For some reason I thought of Dawson's eight-hundred-foot drop.

"What are you thinking?"

"I dunno," I repeated, but something was there. Something was right in front of me and I couldn't figure it out. Then again, maybe I was just stoned.

I decided I was being a tweak and headed into the house. As I stepped over the threshold every single cut, slash, gash, scrape, contusion, and bruise flared at the same time. I stumbled forward into the dark house, unable to ignore the pain. Mo'Lock grabbed hold of me, flipped the light, and shut the door. At my feet I saw tiny pieces of shattered glass. It didn't take long for either of us to realize we were not alone.

Dave, the vampire I should have killed earlier, was waiting for me in Sam's living room.

He was to our right, standing next to the window he had obviously smashed through to get in. I'd thought he was ugly in the shadows of the Houdini house. In the dank yellow light of Sam's living room, he was absolutely fucking hideous. He had rough skin as white as boiled chicken meat, and this gross little upturned nose filled with ancient vampire nose-hair. Mo'Lock and I stood still and said nothing. It was a standoff.

I couldn't take my eyes off his nose and I knew it was because I was high. He looked like a rabid pig in a suit. As soon as that thought entered my head, I laughed. The vampire was about to make his move, but my chuckle stopped him cold in his tracks, confused. It caught him completely off-guard and gave Mo'Lock the opening he'd been waiting for.

The ghoul lunged at the bloodsucker and tackled him mid-torso. They hit the wall hard, shattering paint and plaster as they fell to the floor. The vampire hissed and kicked and clawed. Mo'Lock held his own, planting a rapid succession of alternating right and left hooks down on Dave's ugly-ass face.

It was dead versus dead. The vampire kicked the ghoul off him. Mo'Lock landed on his feet. Dave did that vampire-rising-from-the-casket thing, rising straight to his feet, absolutely rigid, without bending a limb. Pretty impressive, actually.

I moved as far from the fight as I could and fell against the wall. My body was freezing up. Suddenly, I felt like I was dying. Either that or a major anxiety attack. The wounds all over my body were throbbing and stinging. Infection, I thought, it had to be infection. Please let it be an infection. I began to sweat profusely.

I turned around, still leaning on the wall, refusing to fall, until my back was resting against the surface. Mo'Lock and the vampire were really going at it, exchanging blows at speeds that blurred their motions. In a flash, the tide of battle had shifted and the ghoul was getting the worst of it. He was staggering back a bit and taking far more shots than he was throwing. Part of the reason was that the stupid ghoul kept looking over at me wriggling against the wall, sweating like some kind of freak.

In an instant, the vampire took total control of the brawl. He grabbed the ghoul by the throat and flipped him upside down in a single move, slamming him head-first onto the floor. The wood slats cracked and Mo'Lock's head split open wide. The ghoul's thick, congealed blood spattered. Dave grabbed the dizzy ghoul's ankles and held him dangling off the ground. Now the vampire had a weapon. He was going to bludgeon me with my own partner.

I could barely move. The pain from the werewolf gashes and bites had spread like a fire burning beneath the surface of my skin. My muscles were so tight I could hardly manipulate my own limbs. All I could do was lean there against the wall and watch the ugliest bloodsucker in the world drag Mo'Lock toward me.

He started swinging Mo' around, at first in a circle, smashing two lamps and a half-full bottle of vodka, then back and forth, right at me.

"Cal, get out of here! Run!" the vampire's baseball bat yelled out.

I leaned there helpless as Dave came at me, swinging Mo'Lock back and forth. I closed my eyes, more from the pain in my body than to brace myself for the blow.

Shit, how much more could it hurt after all I'd been through?

BAM!

Very, very much.

The first blow slammed me to the ground. The second missed, but took a chunk out of the wall above my head. Poor fucking Mo'Lock, getting smashed around like that. I knew he couldn't be killed, but shit, it had to be pretty fucking unpleasant.

I was on the ground trying to crawl away. BAM! Another narrow miss above my head. The vampire was laughing, the ghoul screaming, and I was on the floor in a knot of pain. It was complete and total chaos. I scrambled weakly to my feet, and turned in time to see Mo'Lock's yowling face coming at mine and—BAM!—I was down. Mo'Lock was out cold. Even a ghoul has limits.

The vampire was laughing. My smashed face was running with blood. My body heaved. My body burned . . . and then it happened.

Clothes tore, muscles rippled and rolled. My eyes shot open, and even through the wash of blood over my face, I caught the vampire's expression as he dropped Mo'Lock and backed away.

He was scared.

I was changing.

I knew instantly what it was and it sure as fuck wasn't any infection. I was turning into a goddamn werewolf! The pain was gone and now most of my clothes were too. I watched the hair grow from my hands and up my arms, sprouting through the pores of my skin on every inch of my body. My bones snapped and reshaped like a dislocated joint popping back into place, and I felt a great strength and hunger growing inside me.

But best of all was watching the vampire shit his pants. That's right, you heard me. Shit ran right down his pant leg and plopped right onto the office floor!

I lowered my head, stood on my haunches, and flexed my new, powerful lycanthrope body. My mind was intact. I was me. It was amazing. I was a werewolf!

So many thoughts shot through my head at once; most my own, but some primal and animalistic. Hundreds of questions, like how was I still in my right mind? But one thought prevailed and rose above the rest: rip that fucking vampire to shreds.

I closed in, up on my haunches. The vampire was panicked. He was moving back and forth, trying frantically to decide where to go and what to do next. But no matter the direction he chose, I'd be on him in a heartbeat, and he knew it. I could see myself rending his flesh, ripping that misshapen nose from his face.

I imagined myself tearing into him. I pictured myself eating . . . and then I froze. Where the hell had that idea come from? I wanted to eat him. The mere thought of it made me drool. That was not good.

My hesitation gave the vampire a desperately needed opportunity. He turned and lunged through the window he'd come in. I reacted instantly, instinctively. No fucking way was he escaping. I wanted blood. His blood.

I ran like never before. My new legs pumped along at speeds I could scarcely imagine moments before. I started on my hind legs, but as I chased him into the more populated area around Ventura Boulevard, I went down on all fours and really let loose with some animal speed. Yet somehow I couldn't bring myself to take Dave down. The chase was too good. The hunt. I didn't want it to end. The sight of his frantically fleeing form, his face turning in fear to see if I was still there was too much to resist. I wanted it to go on forever.

Unfortunately, we were attracting a lot of attention as we sped through the streets and sidewalks of Studio City, although I was hardly aware of it. People were jumping out of our way, screaming and running indoors. I glimpsed my speeding reflection in a store window and saw just how frightening I looked.

I was huge, bigger than any wolf or dog could possibly be, and muscular like a man with animal-jointed limbs and a thick coat of black and gray hair. My eyes were piercing and alive, gleaming through my dark, furred face and extended snout. I was the perfect blend of animal and human. All these years hunting monsters and here I was a monster myself—and loving it!

The chase went on for a good mile and I didn't lose pace with him once. I blocked out the chaos around me and focused my acute senses. There was nothing I couldn't see, nothing I couldn't sniff out. Without looking, I knew that we had covered one mile, passed two hundred and twenty-three pedestrians and another three hundred and twelve people inside their cars. I felt their fear as they saw me, and their relief as I passed. I smelled their blood and wanted to taste it. At that moment, I knew that my current lucidity wasn't going to last. Eventually the bloodlust would take over and the human in me would disappear. It was a suddenly sobering thought in a moment when I felt the best I'd ever felt.

Fuck it. I couldn't do anything about it tonight. I might as well have fun and rid the world of one more bloodsucker.

I ran on, tireless. My nose focused on Dave and I sensed his fear of me suddenly subside. Something was wrong. He was leading me now. We were leaving Studio City and heading straight toward the L.A. River. I almost slowed down, knowing I was almost certainly running into a trap. But I was too far gone to be scared as my bloodlust welled to a breaking point. Trap or no trap, I was going to shred that vampire into tiny little bits and pull each and every nose hair from that ugly pug-nose.

We ran into a park as close as a foot apart. I could almost reach out and poke him with a claw. I smelled the trap, picturing it in my mind before I actually saw it.

We were running downhill, toward the huge, cement aqueduct that snaked throughout Los Angeles. Dave leaped a wire-mesh fence; I tore through it. Ahead was a clearing. At the bottom, the vampire took a sharp left, then swung around and faced me as I came to a halt. I could smell a presence around us. We were surrounded, but I was too focused on Dave to figure out how many or exactly where they were.

I sniffed the air and caught a whiff from the trees. The sound of water echoed through the cement channel. We stood facing each other in the pitch-black darkness of the park.

"Well?" I barked. "Your move, pig-face." My voice was gruff and phlegmy. My half-animal throat wasn't built for speech.

The vampire lunged. I stood my ground and cut him short, slashing his throat open with a swipe of my left while slashing his chest with my right. He reeled sideways and I slashed again, catching his shoulder. He was hemorrhaging stolen blood. Whatever he thought was going to happen, didn't.

I could smell panic rising in him again. Realizing his plan wasn't working, he began to back away. I advanced, snarling. He stumbled away, holding his throat as blood spewed through clamped fingers.

Behind the vampire's back, the cement river with its fetid water was close, and Dave knew it. He began scanning the tree tops. He wanted me to look, but I wasn't having it. I was locked on him as I rocked from side to side, pacing in place, waiting for the moment that I would tear him into an unrecoverable pile of fleshy undead pieces.

I stepped forward and growled.

"Where are you?!" Dave cried out, and the trees began to rustle.

My radar-like senses went haywire. Suddenly, there were a hundred objects coming at me from every direction. I couldn't focus or get an exact fix on who or what I was smelling. I had seconds to act. I jumped forward and pounded the vampire with all my werewolf strength, which was evidently considerable. He flew through the air, flipping, turning, and screaming like a discarded doll, and landed head first in the running water inside the cement aqueduct.

It was a gamble. Running water affected only the most superstitious vampires. But considering Dave's age and his reaction to the makeshift cross, I hoped for the best. I hit pay dirt. He began to sizzle and steam like the Wicked Witch of the West, but I had barely a second to enjoy it before the screaming creatures from the trees finally found their target.

They were on me at once, hundreds of them, none bigger than a small cat. They frantically clawed and scratched me, pulling my hair and biting with sharp, needle-sized teeth. I slashed and pulled them off the best I could. They were like small gibbons, but bald and pink, with teeth so large I couldn't see how they fit into their tiny mouths. Their eyes were black, completely absent of pupils. And they were mean as fuck. They wouldn't stop. I ripped and slashed them to pieces, twisting their necks and killing them one by one, but there were too damn many of them. No matter how many I killed, there were ten to take its place.

Meanwhile, in two feet of moving water, Dave was dying slowly as he screamed for his creatures to kill me.

"Avenge me, my pets! Kill him!"

On the verge of death after hundreds of years, he still had time to be a melodramatic pansy. Incredible.

I wasn't doing much better. I was bleeding and taking heavy damage. They focused on wounds they'd made, tearing deeper and deeper into the tender flesh. I howled, spun, and slashed, but I was losing.

I fell to the ground reeling and shook like a wet dog. They clung hard to the wounds, refusing to let go. The pain was so incredible, at first I didn't even realize I was suddenly hearing the creatures themselves shrieking in agony. Something was hurting them, something other than me. But it was too late. I collapsed on my side from loss of blood. I thought I was a goner for sure when I felt someone beside me, ripping the little monkey-vampires off.

When I finally looked up, I was surrounded again, but this time by friendly faces.

The first face I saw was Junior. Gradually, more came into focus; Benito Cruz and other neighborhood half-vampires, Mo'Lock and a gang of ghouls, including Emek. They all stood there staring at the injured freak I was. Luckily, due to all the excitement, I was no longer high.

Benito stepped up and helped me to my feet. "Man, you look fucked up, dude!"

I said thanks, but it came out more like "franks." The wolf throat didn't want to cooperate and I wished I was human again.

As soon as the thought entered my brain, I felt my body begin to transform. With a crowd of gang-banging, semi-turned vampires and a few dozen L.A. ghouls watching, I went from total dog-boy to an upright half-man/half-wolf with a snout and fur-covered body. My clothes were completely gone, but my holster and gun had managed to hang on.

One of Benito's boys named Julio started laughing. "Dude, I think you looked better before!"

Everybody yucked it up at my expense until Mo'Lock came to my side and looked at me with an unreadable expression. The crowd milled around the grassy park. Nobody moved. The excitement was over. I didn't understand what the assembly was about. Something was up, and I has a sinking feeling I was the main attraction.

Mo'Lock stood over my wounded, furry body and took me by the shoulders. "Cal, how are you? How do you feel?"

"I feel like a guy who just turned into a fucking werewolf," I said, not altogether thrilled with the prospect of what I saw developing around me. The ghouls and vampires were watching me closely and I didn't like it. They were looking for something.

"A floodgate has been opened, Cal. We're all sure of it—we can all feel it." Mo'Lock gestured to his compatriots.

"So, what's that got to do with me?" I pushed him off me.

"You're part of it now, Cal. You're one of us."

"The fuck I am," I said.

I broke away from the group, feeling their eyes following me as I walked to the edge of the water to wash my wounds and drink. I had to resist the urge to lick myself, which only pissed me off more. At the stream's edge I got down on all fours and sniffed the water, then lapped up a few tonguefuls.

"There is a rash of unnatural incidents occurring all over the city. Emek was correct. Something big is happening." Mo'Lock came up behind me. "Cal, the city needs you."

I craned my head around. "Who're you, Jimmy Olsen?"

I went back to drinking like a dog. The taste of the water was foul, dead, like there was more in it than just the rot of the city.

I should've seen it coming. Of course he wasn't dead. That would be too easy. I leapt up on my haunches, but it was too late. Dave came flying at me from the water, wailing like a freaking banshee.

He was almost completely skinned. His flesh had melted from the bone. I didn't want him to touch me and fell backward against Mo'Lock, who was no less repulsed than I. The crowd of ghouls and vampire bangers screamed and scattered around us. I rolled, avoiding the bloody bone-hands that reached for me. Mo'Lock wasn't so lucky. As I jumped up, I saw the vampire lift the ghoul off the ground and toss him away like a rag doll. Mo'Lock hit a tree and slid to the ground headfirst.

That was it. I was pissed off.

I moved toward Dave. He was little more than a dripping skeleton. He had only one eye in his skull, which he was using to scan the ground where the shredded bodies of his monkey-things lay scattered. He backed away, but there wasn't going to be any goddamn chase this time. I moved fast, and slammed my fist straight into the side of his skull. It exploded like a tomato in a microwave, glorious fireworks of bone and blood.

The headless vampire stood in place, swaying for a moment, then collapsed in a heap of bones and slime. It was over.

The half-vampires and ghouls began to come up to me. One started clapping, then another. Soon the entire crowd was applauding, including Mo'Lock. It really got to me, so I reared back my head and howled at the sky.

Then I stopped. What the fuck was I doing? I couldn't live like this—as the very thing I'd made a living hunting and destroying.

I gestured for everybody to shut the hell up, and turned to Benito and Mo'Lock. They were waiting for some kind of answer from me. First I had to take care of business.

"If something is happening, I'll be your personal bloodhound. Everybody keep their ears to the ground. If there's been a sudden surge in paranormal activity, there has to be a reason and a source, so let's wait and see what happens, okay?"

The crowd all nodded to each other. Benito turned and gave a signal to his boys and they began to head out.

"Right now all I want is a thousand beers and some sleep."

Mo'Lock and I walked the other way as the crowd dispersed. I turned full-wolf and dropped to all fours without even realizing it. I felt a terrible sense of dread and loss, a sadness I'd never felt before. I should have been exhilarated with all this power, but I wasn't. It felt as uncomfortable as an itchy sweater. The werewolf thing was cool, but it wasn't me.

For now, I knew I could somewhat control my transformations between human and lycanthrope, but what would happen when the bloodlust took over? I could lose control. I couldn't live with that.

"Will I ever be a real human again?" It came out sounding a little more desperate than I'd intended.

"I'm not sure," said the ghoul. "Have you ever heard of a cure for shape-shifters?"

"No. But if there is, I'm going to find it. I have no intention of spending my life resisting the urge to eat everybody I meet."

"And I don't want to have to take you for walks."

"Fuck off."

Back at Sam's place, a miracle occurred. The Red Sea parted, one loaf of bread became a thousand, the sky rained frogs, and in the year 2003, the United States Postal Service actually managed to deliver a package.

Mo'Lock and I had been back for less then an hour. I'd shifted back to human form and showered. All my original wounds were healed, now replaced by injuries made by little monkey-vamp bites. I couldn't catch a break. I was doomed to be covered with stinging, painful wounds for the rest of my life.

Mo'Lock and I came as close as we ever do to arguing about the whole floodgate thing he and Emek had been going on about. I had my ideas and they were nowhere near as sinister as his. While the ghouls thought there was some kind of monster apocalypse coming, I thought there was a single cause for all of this. I didn't want to say anything until I was sure, though.

That's what triggered the fight.

Mo'Lock hated that I didn't share my every thought with him. Fuck him. This wasn't *Oprah*. This was my fucking life. I'd talk when I wanted to talk.

Finally, he got pissed off and stormed to the door. He almost tripped over the large, battered box on the step. Mo'Lock forgot he was mad and picked up the parcel.

There was no movement or sound coming from the battered carton. I feared the worst and immediately tore at the tape.

The top layer was all crumpled paper and little Styrofoam peanuts. I pulled the paper away, sending peanuts flying. For half a second I thought the box was empty.

"IT'S ABOUT TIME YOU FOUND ME, YOU STUPID MOTHERFUCKER!" blared from the box, accompanied by the foul stench of an unbrushed mouthful of nasty old teeth.

The ghoul and I had to back away. It was that bad. I tried to get Mo' to pull the screaming head out, but he pushed me forward. I held my breath and reached into the box. Inside I felt the hot, sweaty, semi-haired, completely scarred head of my old buddy Sam Burnett and lifted it to freedom. Half-melted packing peanuts peppered his face, and Styrofoam fragments were all over his mouth. He'd been eating the packing peanuts to survive. I would have laughed, but that was some fucked-up shit.

As I rested the head on the coffee table I shot the ghoul a look. "Mo'Lock. Listerine. Bathroom. Now!"

Sam was ranting, screaming, and throwing insults at a machine-gun pace as I made a comfortable resting place for him on the table. The words I could take, but the breath? Damn! Finally Mo'Lock came running back with the bottle of mouthwash. I grabbed it and poured it into Sam's mouth. He resisted at first, but finally gargled.

I felt like I'd deactivated a nuclear missile.

"So you fuckheads destroyed my house yet?"

I smiled. "Oh, and thank you for traveling cross-country to help my sorry old ass, and . . ."

"All right, all right!" Sam yelled. "Fill me in. Where's my body? You deal with Billy yet?"

I fish-eyed the ghoul. "No. We've been waiting for you."

Sam flipped out. Well, as much as a solo head can flip out. "What?! You mean to tell me you've been out here for a week plus and you've done nothing about finding my body?! What the fuck have you been doing?!"

"Been pretty busy, actually."

"Shut up!"

He was one angry head, but he didn't know the details. I filled him in on the flurry of activity, from the hipster werewolves to the showdown with Dave. I ended by updating him on the fate of his sheriff buddy. Sam took it pretty well. He screamed and yelled and somehow managed to turn his face red as a ripe tomato.

"How could he have fallen from that high in the middle of nowhere?" he asked when he had finally calmed down. "Any reports of flying beasties?"

"I don't know, Sam," I said. "Give me a chance to think. There's a pattern here somewhere, I can feel it. I'm pretty sure that Billy is a key element."

"You think so, shithead?"

I turned and pointed right in Sam's face on the coffee table. "You better start showing a little respect, or so fucking help me, I'll punt you all the way back to D.C."

Sam smiled. "There you go. That's more like it."

When I turned, Mo'Lock was glaring at me. "You talk to him. Couldn't you have told me?"

I started to tell him to fuck off, but he was right. I nodded and gave his shoulder a little slug. "No reason at all. Sorry."

I looked in my pockets for anything to give me a buzz but came up empty. Things were getting fucked up fast. I started getting cravings. On top of it all, I was a part-time werewolf. I could feel their eyes on me, but I ignored them and lit a cigarette. I dug through my desk and found the last of the stash of meth that I kept taped under the top drawer. It had survived the move.

I put the little glass bottle up to one nostril, held the other closed and snorted the crystals into my head. It stung, but within seconds I felt the effects. I chased it with a drink. Now I was ready for work.

Mo'Lock was frozen at the front window. I watched him until one of his eyebrows rose. He turned his head toward me and pointed with his thumb. "Cops are here."

I looked up, and sure as shit there were two LAPD blues getting out of a squad car in front of the house.

"Goddammitmotherfuckingshit," I muttered. I wiped my nose with the back of my hand. "Cover the head!"

Mo'Lock grabbed a dish rag and started to cover Sam's head until Sam spoke up. "Mojo, Moby . . . whatever the fuck yer name is," he yelled, "don't cover me. Look at the cops again."

Mo'Lock looked out the window once more as the two blues walked slowly up the sidewalk. I watched a slow, almost sinister grin grow across his lips, and I knew what Sam wanted him to see. They were ghouls. LAPD ghouls.

One was clean-cut, tall, and blond with a short crewcut. His badge read Hamm. The other was African-American, clean-cut, with light eyes and a shaved head. His badge read Shooter. The blond looked from me to Mo'Lock to the head on the table and nodded.

"Sam Burnett. We need to talk to you."

The head on the table was happy as hell to be the center of attention. "Good to see you boys. What's the rumpus?"

The ghoul cops looked at each other, confused. I stepped up and introduced myself and Mo'Lock and took over the conversation. "What's the trouble, officer?"

Shooter looked at me. His eyes were bright and dead at the same time, with a cold stare that gave me chills. My guess was that this is what you got when you combined the laid-back ease of a ghoul and the manic reality of a cop. What I couldn't guess was if it was a good thing. I was used to the East Coast type of ghoul.

"The Griffith Park Observatory," Shooter said, speaking like a machine. "There's some sort of disturbance up there. We have significant undead numbers on the force and we've managed to keep most of this below the radar of the humans. But if something isn't done soon, the results could be devastating."

I gestured for more. "What sort of disturbance?"

Hamm pulled out a Polaroid and flipped it to me. I caught it and looked at the snap as Mo'Lock peered over my shoulder. It was a shot of the observatory. I'd seen it before in films and TV, but now it looked different. The building was completely covered with scaffolding, but I'd heard it was shut down for renovation. No mystery there.

But the something else had no easy explanation: There was a black tear floating in midair, just above the yard of the historic building. A black, floating hole and something was crawling out of it.

Before I could ask what it was, Hamm handed me another photo that showed what the hell that "something" was. It was red, with bat-like wings, horns, and spikes all over its body, and the burning eyes of a demon. I didn't think I was going out on a limb guessing the floating tear was some sort of portal.

In the second picture, the red demon was airborne just outside the rip. It didn't take long for me to put two and two together, but Mo'Lock beat me to the punch.

"This would explain what happened to Sheriff Dawson."

"Let me see!" Sam screamed from the table.

Mo'Lock lifted Sam's head and hoisted him for a look, but something caught his eye before he saw the photos.

"Wait!"

Mo'Lock stopped at the open front door where Sam was looking outside at the dirt-covered yard.

"What's up?" I asked.

"Not much," he said, "but last time I was home I had a fucking lawn."

We were all outside looking at the raked dirt surrounding Sam's house, but beside the inarguable fact that someone had stolen Sam's lawn, there wasn't a lot to see. I recalled my earlier thoughts of Dawson. With the flying demon added to the mix, I had an angle.

"Sam, you have a ladder?"

"Yeah, it's in the gardening shed with my other supplies," Sam spat. "No, you stupid fuck, I don't!"

I ignored the sarcastic head and asked Shooter to give me a leg up to the porch overhang. From there I could get to the roof. I had a hard time climbing at first, until I remembered the little bug I'd picked up. I concentrated hard, seeing if I could transform only a little. I didn't want to become a full werewolf and ruin another set of clothes, but I needed the added strength and agility. It worked. My body stayed the same, but my teeth and snout turned slightly doggish. Thank God nobody could see me.

Once on the roof, I looked down at the dirt and my hunch bore fruit. There were markings in the dirt, strange lines and squiggles going all the way around and forming a circle. Suddenly my current run of bad luck began to make sense.

"Hey Sam, what did the kid use to trap you?" I yelled down.

Sam paused. "I told you . . . a magic circle."

"Well, one guess what's surrounding your house."

We destroyed the circle. Hamm and Shooter worked side by side with Mo'Lock and me as we kicked and spread the dirt, destroying every last symbol etched into the earth. Sam rested on the porch by the door.

When we finished the yard, I started giving orders. I told Mo'Lock to go to the observatory with the LAPD ghouls and see what could be done about the tear in the air. "At the very least try to capture or kill whatever comes out of there."

"We've been trying," Shooter said.

"Try harder."

Mo'Lock stepped up. "What about you?"

"The head and I are going to pay a visit to Billy's house."

"What if he isn't the cause of all this?" the ghoul asked.

"I can smell his stinky teenage sweat all over this dirt. It's him all right, and I'll lay money that he's behind the tear. Looks like devil boy isn't just happy messing with this dimension. Now he's breaking into others."

"He might destroy Sam's body if you get too close."

I smiled. "At this point, that's a gamble I'm willing to take."

From the porch Sam yelled, "Hey, fuck you!"

"Besides," I went on as I grinned, "I don't think Billy's ready for what I've become."

Mo'Lock nodded. "Human magic versus monster magic."

"Two different applications." I smiled wide and showed my new canines. If I concentrated, I could make them shoot in and out of their sockets.

I might have been fucked up, but I had this werewolf thing by the balls.

Mo'Lock and the undead cops left for Griffith Park, so I picked Sam's head up and headed into the house for some supplies.

Once again I needed to suit up for a fight with an enemy that had the upper hand. I hated that. But I had a few things on my side, not the least of which was how pissed I was that the little fucker had put a curse on the house and almost got me killed no less than three times. I was gonna bitch-slap that prick like he'd never been bitch-slapped.

Inside I loaded up the .38 and packed a spare. Unfortunately, with this type of scenario there wasn't really much specialized equipment. Holy water, silver bullets, and all that were only for certain sects within the monster community. I did take a small anti-magic amulet with me, just in case, but I prefer not to rely on things like that. As far as I'm concerned, it's like using the enemy's weapons.

Besides, we were dealing with something very different; the human monster. All I could really bring to the party was some heat and my brains. Oh, and my leather sap, in case the whole thing could be solved by a crack to the skull.

I put Sam in a box with a towel and prepared to head out, but as I lowered him into the box, an ominous and familiar click came from the open front door. I was frozen, holding the head and staring dumbly as Sabrina lowered her camera and grinned like a fiend.

"Monster hunter kills competition," she said. "I can see the headline now."

Then Sam opened his eyes and yelled, "Can't you see we're busy!"

Sabrina almost dropped her camera. She staggered into the house and then back against the wall for support. I prayed she'd faint so we could make a break, but she was too tough. She gathered her composure with a few deep breaths. Within fifteen seconds she was cool, calm, and ready for another shock. That tore it—I liked her.

"We have some metalhead in Sherman Oaks that's been playing with satanic rites and interdimensional tampering. Possibly conjuring curses—the whole gamut of nasty evil," I said, lowering Sam into the box once more. "Sounds like the kid started out playing, but we have a trail of bodies . . ."

"Brian Hogue, Carl Potter, and Sheriff Dawson," Sabrina said as she came up to me. "They were the apparitions outside my window."

I shot her a quick glance. "Dawson too?"

"Wha—? Who? Dawson?! I thought he was dead!" Sam was freaking out in the box.

I waved for Sam to shut up.

I grinned. "So, they appeared again?"

She grinned back. "This time I went outside and confronted them. They wanted my help."

"Could this get any fucking weirder?" Sam yelled from the box.

"They talked to you?" I added.

She stepped closer to me. "That's all they wanted. They'd gained some power working with Billy, learning Satanic rites. They used the last of their power to contact me and tell me how they were killed."

"By curses Billy Fuller put on them?"

She nodded slowly. "Yeah. Sounds like they were all buddies. They experimented with the whole witchcraft, devil thing . . . then Billy screwed them. Hogue and Potter were just into it for kicks. Fuller got serious." She was staring at me as she talked.

I swallowed hard. Suddenly, it was getting hot. Something about her confronting the apparitions, I don't know, turned me on.

"Why was Dawson with them?"

"Some spirit world unity. Victims bound together, united in exposing their killer." She was whispering.

"Oh," was all I could muster.

We had both moved forward. We were close, inches apart. My whole body was about to start shaking, so I just did it. I leaned in and kissed her and, thank God, she did the same. It had been a long time since I'd kissed a woman, but it never felt like this. Kissing Sabrina felt right.

After a long pause, we parted. We both smiled and laughed, shy like kids. It was the perfect moment, a moment about to be shattered by a pissed-off head.

"This is all very touching, but in case you haven't noticed...I DON'T HAVE A MOTHERFUCKING BODY AND I SURE WOULD LIKE TO GET THIS GODDAMN SHOW ON THE ROAD!"

I closed the box. Billy could wait another hour.

Sabrina wanted to come with Sam and me to Billy's place in Sherman Oaks, but I didn't like the idea. The kid was way too dangerous. Luckily when I told her about the rip and the demon that had been spotted coming out, she decided the observatory had better photo opportunities.

I watched her walk to her Beetle and glance back at me no less than three times with a stupid grin plastered on my face that was impossible to erase. I hardly even noticed Sam yelling from inside the box as I carried him to my car, but once we started driving he was hard to ignore. He didn't shut up the entire trip. He bitched about how I treated him, he bitched about being severed from his body, he even bitched about being hungry and having to piss.

That's when I pulled the car over.

"What do you mean you have to piss?"

"I gotta piss and I'm hungry."

"You felt this before?"

"Not like this," said the head in the box.

I licked my lips. "Could mean we're close to where your body is being hidden."

"It could mean Billy is shoving corncobs up my ass," Sam blurted. "Let's move, asshole!"

I drove off the shoulder and took an extra sharp turn so Sam rattled inside the box like a melon. We drove straight to Billy's house, a small but nice place in a quiet, middle-class neighborhood. It was kind of on the sleepy side, but kind of on the snooty side, as well.

The Fuller house was a one-story rancher with green shutters and matching trim. I parked a few doors away and left the head behind with the windows rolled down for air. I needed both of my hands to work. This was dangerous work, not fucking football.

There was only one car in the Fuller driveway, a rundown, older model sedan. In fact, of all the houses on the block, the Fullers' looked the worst. It was obvious there was trouble inside. Homes have a way of outwardly showing the distress of their occupants. Whether it's an unkempt lawn or a thick layer of pizza menus on the doorknob, I've found that people always have ways of crying out without actually making a sound.

I tapped lightly on the door. Nothing. I tapped again, then rang the bell. Within seconds I heard movement, a muffled female voice, and the door being unlocked from the inside.

A middle-aged woman wearing a Denny's waitress outfit answered the door. She had a pretty face, but wore a tired, haggard expression. You didn't have to be a psychic to read this one: divorced, trying to survive on her own and keep the house by going back to work. Waitressing was the only thing she could find and it was killing her. Plus, she had Billy for a kid. I felt bad for her.

As soon as she saw me, she slumped and sighed.

"Oh dear, what's he done now?"

She thought I was a cop. I let her. "Maybe you can tell me, ma'am."

"Call me Doris," she said. "Come in. I was just making some Sanka."

It was a normal house in every way, but oddly dated. The living room was off to the right of the foyer. The entire color scheme was dull orange and brown. There was a TV, a couch, a lima bean–shaped coffee table, and a painting depicting a snowy lake scene with a gold frame frosted with white. It screamed *Better Homes and Gardens* circa 1977. It reminded me of the house I grew up in. As soon as I saw the giant wooden fork and spoon hanging on the kitchen wall, I felt right at home. We sat down at a small, round, Formica-topped table while Doris Fuller poured two cups of steaming hot instant joe. I couldn't take my eyes off the wallpaper. It was yellow with a velvet paisley pattern.

She smiled at me and lowered her eyes, as if waiting for more shit to be dumped on her head. I knew she had no idea of the evil being generated in her home. In fact, I was amazed I hadn't felt anything. Usually when I stepped into a threatening atmosphere, I could feel a strange tension in the air, or lately, in my wounds. Here I felt nothing. It was clean.

"Things have been terrible around here, what with all the deaths. Poor Billy has been so depressed," she sighed. "Frankly, I'm worried."

"Well, that's why I'm here, Doris," I said in my best soothing voice.

"I know, I know. It's about the Wayside Cemetery, isn't it? I caught him sneaking in late last night and he told me where he'd been. I gave him what for and he promised me he'd stay away from there once and for all." She ended with a sip and smile, leaving a red ring on the rim of the mug.

Wayside Cemetery.

That had to be where Sam's body was stashed.

I pretended to sip the hot swill. "Well, Doris, it sounds like you have things well in hand here. Is Billy home by any chance?"

She gave me the "go on" gesture. "Yes. The little bugger caught himself a devil of a cold last night. He's asleep upstairs, so if it isn't absolutely necessary, I'd prefer it if we just let him be."

"I guess there's no reason to bother him," I said, standing. "Just make sure he stays out of that cemetery, okay."

I smiled and gave her a wink. Big mistake.

She hurried after me and tried to block my way out. "I didn't catch your name, Mr. . . ."

"McDonald, ma'am. Cal McDonald."

"Is there a Mrs. McDonald?"

I sidestepped her and tried to smile, but she had me cornered. "No, there isn't."

She smiled and poofed her hair net. "Maybe you could stop by again for something a little stronger than Sanka."

I bowed my head. "That would be nice, Doris," I offered weakly, ducking out of the house like a cat on fire. I had to wave back at her fifteen fucking times before she finally closed the door.

Back in the car, I updated Sam, and we waited half an hour for Doris to leave for Denny's. As soon as her car turned the corner and disappeared I went into action. I went to the back door of the house and jimmied the sliding glass door, then crept down a narrow hall until I saw a door with a "No Humans Allowed" sign.

I placed the anti-magic amulet around my neck. If the punk tried anything it would bounce right off me, but I still felt like a jackass wearing it. All I needed was some sandals and patchouli and I was ready for the smoke-in. I also had my newfound werewolf power as a backup. Between the two I figured I could take the kid down and put an end to this bullshit once and for all.

I tried the doorknob and it gave, revealing every teenage reject's room rolled into one. Posters, mostly metal and industrial bands, covered the walls and ceiling. Trash littered the floor. There was a purple plastic bong and beer bottles, and an ashtray full of butts and spent matches. The bed was a single mattress tucked between the TV and the stereo.

The mattress was stuffed with sheets and pillows to make it look like someone was sleeping in it. I intentionally stood there and stared at the bed, looking as dumb as I could. I even went a little slack-jawed, but what I was really doing was increasing the wolfishness of my ears and eyes just enough to read the room without looking around. Because, despite appearances, I wasn't alone.

There was a closet to my right. I could feel Billy eyeing me through the wooden slats.

I decided it was time he had a little scare of his own. I took out my backup piece, a .45 with a handy-dandy silencer, then stepped over to the bed and unloaded the entire clip into the pile under the blankets. I riddled the fake body until the room was filled with smoke and feathers.

After the last shot, a whimpering gasp came from the closet.

I turned and leveled the gun on the closet. "Get out here."

Billy Fuller came out. He was as skinny as a flagpole. His hair was long and greasy and acne covered his cheeks. He wore a Skid Row T-shirt. He was not only evil, but horribly behind the times.

Billy was shaking, but his eyes were darting from side-to-side. I could see he still had a trick up his sleeve. Even so, I was shocked when he came at me, stopping within a foot, raising an amulet of his own, and chanting.

"*Ammul Kanna Keela!*"

I yawned and showed him the charm around my neck. "Sticks and stones, punk," I barked, slapping him so hard he flew against the wall. My hand had a thick coating of Clearasil across the palm. I walked over and lifted him up by his T-shirt.

"I'm gonna ask you this once, kid. If I don't get the answer I want, I'm gonna shove the gun up your ass and play butthole roulette. Where's the incantation you used on Sam Burnett?"

Billy peed himself. "I threw it away."

The pipsqueak still had some fight in him. He was so small. I had to remind myself that he was also a killer.

"Don't bullshit me, Billy," I said, pulling his face close to mine. "I know if you throw away the incantation, the curse won't work. I've been at this a lot longer than you, so don't bullshit a bullshitter."

I gave him a quick yank. Our noses touched, and for a single instant I allowed my face to shift to a wolf, then back again. I just wanted to give him a peek.

"Where's . . . the fucking . . . incantation?"

He was beaten. The kid pointed to the bong. I threw him onto the bullet-riddled mattress and turned the bong over. Taped to the base was a small piece of parchment with some mumbo-jumbo scrawled on it. I took the paper and turned to Billy as I reloaded my piece.

"The body. It's at Wayside Cemetery, right?"

Billy nodded.

"Where?" I slammed another clip into the .45.

He shook and started to cry. "There's a tomb for the dick who founded this piece-of-shit town. I left it in there."

"Good boy. Now listen to me," I said reholstering my heater, "You're gonna clean yourself up good, then you're gonna march yourself down to the sheriff's office and turn yourself in. You're a kid. You'll get the easy treatment and a lot of attention. You'll be the most popular psycho in the state."

The kid stared at me blankly.

I waved. "Hello? You understand? Otherwise, I come back with Sam in one piece. Believe me, that old son-of-a-bitch will tear you apart. He isn't as understanding as me."

Finally the kid nodded. I turned my back, knowing if the kid didn't try anything with my defenses down he'd do as I told him.

"*Satana Karise!*"

A bolt of pain shot through my body like electricity. I yelled and fell to one knee. The little fucker had no intention of letting up.

When I turned back, Billy wasn't alone. We had some company. A red, winged creature stood behind him, in front of a black portal ripped into the air. I stood back up and looked at the kid. He was smirking, his greasy hair slung down over one eye. My blood boiled. Who did this little punk-ass bitch think he was?

"Nice try, mister. But I have friends now—real friends—and they'll protect me against you and anybody else who tries to stop me. We made a deal."

I stared up at the demon, maybe the same one who'd dropped the sheriff to his death, and I could see by the look in its narrow eyes the kid was right. If I wanted Billy Fuller, I'd have to take on the creature first. I put my piece back in the holster and began to selectively transform myself. My hands changed to claws, my jaw sprouted wolf-teeth, and I increased my bulk just enough to not tear apart my clothes.

I was ready for a fight.

The creature took Billy by the shoulder and stepped around him. It rattled its wings and licked its long nails.

I waited.

It made the first move. It came at me shrieking and tackled me head on. I took the blow and fell backward, but managed to rake my claws across its lower back. It yowled and rolled off me. As it turned back to attack, I slashed its throat wide open. The shrieking stopped. Blood sprayed.

The demon tried to struggle away, but I knew I had it down for the count. I lunged on top of it and brought it down hard. I tore at its wings, pulling one completely out of its back. Finally, the creature stopped moving.

Just to be sure I'd killed it (and to put a scare into the kid), I pulled out my piece and blasted a slug into the demon's head, blowing its supernatural brains all over the shag carpet.

Victorious, I stood and shook the blood from my body like a dog after a bath. But I'd miscalculated.

Billy Fuller was gone, and so was the rip in the air.

Before I left the Fuller house I covered the dead demon with a sheet and took a hit off the kid's bong. I knew I'd sort of freaked the last time I got high, but it looked like the kid had some pretty good stuff.

I told Sam what happened on the way to the cemetery. Billy Fuller had more tricks up his sleeve and we had to stop him before he realized how much damage he could do. If he'd actually made a deal with some sort of demonic power, the repercussions could be catastrophic for both the kid and Los Angeles.

Sam, of course, was an unstoppable ballbreaker about the whole thing.

"Well, little Cal fucked up again. I woulda killed the little fucker when I had the chance."

"Lay off. I ain't killing no little kid, no matter what he did," I said, driving through the cemetery gate.

"You are such a pussy. I don't know how you survive."

That was it. I slammed on the brakes and stopped the car. The box with Sam in it went flying to the floor.

I grabbed it and leaned in. "I just saved your ass, old man. Don't you think it's about time for a little respect?"

Sam's head rolled its eyes. "Sorry."

"And?"

"Thank you."

I nodded and grabbed the box. The tomb was right in the center of the otherwise plain graveyard. It had a big steel door, chained shut. The padlock was brand new, so I knew it was Billy's doing. I blasted the lock with the silencer and pushed the door open. Daylight flooded into the crypt.

Inside, on a white stone block, was Sam's headless body sitting like a guy waiting for the bus. It was slumped over, and the raggedy old suit it wore was covered with mud and dust. I took out Sam's head and placed it next to the body, and then made the first in a series of big mistakes.

I touched the body.

The damn thing flipped out. It went completely fucking nuts, swinging its arms and running around the tomb like a spastic child on fire. It was out of control, running in circles. I tried to grab it but it was too much to handle. Sam screamed. I screamed back. The headless body decided to bolt out of the tomb, making a blind run for it.

"Careful! Don't hurt my fucking body! Catch it!" Sam screamed.

"I'm trying! I'm trying!"

I chased the body all over the graveyard as it juked and hurdled headstones. How it knew where the obstacles were was anybody's guess. I finally got pissed and ran at the thing full speed. I tackled it, then held it in a bear hug and hauled it back to the tomb. Once inside, I pinned it securely next to its head.

"Now burn the incantation!"

"I know what to do, Sam."

"Burn it!"

I lit the parchment. As it burned, Sam's head began to levitate as the lines of time and space sparked and smoked. By the time the small paper was ash, Sam and his body were reunited—all five foot four of his cranky ass.

"Man, I gotta piss like nobody's business!"

"Hold it. We gotta get up to Griffith Park and see what's happening up there."

"I ain't doing anything until I piss and get some food!"

Fine. We stopped at a burger joint on the way to the park. Sam drained himself and ate five hamburgers without taking a breath. After nearly choking to death, he was ready for action.

"Let's go kill this little bastard," Sam smiled. Every scar on his messed-up head moved like a thousand tiny grins.

I was about to pull away from the burger dump when suddenly everything went black. And I mean everything, including street lights and the sun. In the blink of an eye, total darkness—like an instant eclipse. Everything came to a halt and for one nanosecond, the world was silent. A beat later, I began hearing screams and car horns in the darkness. It was as black as a starless midnight sky. People were panicking.

A car, practically on two wheels, came smashing through the side of the restaurant wall and landed on top of a table of six with a thunderous, smoking crash. There was blood and smoke and screaming everywhere. I yelled for someone to call an ambulance.

As we moved through the unnatural dark, the entire city was in chaos. There were screams and crashes everywhere. In the sky I heard helicopters, but couldn't see them. People were running into the streets and getting struck down by cars. It was horrible.

Though we wanted to, we didn't allow ourselves to stop and help. I looked over at Sam as we drove toward the park. There was a horror in his eyes I'd never seen before. Maybe the ghouls had been right all along. The floodgates had opened. The day of the monsters was upon us, and it was all that little fucker Billy's fault.

Maybe, if we hurried, we could do something about it. If not, we were in for a long period of darkness, and most likely, the end of life as we knew it.

I drove through the darkness like a madman, from Sherman Oaks to North Hollywood, but just as I prepared to make the turn to the observatory, I saw a nightmare. Just ahead of us, a woman was being dragged from her car by a red, winged creature identical to the one I killed. I slammed on the brakes and came to a sudden stop, catching the woman and the creature in my headlights.

As I ran toward the action, the creature stopped, and tried to take flight. I lowered my .45 and aimed.

BLAMM! The shot tore through the side of the demon's face. It released the woman, who wisely ran away in a screaming panic. I shot again. This time I hit it square in the forehead. It dropped to the pavement like a big wet rag, but I didn't get two seconds to enjoy the victory. Sam tapped my shoulder and pointed up. The black sky filled with flying creatures.

"You have an extra piece?"

I handed him my .38 snub-nose.

"What are we gonna do?" I'd never heard that tone in Sam Burnett's voice. It was fear, plain and simple. Fear and helplessness.

"I don't have a clue."

But I knew whatever we could do had to start at that rip in the air. Somewhere in that black hole was the answer. As we got back to the car, three demons landed and stole away the body of their fallen comrade. Before they flew off again, they looked at me and hissed.

I reached for my gun, but Sam grabbed my arm. "Don't waste your time, son. Let's get to the observatory."

He was right. I peeled out of there, doing eighty down a residential street until I cut back onto Alameda. And then once on Victory, I opened her up to almost a hundred. Every time Sam looked up he saw creatures flying in all directions. Some of them had people in their claws.

I turned on the radio.

"... UNKNOWN SPECIES OF CREATURES NUMBERING IN THE HUNDREDS ARE ATTACKING AND KILLING CITIZENS. THERE IS NO WORD ON WHAT THEY ARE OR WHY THEY ARE ATTACKING ..."

It was madness.

I changed the station.

". . . CITIZENS ARE WARNED TO STAY IN THEIR HOMES ..."

I turned off the radio. Christ.

Just as I saw the hills of Griffith Park ahead through the bleak haze of darkness, I noticed movement on the streets. Instead of listening to the radio reports, people were coming out of their homes and into the streets. Suddenly there was a crowd in front of me. I slammed on the brakes and skidded within an inch of killing more than a dozen people.

But they weren't people. It was Emek and a group of other ghouls. Emek came around to the window.

"What's the word?" I asked.

"Complete chaos."

"I'm heading up to the observatory. Can you and your buddies deal with the . . . whatever the fuck they are?"

Emek nodded.

"Thanks. Sam, head back to your place," I said as I began to shift to my wolf form, "I'll go the rest of the way on foot."

I was gone before he even answered.

I dropped on all fours and ran into the park as fast as my legs would carry me. I could smell action ahead. The scent of Mo'Lock and Sabrina guided me to the top of the thickly wooded hill.

The observatory came into view at the crest of the hill. There was a small crowd waiting. Mo'Lock stood by Sabrina near the main building, speaking with the two LAPD ghouls. At the gate of the observatory grounds other cops guarded the roads. I assumed they were ghouls too, but it was the floating black hole that I was most interested in. That was my way to get to Billy and put an end to this madness once and for all.

Mo'Lock, Sabrina, and the cops approached me as I rose to my feet and shifted back to human. Sabrina was looking at me strangely, but I couldn't tell if she'd seen me in wolf form or not.

"Anything happened here? The valley is bedlam."

"A bunch of those red things flew out," Mo'Lock said, "but we couldn't do anything. It was right after it went dark."

Sabrina smiled. "I got the photos to prove it."

I smiled at her. If she saw me shift, she wasn't letting on.

Hamm and Shooter looked worried. "We have a report of another hole in South Central," Hamm said.

Shooter finished. "If this spreads much further, we won't be able to do anything to stop it."

I looked at the rip. "Mo'Lock, give me a leg up. I'm going in."

"I'm going with you," Mo'Lock insisted.

I pulled him aside and whispered. "Not this time, buddy. I think this Billy kid made some sort of deal with an evil force… a spiritual force. I don't think someone of your undead nature should be messing around in there."

Mo'Lock looked to see if anybody was listening. "Are you saying the hole is the gateway to . . ."

"I'm not saying anything for sure. But if it is, you could put yourself in danger, not having a soul and all."

The ghoul thought about it and then nodded. "I'll be here if you need me."

"You always are." I slapped his arm. "How about that leg up?"

I walked to the edge of the floating hole in the air. The lowest point of the opening was about two feet above my head. I stared up at it then glanced over at Sabrina.

"See you when I get back."

She tried to smile. "You better. You owe me an interview."

Mo'Lock hoisted me up to the opening. I grabbed the edge. It felt hot and spongy-wet, but I was able to get a grip and pulled myself up and over. The next thing I knew, I was in a black expanse and the hole was gone. I was in.

There was nothing but total darkness. I could have been in a stadium or a closet. I couldn't tell. It wasn't the kind of darkness I was used to, but a thick, airless dark without any sign of light or sound. With no plan to speak of, I began to walk into the darkness but no matter how long I walked I couldn't tell if I was making progress. As far as I knew I was walking in place. There was no horizon, no way to judge where I'd been or where I was going.

I stopped, feeling the futility of just walking, and decided to try something. I took out a cigarette and lit a match. The fire swelled up and for an instant I saw something very strange . . . the barest glimpse of stone walls and smoke. As I stood there smoking, I began to hear a sound nearby. It was a voice laughing.

"Billy?"

There was no reply, but the laughter got closer and began to move around me in a slow circle.

"I know it's you, Billy," I called out. "I know you're there."

The laughter stopped and I squinted as a figure appeared just ahead of me. It was the kid. He walked out of the darkness and stopped a few yards away.

"You can't beat me in here, mister," he said.

"Oh yeah? Why's that?"

"I've got friends in here."

"You had friends back home, too," I said, "but you killed them."

There was a very long pause.

"They got scared. Brian said he wanted out."

"Out of what, Billy?"

Billy stepped closer and I could see now that he had changed. His skin was rougher. Instead of acne, his arms and face had sprouted dozens of tiny gray horns.

"The pact. We made a deal and Brian wanted out. You can't just break a deal."

I took a hit off my smoke, keeping it nice and casual. "Yeah, I can see that. What was the deal?"

Billy laughed. "Simple, a little blood for some power."

"So you got the power and all you could think to do with it was hurt people."

That pissed him off. He stepped a little closer, and for the first time I could see that we weren't alone. There were shapes moving in the background, hundreds of them.

"None of this would have happened if your old friend hadn't come snooping around!" Billy spat.

"Maybe, maybe not."

I used my last cigarette to light another. I offered one to the kid. He shook his head.

"So now what, Billy?" I gestured around to the crowd closing in on me. "You and your friends going to kill me too? Then who, your Mom?"

Billy looked genuinely stunned. "No! Why would I kill my mom?!"

"Well, those things—your buddies—are out there causing a lot of trouble. I had to shoot one to stop him from dragging a woman out of her car. What'd you think he was going to do to her?

Kill her, rape her, eat her? Could have just as easily been your mom on the way to work."

Billy twitched.

I'd planted that seed of doubt.

In the background, the shapes shifted restlessly. They seemed nervous. A large figure pushed through, coming up behind the kid. I took a step back. The shape was huge and muscular. It was a living shadow, a wall of blackness standing behind the boy who had sold his soul.

"This the deal maker?" I asked.

Billy nodded slowly. His skin looked as if it was clearing. The shape didn't make a sound.

"How'd you get in touch with the big guy?" I asked, trying to keep the conversation nice and easy.

Billy swallowed nervously. "Got it from a book of incantations."

"Sure you weren't listening to the rock 'n' roll records backward? Smoking the moon cabbage?" I winked.

Billy cracked a smile.

"By the way," I went on, "I took a hit off your stash after you took off. Hope that's cool with you."

That got me a full grin. There ain't a teen on the planet that can resist the pot-smoking adult. In his rebellious, confused brain, that made me the coolest thing since, well, the last dope smoker he met. It was just that way at that age. Luckily for most, it passes— unless you're me.

His horns looked like pimples again. I had him. I knew the deal: I'd dug around witchcraft as a kid, too. I'd played with the Ouija board and levitated my pals on the tips of my fingers. All kids do it, but this kid went too far because he was tempted. Because some evil fuck gave him a taste of true power.

Suddenly the huge dark shape put its giant, shadowy hand on Billy's shoulder and spoke. "This one is mine."

I flicked my butt and lit another. "That doesn't work for me."

"Then you will die in here."

I feigned fright and took a long drag. "Tell you what, let the pimple factory go. I'll stay here and fight you. You win, you get me and can pretty much do whatever you want after that. Do we have a deal?"

The dark shape laughed.

"I asked you if we had a deal," I added, padding the plan. "I know you're a man who follows deals to the letter. You're bound to them, aren't you? You and me, in front of all your buddies, in plain sight. To the death."

The shape laughed again and shoved Billy at me. The kid slammed hard against my body and looked up at me. He looked scared. I didn't blame him. So was I.

"You stay here," I told the kid, "If the hole opens, jump through it."

Billy nodded, near tears. "Okay."

"But you're still in big fucking trouble."

"I know."

Billy stepped away as I looked up at the huge shape. He was about eight feet wide and just as tall, with arms the size of tree trunks and legs to match. He was all shadow, without features, but even through the darkness I could see the familiar horns and cloven feet. The shape was allowing me to see this. It was part of the illusion, but I didn't give a shit. He was just another whining spirit to me, and I knew his weak spot.

The shape roared and came at me. I ducked sideways and transformed faster than I had before. This time it was for real. I went full-blown werewolf as my clothes shredded from my body. As the shape lunged I rolled and kneed him in the gut, sending him to the floor. The crowd gasped in unison.

The shape wasn't down for long, though. He stood right up and smashed down on my head. If I'd been a cartoon, he would have turned me into an accordion. But, being flesh and blood, he broke bones and drew blood. I rolled with the slam and tried to rake his belly. My claws passed through air. Either he was fast or my plan was on course.

Before the next blow could be thrown, I raised my hands. "Wait, wait, wait!"

The shape stopped.

"You're cheating. We had a deal. You are bound by your deals."

The shape loomed silent. The crowd muttered. I glanced at Billy to see if he was okay and he gave me a nod. That's kids for you; one minute they're trying to kill you, the next minute they're your pal.

"What do you mean?" the shape bellowed.

"You're cheating."

The shape looked stunned. "I am not."

Then he let loose with the hard stuff. I knew he would. I just had no idea how much it would hurt.

He waved his hand without touching me. My flesh exploded, ripping beneath my furry pelt. Suddenly I was covered in blood, staggering in unbelievable pain. I fell to my knees. The shadow was shredding the skin from my body.

I looked up at the shape for a split second and saw a milky film between us. It was there! It was the lie. He'd broken the deal and the illusion flickered.

Then he waved his other hand. I heard, then felt, bones snapping inside my body. I cried out. I couldn't help it. The pain was unreal.

"I knew this would be easy," he said, "but not this easy. It's hard to believe you're the one I feared would ruin my plans." His voice was thick and cocky, but like all of these assholes, he just had to talk. "It was my idea to show the boy how to use the circles. It was me who trapped you and sent your life spiraling into hell!"

I rolled in my own blood. "It wasn't that big a change, really."

He waved his hand and my fur tore open across my belly. I was hurting and bleeding out fast. If I was going to make this work, I had to do it fast.

I screamed up at him. "You broke the deal!"

He stopped.

He knew I was right. He knew he had a secret.

I pulled myself to my feet and used every ounce of strength to concentrate on my werewolf power. I felt my wounds stop bleeding. I felt the wounds seal shut. As long as I was a lycanthrope, I could regenerate—at least until I lost too much blood.

But the shape saw what I was doing and motioned at me. I felt my blood run cold. He was taking away the virus that made me werewolf. He was curing me of the curse and killing me at the same time. Once human I would die easily, and he knew it.

I stood there wearing nothing but blood and my gun, pointing. "You are bound by the deal! The deal was YOU and me! YOU and me!"

The shape lowered its arm quickly as if some other force pushed it down. Then after a long silence the shape said, "This is me."

I grinned and shook my head. "No it isn't. Show your true self. That's the fucking deal. I said plain sight. That means showing your true self, you bastard!"

There was a stunned silence as everybody froze in the shadows. There are few things that bind devils and demons, but one is the sanctity of the deal. I got this one on a technicality.

The huge shadowy form was an illusion for human eyes. I knew it. He knew it, and now everybody knew it. I set him up when I made him agree to fight me in plain sight. I used my wolf form, sure, but I never denied my power. Plus, he felt it inside me. The shadow, on the other hand, lied by omission. Slowly, the illusion faded and I saw the true Deal Maker on the floor in front of me.

I stared down at the master of darkness, revealed. No more than a foot tall, he looked like an overcooked rump roast with little black sticks for limbs, tiny, red eyes, and slits for his mouth and nose. Even though I was in pain, I started laughing.

The little thing on the ground waved its tiny stick arms at me. "So now you know. Still, I will prevail! I have always lived! And I always will! What can you do to me that hasn't already been tried? You win this time, but I'll be back and . . ."

The little thing on the floor went on and on. Billy was in shock at the demon he had served. I gave the kid a nod.

"You do it," I said. "I'm too fucked up."

Billy stepped forward and raised his foot high. He brought it down on the rump roast demon and splattered him all over the void. I scanned the darkness. All of the winged shapes had receded back into their demonic realm. Today's invasion of the living world was officially a failure.

I patted Billy's back as he helped me limp to the opening. "In case I didn't mention it," I said, "you're still in a shit-load of trouble."

"I know."

"I mean, you can't just go around killing people."

"Yeah," the kid said, "but I bet you've killed tons of dudes."

He had a point, but I wasn't buying it. "Don't even."

Through the rip I could see the trees of Griffith Park and the shimmering view of the city below through the crack. Billy stopped at the opening and looked up at me.

"Man, what am I gonna do? They're gonna fry me."

"Just tell them the truth. Tell them the devil made you do it."

I'd like to tell you there was a grand reunion outside the rip, but if there was I'm not the one to ask. I fell out of the hole and hit the grass naked and unconscious. Mo'Lock told me later the only word I said was "Ow."

I woke up in a hospital bed three days later with twenty-three broken bones, four hundred and seventeen stitches, and more bruises, contusions, twists, and pulls than any doctor could count. Both legs and one arm were in a cast, as was my pelvis. They had me in one of those steel halos with the screws. On the upside, I had a morphine dispenser that I drained daily.

Because of the strange nature of the crimes and no solid evidence linking him to any deaths, Billy Fuller was sent to an institution for mental observation until a trial could be held. Evidently the kid was following my advice; he'd told them the truth.

Of course, they thought the kid was fucking nuts.

Good for him. I hoped he took advantage of his second chance. If he didn't, I'd kill him. I sent him a little note saying so.

When I woke the first time, Sam and Mo'Lock were there waiting for me. Sam was picking a scab next to the nub on the left side of his head he called an ear. Mo'Lock was sitting there, watching me. If it had been anybody but a ghoul, it would have been sweet. Instead, it freaked me out.

"How are you feeling, Cal?" he said the nanosecond my eyes opened.

"I've been better." I reached for the IV and gave the button a push. "Better now."

I felt fine.

"Look at you lying there, you big pussy!" Sam walked to the side of the bed. "I got hurt too, ya know. You don't see me lying in bed!"

I laughed. Mo'Lock didn't get that he was joking and glared at the old man.

"How'd everything work out?"

"Like nuthin' ever happened. The cops cleaned up all the bodies and intercepted most of the reports. A few stories snuck under the radar. The networks reported that an unexpected eclipse occurred and a gang of toughs attacked some folks. Once again we're in the clear because people would rather keep their heads in the sand."

"What about . . . ," Mo'Lock struggled to find the words, ". . . the werewolf?"

"Gone. Whatever that freak did to me in there, he stripped me of the power."

Everybody got quiet then, and it had nothing to do with me. It was about what I'd fought. Nobody wanted to face what and who it may have been. It was Sam who finally broached the topic with his usual grace.

"So you think it was the devil-man himself that whupped you?"

I shook my head. "Doubt it. I'd like to think the big guy wouldn't be that easy to beat. If it was, then I'm the luckiest fucker walking the earth."

Everybody agreed, but all the talk was getting on my nerves. I turned up the IV flow.

Sam had one more thing to ask as I slipped into a drugged-out haze. "Look," he said nervously, "I'm thinking I might move around a bit. You know, get away, see the world and all that crap. I was wondering if you were planning on sticking around L.A. for awhile and . . ."

"Yes," I said, "I'm staying. Thith placccccce is . . ."

And that was the end of that.

The second time I came to was better. It was the following day, and I woke to a hand caressing my face. When I opened my eyes, Sabrina was sitting on the edge of my hospital bed. She had a smile on her face and a look in her eyes as she watched me I'd never seen in my life.

"Hey."

"I was wondering if we could do that interview now." She smiled and ran the back of her hand against my cheek.

I nodded. "Sure."

She wriggled on the bed and took her pad and paper, pretending she was about to take notes. "First question: is your name Cal McDonald?"

"Yes."

"Second question: are there really monsters?"

"Look at me."

She pretended to make a checkmark on her pad.

"Okay, and the last question: do you like Sabrina as much as she thinks she might like you?"

"Yes."

She threw the pad aside and leaned close. "Sam Burnett said you were going to stick around awhile. I think that's pretty good news."

"You're just saying that because I have screws in my head."

She kissed me. "I think we could make a good team, don't you?"

"You'll have to check with Mo'Lock on that one. He can be a tad possessive."

Sabrina reached into her bag and pulled out the latest issue of *Speculator*, hot off the press. On the cover was a grainy photo of Mo'Lock and the headline "Confessions of the Undead."

I laughed so hard it hurt everywhere. Sabrina leaned over and pushed my medicine release button. She was the woman of my dreams.

I looked her in the eyes as the haze began to come over me again. "I believe I can hang with you," I said.

She reached out and touched her fingers to my mouth as I faded. I fell asleep with a smile on my face. For the first time in years, I didn't dream about monsters.

DIAL M FOR MONSTER

THE DEAD DON'T DIE

By the time I got the call most of the town was already infected. That's the way these things happen. If I got the calls sooner I might be able to save more lives, but I never do. The dumb fucks usually go through the usual law enforcement agencies—who of course have no clue how to handle undead outbreaks—and the problem winds up eating through and spreading.

Near as I could estimate the first zombie rose from the dead on Tuesday, in the first week of June. By that Friday, the dead outnumbered the living, and the mayor of Mendez, California had eaten most of his staff, including his wife and twin daughters.

The place was a fucking bloodbath.

I got word of the outbreak through some ghouls, who had heard about it from a vampire fleeing the scene. Even vampires can't deal with zombies. They are without a doubt the most brainless and aggressive freaks on the scene and they'll take a bite out of anything even remotely fleshy.

The key was to move fast, before the problem spread to another town. Luckily Mendez was isolated. It was a little shit-hole west of Los Angeles. From the air (I flew over it once) it looked like a perfect circle surrounded by trees, with an outer ring of dessert wasteland. If a zombie infestation broke out, this was the place you'd want it: remote and easily contained.

I asked Mo'Lock to gather up as many of his freaky ghoul friends as he could. In the end we wound up with two busloads of dead postal workers, UPS drivers, and movie producers, packed in and ready for action. It's always easy to round up a crew of ghouls in L.A. They're fucking everywhere, like rats and strip malls.

The buses were surprisingly simple to swipe. A couple ghouls Mo'Lock knows work in a lot where they park them for repairs. They scrambled a couple of manifests and the next thing I knew I had two Greyhounds parked outside my house. Some joker had changed the destination signs above the outside drivers' windows so they read "Straight to Hell." As soon as the sun went down I had ghouls loading in by the dozen.

For once they all listened to me and brought their own "gardening tools," as I requested. Some had axes and picks. Some brought pikes and hoes. One jackass brought a rake.

Unfortunately, no LAPD ghouls could make it.

Most of them work the night shift.

I led the convoy out of L.A. in my Catalina. Mo'Lock drove with me. I loaded the space between us on the front seat with some beer, had whiskey and Vicodin already in my belly and music blaring on the stereo. Mo' kept trying to talk to me as we barreled along the freeway, but I couldn't make out what he was saying over the music. The ghoul was thoroughly annoyed.

Finally I gave him a break and turned down the volume.

"You say something?"

The ghoul stared at me a full thirty seconds before saying, "I asked you if you had a plan."

I lit a butt and nodded. The smoke snaked right into my eyes, causing me to temporarily lose control of the car. I swerved hard left, doing around ninety, and covered my tracks by acting like I was changing lanes. In the rearview I saw the buses keeping pace like two huge ships slicing through black concrete.

I couldn't help but imagine what would happen if they wrecked. Bodies, hundreds of them, would fly all over the highway, scattered like rice at a wedding. Only when the paramedics showed, all of them would be getting up without a scratch.

That would be fucking hilarious.

Mo'Lock repeated the question. I shrugged. Sure I had a plan. About as much of a plan as you can have when the dead are rising and devouring the living.

"I want you to get your buddies to circle the town," I said. "Form a perimeter to stop the outbreak from spreading."

"And what will you be doing?"

I glanced over at the ghoul and grinned. "I'm going in."

Mo'Lock nodded, but I could tell by the way he looked out the window he wasn't sure what I meant. Cool by me. That shut him up for the rest of the trip to Mendez.

I had the convoy stop just outside of town and gave out instructions. I wanted the ghouls to park the buses on either side of the town, and then fan out until they met up again, forming a wall of dead to contain the undead. The ghouls liked the plan. They all nodded and shook hands as they reloaded the buses with their pitchforks and axes.

As the buses drove away in opposite directions, kicking up clouds of dust, I scanned the area with a pair of night vision goggles. The good news was that I couldn't see anybody. That was also the bad news. It meant either everybody in town was dead, undead, or in hiding. I hoped for the last.

While I waited for the ghouls to set up the perimeter I went to the trunk of the Catalina and went into the "Lock and Load" routine.

I took two double-barreled 12-gauge shotguns. One was sawed off, the other wasn't: for long- and short-range blasts. I also loaded up my .45 and a .44 Magnum. I finished by weighing down with ammo attached to two ammo belts. I looked like a complete asshole.

After a bit longer than I would have liked I got calls from ghouls all around the outskirts of Mendez. The containment perimeter was in place. They were meeting resistance in the form of lumbering flesh-eaters. I told them to take them out, remove the heads if possible, and just make sure they didn't get past them.

Now it was my turn. I had to get in there and figure out how this thing had happened. There are a number of ways zombies are created, ranging from the intentional creation like voodoo and all that crap, to accidental like what went down with radiation, in Pittsburgh, back in the late sixties. Once I found the reason, I could figure out the cure, if there was one. If there wasn't a cure, then we had a lot of heads to blow off.

I drove down the main road into town, passing one partially devoured body and a "Welcome to Mendez" sign. I stopped the car and got out right after the sign. If there's one place you don't want to be in a zombie outbreak, it's in a confined space. I stood a much better chance on the streets.

At first I didn't see much, just a bunch of small-town, redneck bullshit like a bingo/square-dancing hall, a seed store, and a diner that looked like it hadn't been painted in . . . well, *ever*.

I came across a few more bodies scattered around the streets. One looked like the local law. He wore a tan sheriff's uniform. His head had been completely pulled off. It was lying in the street, most of the flesh ripped right off the skull. There was another corpse outside the diner, a woman and a small headless shape next to her. Her kid, I assumed.

On the streets I saw drag marks of blood, as well as drag marks made from shoes. That accounted for the lack of bodies. The zombies, wherever the fuck they were, had probably dragged the bodies off to a nice shady spot to eat.

"Hello!" I yelled. "Helloooooo!"

I listened to my voice bounce around and disappear, but nobody answered. I pressed on and looked for anything suspicious. I went inside the diner. What had looked empty outside was anything but, inside. There were devoured bodies all over the floor, piled one on top of the other. Most of them had their heads torn off and their skin was stripped clean to the bone around the arms, legs, and some of the torso. There were a couple who still had heads. I steered clear of them, in case they came back.

Back outside the diner I sucked a lungful of fresh air and scoped the scene. It was odd. Usually these outbreaks were like zombie riots. They were everywhere. Not in Mendez, though. The place was a ghost town.

I checked the bingo hall and had a little bit of luck. There were four zombies fighting over the body of a young woman. They were tearing her to shreds, pulling and shoving and grunting. When a piece would break off, a zombie would huddle on the floor like a caveman and suck down his hunk, then get back into the fight for more.

I stood there a full minute before one of them smelled me. When it looked up and sniffed the air I stepped quickly across the floor, planted the sawed-off against the bridge of its nose, and blew his head clean off from the lower jaw up. The other three started moaning and flailing and came at me faster than I'd ever seen zombies move. I shot two with the Magnum and the third with the long-barreled 12-gauge.

I thought I was done in the bingo hall, but I wasn't. The girl they'd been tearing apart, despite massive quantities of tissue loss, began to move. When I glanced at her, she was gnashing her teeth in my general direction. I stared into her eyes. They were shocking:

focused on me. That, and the flesh eating, eliminated any voodoo possibilities. These freaks were probably the result of someone's wrongdoing, or radiation.

I didn't want to shoot the girl, but I couldn't risk the spread so I put a .45 slug through her head. There was a bit of a spray from the exit wound, but despite the wedges of missing flesh, she looked like she just fell asleep.

I left the bingo hall knowing a little more than I did the minute before. I knew I wasn't looking for a person. What I needed to find was the location of an explosion maybe or some sort of radiation leak. I combed the rest of the two-block area called "downtown," then proceeded to the larger residential streets.

That's where everybody was.

The tree-lined suburban streets were littered with zombies shambling all over the place like drunks at a block party. They were eating scraps from well-picked bodies and pounding on doors of sealed-up homes, so there must have been survivors. At least I hoped there were. From the looks of the sheer numbers roaming the street, I had my doubts.

I chose the most direct route and started walking right up the middle of the street. These weren't undead who were cursed or under a spell, so there was no chance of bringing them back. They had to be killed. Every single one could pass on the infection. This was also another reason to get the job done before the Feds or the military showed up and tried to "sample" the infection, whatever its origins, for weapons testing. What fucking idiots.

I started blasting as soon as a zombie stepped in range. The first one took the shot in the neck and kept coming. I adjusted my aim and smeared its head all over the street. As soon as I dropped number one, the whole army of dead turned and saw me.

"Come on fuckwads!" I yelled. "Time to die again!"

They came to me like ants to cookie crumbs.

Just call me king of the assholes. What a stupid move.

I took the first wave in stride, blasting one, two, three and four flesh-eaters with the shotguns. I maneuvered through the shambling crowd by turning constantly as I walked, always firing. When I needed to reload, I'd kick a few out of the way and sprint to a clear area. It took the brainless dead a while to find me again, but these freaks were pretty fast. I had to keep on the move or I would easily get overwhelmed.

As I ran to a clearing near a house with a white picket fence I cursed myself for bringing the shotguns. They were effective, yes, but reloading took too long and opened me up to attack. As if to illustrate my point a quartet of dead came lumbering at me from behind the house. It was a family, the residents of the house I presumed: father, mother, daughter, and son. A family that dies together, dines together, I guess.

The boy—couldn't have been more than eleven—came at me and tried to attach himself to my thigh, but I slammed him in the face with the butt of the shotgun right as he went in for a chomp. The sister came next. The small ones moved faster. I threw her to the lawn next to her zombie brother and turned them both into ground beef with the sawed-off.

I turned my attention to mom and dad, raising a weapon toward each, but as I did I realized the crowd I'd run from had caught up to me. Suddenly, I was surrounded. Normally I'd take a dive and bring them down at the knees, but these were flesh-eaters. You don't want to be stuck at the bottom of a pile with these motherfuckers. Instead I fired off some shots and then used the shotgun like a bat and cleared a path.

But nothing I did shook them. No matter how fast I moved, they were there, relentless and hungry. I was probably the only fresh meat on the streets so within a few minutes I was the pied piper of the dead, leading a parade of slobbering zombies in a circle around the block. Every couple of feet, when I felt like I had some distance, I'd turn and blast the ones at the head of the procession to shorten the line a bit.

After about an hour of running, stopping, turning, and blasting, I had made a significant dent in the ranks of the living dead of Mendez. I reduced the small army of transformed townsfolk into a scattered mess of headless bodies.

There were still a few wandering here and there when I spotted the thin trail of smoke rising from the trees. My best guess was that it was the next block over. I reloaded all the guns and then followed the trail. It wasn't much smoke, probably a kitchen fire started when the cook got eaten or turned, but with a pause in the living dead onslaught it was the next best thing to a lead.

The trail led me to the next residential block. It looked exactly like the previous—mid-range family homes, mostly Spanish style— except this was block wasn't covered with bodies and brains.

But it was still early.

The smoke trail seemed to be coming from the roof of one of the few two-story homes on the street. I couldn't tell from where I stood so I climbed up a car parked in the street. From the roof of the car I could see the house across the street, the smoke, and the hole in the tile it was rising from.

Bingo.

I double-checked my weapons and then called Mo'Lock to get an update. It took a couple of rings but he eventually picked up.

"Mo'," I said, "It's Cal. What's the report?"

"Um . . . not much."

"How's the perimeter holding up?"

"Fine."

I took a deep breath. "How about some details? Have you and your buddies run into any zombies?"

"No."

"Not one?" I asked.

"Not one."

I gripped the cell hard in my hand. "So, while I've been in here fighting for my goddamn life, you guys have been—"

"Securing the perimeter."

I kicked the car and put a massive dent in the door, then I threw the cell as far as I could toward the woods surrounding the town. I hoped I fucking hit one of them.

Without backup I walked to the house with the smoke coming from the hole in the roof. The front door was wide open, and from the dirt and blood all over the front porch, it looked like there had been a lot of traffic in and out of the house during recent events. I couldn't hear anything from inside, but a strange heat emitted that put me on edge.

I entered the house slowly, with shotgun barrels out in front. Inside was dark, and the blood on the porch continued inside as well. In fact, the foyer floor was so blood-covered that it would have looked like a paint job if not for the spatters on the wall and the drag marks and footprints. To my right was a staircase, not so bloody, but I went up since that's where the hole originated.

The place had kind of a Victorian/*Psycho* thing going on. Lots of dark wood on the floors and walls. I plodded up the stairs to a hallway and started checking rooms. It was clear until I hit the master bedroom.

It was there I found the hole in the ceiling.

But the hole, about the size of a large pizza, didn't stop at the ceiling. Whatever came down through the roof had kept right on falling. I walked to the edge of the hole and leaned over. From the looks of it, the hole went clear down through the ground floor and into some sort of basement or wine cellar. It was dark, and from this height I couldn't see much more than the smoke that rose toward my face, twirling and winding like a transparent snake toward my nose.

I avoided the smoke, covering my nose, and made sure I didn't inhale. Call it a hunch, but I suspected the smoke was a part of this mess. Up close it had a green tint to it, and it moved slower than normal smoke, like milk diluting water. Like it had purpose.

I backtracked down the stairs to the main floor and searched quickly for a basement door. There wasn't one, so I walked to the back of the house, through the kitchen where it looked like someone had been baking when whatever fell through, fell through. There were pots and pans out, measuring cups, the works.

I passed through the kitchen and outside through a wood-framed screen door. The yard was fenced in: white picket, of course. There were also clothes hanging on a line. The scene was beginning to remind me of a Norman Rockwell painting. Well, a Rockwell painting with the living dead tearing grandpa's gut out.

To the right of the screen door was one of those *Wizard of Oz* storm doors cutting into the ground and part of the house. The door was open.

I glanced down into the cellar. It was dark, but leading in *and out* of the darkness, on the stairs, were bloody footprints. It looked like this cellar had seen a lot of traffic since the outbreak. I tore some fabric from a sheet hanging in the yard and made myself a mask to keep the smoke from getting in my nose and mouth, and then I checked my shotgun and started down the stairs.

I paused briefly about a step and a half down. There was a sound in the air, a distant flutter. It was either someone heading this way, or the wind. I didn't give a shit which.

I walked down the stairs to the cellar, pausing briefly on the last step while my eyes adjusted to the darkness. Once adjusted I could see that the basement was little more than a dug-out hole, with cement walls and floor, used to store the water heater and air conditioning unit. Over time a considerable amount of other junk had been added, including bikes, old exercise equipment, and bundles of newspapers and magazines.

On the far side, away from the stairs, I saw the smoke. Above the smoke, light broke through the hole in the ceiling.

I moved forward and stopped immediately. I heard shuffling coming from behind a stack of papers blocking my view of the area. I knew that shuffling. Nothing sounds quite like a dead man walking, the unnatural dragging and stomping as one limb is pulled ahead to support the other.

I stood my ground as a zombie appeared around the corner, moving away from the area around the hole I'd yet to reach. He was a middle-aged man, bald, and wearing an apron from the local market. Smoke rose from his dead eyes as he stumbled through the darkness looking for a way out or something to eat.

He spotted me. I let him shamble toward me. From six feet away, I guessed I had thirty seconds to study him before he reached me. He was slower than slow. I looked at his eyes and saw the smoke swirling in and out of the space between eyeball and socket. It was as if the smoke caused both the death and the zombification. I'd never seen this. I was intrigued.

Unfortunately, baldy got too close, so I had to remove his cranium with the shotgun. His headless corpse fell within an inch of my shoe tips. The same green tinted smoke rose from the bloody stump of his neck.

I stepped over the body and, as I reloaded, moved fast to the area below the hole in the ceiling.

There was a person there on the ground beneath the hole, an old woman with a white beehive hairdo. I saw now what had come through the house. It was a small glowing hunk of space rock; a meteor, I guessed. It was embedded in the woman's chest, and from the looks of her twisted limbs it had hit her in the bedroom and dragged her clear down to the cellar. She wasn't dead, but she should've been.

Though most of her old bones appeared shattered from the impact and fall, they still moved. Especially her head. It bobbed and writhed on mutated muscle and flesh. Her eyes were wide and green as fresh-cut grass. Her mouth, gummy with clear slime, opened and closed like a hungry baby bird. She was fucking disgusting.

I kept my distance. I was reasonably sure this was where the outbreak began, but now I had a hunch there was more to it. Somehow the old lady drew living people to her and sent them away as flesh-eating zombies. And that rock melted into her guts had something to do with it, but how or why was anybody's guess.

So I decided to ask.

"You have two seconds to explain yourself," I said, "before I commence blowing your head all over the room."

The beehive bobbed and rolled. The neck was broken, but somebody forgot to tell the head.

After a second or two of drooling and slobbering (the old lady, not me), I lowered the shotgun at her head. There wasn't going to be any explaining. The thing on the ground was just a freak of nature, a radioactive, zombie-making, freak of nature.

Then . . .

"Wait . . ." the thing said. Its voice was garbled, slimy.

I kept the barrel on the head. "Speak."

"We . . . have . . . come . . . a . . . long . . . way." The thing spoke as its eyes rolled and smoke puffed from its mouth like a sickly tugboat.

The thing went on to explain, in a voice that sounded like a speaker drowned in a barrel of snot, that *they* were a race from somewhere and a terrible disease took over their planet, or some such shit, and here they were.

"Spreading the disease on our planet," I said. "Thanks a ton, asshole."

The beehive bobbled and garbled. If it was an apology, I didn't like it.

"So, where is this planet of yours?" I asked.

The arm of the spattered old lady rose out of the slime and rot like the limb of a mantis, and then dropped onto the meteor embedded in her gut. "Home . . . is here."

Wow. I stared at the writhing body and the rock, the planet in her gut. What an unbelievable turn of events; an entire planet falling to Earth, hardly the size of a basketball. I'd seen some pretty amazing stuff in my time, but this took the cake. Absolutely astounding.

I almost felt bad when I blew its head all over the cellar.

As I exited the basement and removed the cloth from my face, I found out what the sound had been before. The old woman's yard was bustling with men in white bio-suits and soldiers in gas masks. In fact, they were everywhere. There were Jeeps and Hummers in the streets and helicopters in the air. Looked like the cavalry had finally arrived . . . too late, as usual.

I was immediately surrounded by soldiers with automatic weapons. They were all barking and yelling at me.

I just smiled. "You guys here to clean up my mess?"

Bang!

I was out cold. If I had to guess, I'd say it was a rifle butt.

When I came to I was in a small office. The walls were gray. So were the floors and ceiling. There was a small table and two chairs on either side. I sat in one. The other was empty. The floors, the whole room actually, hummed and vibrated. I realized then that it wasn't a room at all, but a mobile interrogation room. The military love their toys.

I wasn't tied up or handcuffed so I lit a smoke and waited for whoever I was waiting for to show up. I had my worries. If the Feds had moved in for the cleanup, anything was possible, depending on what they found, or thought they found. I didn't want to get mixed up in any Area 51 bullshit. I also didn't want Mo'Lock or any of his buddies getting pulled in for questioning. That could lead to big trouble.

About two and a half smokes after I came to, I had company join me in the mobile room. It was an older man, escorted by a couple guards. The older man wore a uniform, but I can never keep which one was which straight, so I'll guess and say he was Army, and from the amount of shit stuck all over his chest, I'd also guess pretty high ranking.

"Mr. McDonald, my name is General Theodore Adams."

"Hi, Ted," I replied.

He was not amused.

He dismissed the guards and sat in the opposite chair without offering to shake my hand. Fine. Fuck 'im.

The general narrowed his eyes at me. "How much do you know about what happened here today?"

"I know I stopped it."

He wasn't amused by that either.

"We have taken the 'object' from the basement and we have it contained," the general said.

I nodded. "Any survivors?"

"We found many of the town's residents hiding in their homes. We're estimating less than half of Mendez fell under the attack."

I pointed at him. "I suggest you destroy that 'object' before you have another outbreak."

"We'll take care of that. Don't worry, Mr. McDonald."

"So you know who I am?"

The general smiled and removed his hat. "My wife has a garden," he said. "She lives for that fucking thing. It makes her happy, but sometimes the garden gets bugs. Do you know what she has to do when she gets bugs?"

"Does she spray?"

"No," he went on. "She buys a predator bug and places it in the garden to go after and kill the harmful bugs."

I looked around. Was there a point to all this?

I shrugged.

The general pointed. "You're the predator bug," he said. "Near as we can tell you don't hurt anybody . . . except the bugs that hurt people, so we tolerate you."

"I'm a bug?"

I knew what he was saying. I didn't really give a shit and it didn't surprise me that they knew who I was. They'd have to be pretty stupid not to keep tabs on me. What I couldn't figure out was if they believed that there were monsters in the world. He seemed to imply they did, but they were fine letting me deal with it.

That made me mad. I was just one guy up against an entire subspecies, a separate populace who hunted humans, and this flippant attitude pissed me off. All I could think was that if I had the military on my side, the monster population of the world could be seriously damaged, if not wiped out entirely. I wondered if they realized how many murders around the world were committed by unnatural creatures?

The general leaned in. "Mr. McDonald, what I'm telling you is you're free to go."

I stood.

"But . . ."

I froze.

". . . we'll be keeping an eye on you."

I shrugged. "Can I offer *you* a little advice?"

The general took a turn shrugging. "Sure."

"You may or may not believe in the things I know exist in the world," I said. "But that rock you pulled out of that old lady's gut is extremely dangerous. I think it would be in the *world's* best interest if you destroyed it instead of taking it away for study."

"I'll consider it."

"You should."

"I will."

"You'd better."

As confrontations go, it was pretty weak.

I walked out of the mobile interrogation room and into a military occupation of Mendez, California. The roads were blocked off, the dead were covered or gone, and everywhere I looked guys in uniforms were talking to survivors. I walked back the way I'd marched through town and found my Catalina parked where I left it.

My cell phone was lying on the seat with a note attached.

It read, "Cal. The Feds showed, so we left. Found your phone in a field. See you back in Los Angeles."

It was signed, Mo'Lock.

I smiled. Who else gets shit on by humans and helped out by the dead? Just me. I started the car and left town thinking about the stupid story the general told me about the bugs and the garden. I guess it was a good analogy of what I do. I don't mind being a bug in the garden, I thought.

As long as I'm the bug doing the killing.

DOLL FACE

Note: This story takes place before the bizarre events depicted in the graphic novel Criminal Macabre: A Cal McDonald Mystery.

When I came to I was on the floor of a jail cell. That in itself was bad enough, but I also had some company.

Some big fat fuck with thick glasses was trying to remove my belt. I didn't know if he was trying to steal or attempting some butt-pirating, and I didn't care. Using the flat of my palm I jammed his nose to one side, and then cracked it loose with the other.

I rolled to my feet and fat boy fell backward against the bars of the cell. I looked around quickly and saw three other cellmates staring, bored, like they'd seen it all before. I decided to give them something they'd never seen.

I finished removing the belt from my pants and pinned fat boy to the bars. I used the belt and tied him by his throat then proceeded to whale on his chubby face until the guards showed up. I hadn't intended on it, but I must've tied the asshole to the door because when the guards pulled open the cell, fat boy got dragged along for the ride. My cellmates cracked up. So did the guards. Everybody was laughing except the asshole. He was unconscious.

When the laughing stopped and fat boy was peeled off the bars and taken away, one of the guards, a giant black guy with light eyes, looked at me and nodded. I nodded back. He was a ghoul. A lot of L.A. cops are ghouls.

"Cal McDonald?"

"Yeah."

"Lieutenant Brueger wants to see you."

I waved goodbye to my cellmates and stepped around the half-circle smear of blood on the floor. I followed the big ghoul. I couldn't help but stare at him. He took up half the hall and almost reached the ceiling and those fucking eyes looked like they could shoot a laser beam.

"What's your name, officer?" I asked. I think my staring was making him uncomfortable.

"Norris."

"Good to meet you, Norris," I said. "Any clue how I wound up here?"

"Disturbing the peace."

"Can you be a little more specific?"

"You threw a gentleman through the window of a sushi bar on Ventura Boulevard."

"Huh. No shit. I wonder why I did that."

The ghoul cop grinned.

"While I'm asking stupid questions, who bailed me out?"

"I believe it was a young lady. A Miss Sabrina Lynch."

"And she didn't stick around?"

The ghoul shook his head.

Shit.

This marked somewhere around the fifth time Sabrina had had to bail me out of jail. She'd been nagging me about drinking, or more to the point, the things I did when I drank too much. I wasn't used to this relationship crap and I sure as hell wasn't used to anyone giving a flying shit about what I did or how much I did it.

Oh well, that was a shit-storm for later.

The ghoul stopped at the end of a long hall and pointed. "The lieutenant's office is the first door on the right."

I stuck out my hand. "Good to meet you, Norris."

He shook my hand with his and my hand disappeared. "Good to meet you as well," he said, "and please tell Mo'Lock I said hello."

Before I could say anything he walked away. How the hell did Mo'Lock know him? Fucking ghouls networked better than Hollywood agents.

I walked to the first door. The door was old style with Lieutenant Gretchen Brueger painted in black on the fogged glass. I gave it three quick taps.

From the other side a female voice barked, "Come in!"

I pushed the door open and stepped inside.

I don't know what I expected, but the young, attractive woman sitting behind the desk was not it. The walls of the office were covered with framed awards and engraved plaques. There was even a key to the city from the mayor. You didn't have to be Einstein to figure out whoever this Lt. Brueger was, she had punched and crawled her way to the top of the LAPD.

She didn't know what the hell to make of me. She gave me a quick once-over and then gestured for me to sit. She didn't offer me her hand.

"Cal McDonald," she said.

I nodded. I didn't say anything.

"So how long are you staying in Los Angeles?" She asked. Her tone dripped contempt.

"I moved here."

"I just read a four-inch-thick file on you," she raised one of her perfectly plucked eyebrows. "And it looks like you spend a fair amount of time on both sides of the law."

"If that's what you want to call it."

She leaned forward. "You spent the night in a cell. What would you call it?"

"A blackout." I smiled.

She didn't.

There was a long, long silence. Almost too long. When I was about to leave, she cleared her throat. I stopped.

"I understand you claim to have dealt with . . . um . . . some unusual things in your life."

I nodded. "I deal almost exclusively with cases involving the so-called supernatural."

"So, you don't believe?"

"No, I just hate the word supernatural," I said. "It implies some sort of otherworldly hoodie voodie and from my experience . . . the things I've confronted are very real—flesh and blood and all that crap."

She didn't want to come out with it and I wasn't about to make it easy. If she wanted to ask me about monsters, she was going to have to spit it out in plain English. I knew it was coming. It always did. These law enforcement types must run into more strange crap, but they always turn a blind eye. A man is found with giant holes in his neck and these pricks will call it a shooting. Who the hell shoots two perfectly placed shots into a guy's throat and with no exit wounds? That's what I call denial. It's like they *refuse* to accept how dangerous the world really is.

Finally she sat back in her chair and tried to smile. Maybe she was about to ask me what she wanted to ask, but I cut her off at the pass.

"How long have you been a cop?" I asked.

She seemed startled by the question. "Seems like my whole life," she said almost to herself more than me. "I come from a family of cops."

"Are you the first to make Detective Lieutenant?"

"Um, no. I had a brother who made it. He was shot in the line of duty—"

"Sorry."

"—and my grandfather made Captain."

"So now that we got all of that out of the way," I smiled again. "How about you tell me why you called me in here. I'm guessing it's more than a shakedown."

Now she grinned. Not much of one, but it was there. "You're not what I expected."

"Oh yeah," I laughed. "What did you expect?"

"A drunken lout, I guess."

"Wait until tonight."

The air in the room was clear. She seemed relatively at ease. I didn't know it but in about two minutes I was the one who would be on edge.

"We have a suspect we're holding downstairs," she said. "I was wondering if you'd take a look at him for us."

I laughed. "Well, if you have a hold of him chances are he's not my kind of freak."

She stared at me. "He walked in here last night. He looked like, I don't know, an accountant or something; glasses, sweater vest, the type of guy you see a thousand times a day and never think twice."

I pretended to nod off.

"Except," she went on, "this guy walked into the station *drenched* with blood."

I opened my eyes. "Drenched?"

"Head to toe, like he'd swam in a vat of it."

"Okay, you got my attention," I said. "What else?"

"He refused to speak, or couldn't, but we arrested him and put him in a holding room for questioning. For five hours straight he just sat there and didn't make a sound, then all of a sudden he starts . . . I don't know how to describe it . . . babbling."

"Speaking in tongues maybe."

"Maybe." Brueger looked at me with an expression somewhere between lost and pissed off. I could see this guy had her good and freaked.

I asked her if they'd tested the blood and they had. The tests came back as strange and inexplicable as the bloody man. It wasn't his blood. It was many peoples' blood, all mixed together. She said the lab told her it would be impossible to separate the samples, but there could be as many as seventy-five to one hundred different possible blood types in the mix.

"And he hasn't done anything but this babbling?" I asked.

"Pretty much, and it's constant, hour after hour."

I scratched my head. "You wouldn't happen to have a drink, would you?"

She glared at me.

"I didn't think so," I said. "Anything else?"

"Well, he did speak a couple words we could understand."

All I had to do was keep my mouth shut to avoid stepping in a big pile of shit, but it's amazing, sometimes the simplest things are the hardest to avoid.

"Yeah, what'd he say?" I said, walking right into it.

Brueger nodded. "He said your name."

Fuck.

I followed Brueger and a cop downstairs. I couldn't tell if the cop was a ghoul or not, but he sure as shit looked like one. But then again, most cops do. We took a back elevator from the bottom floor and went down one more. It looked like some kind of dungeon.

"What's with this place?"

The cop turned to me. He had huge wide-set eyes and a nose like a boxer. "They used to bring perps down here in the old days, if you know what I mean."

I did. This was where they used to bring people to beat confessions out of them, and by the blood smudges on the walls and floor, the old days weren't so long ago.

Brueger tried to sanitize. "The new cells and interrogation rooms are in the next building. They're much nicer and more modern."

The boxer-faced cop gave me a wink. I just looked back at him with a dull stare as we rounded a corner and came up on two cops standing outside one of the many doors lining the dingy hallway. One of the cops was Norris. He nodded when he saw me.

On the other side of the guarded door I could hear a muted voice. At first I thought it was two people talking at once, then as Norris cracked the door I realized it was one voice speaking at an impossibly fast speed. It sounded like an auctioneer on crack.

I glanced at Brueger. She stepped by me and pushed the door open all the way. Inside was a plain gray room with a table. There were two empty chairs and a small, skinny man sitting on the other side, handcuffed, his lips moving like a hummingbird's wings. His face was long and thin with a bizarre patch of hair right on top of his pointed head. He wore tan old-man pants and a red short-sleeved shirt. His arms were covered with either freckles or age spots.

He stared straight ahead at his own reflection in the two-way mirror. If he knew we were there, he gave no indication.

"That's all he does," Brueger said. "Any clue what the hell language he's speaking?"

I listened to the furious babble of the skinny man for a second and then glanced at Norris. The language, if you want to call it that, reminded me of the speed-English ghouls spoke in when they talked to each other. This was different. Brueger noticed me looking at the ghoul-cop. I quickly looked away. I knew how hard it was for the dead to blend with the living. I didn't want to blow his cover.

"Are you recording this?" I asked Brueger.

She nodded.

"Show me."

I followed Brueger to the room on the other side of the mirror. Inside a female officer, human, monitored the recording equipment set up on the table. Brueger introduced us quickly and then handed me off.

"You noticed the rhythm?" I asked.

The female cop nodded. "Yeah, whatever it is, he's saying it over and over."

"Have you tried playing it backward?"

The female cop looked at me and turned as red as I've ever seen someone turn.

"No sir," she said.

I smiled. I wasn't trying to show her up. Sometimes the simplest fixes are the last ones you try.

After a couple clicks on her keyboard, the cop played a piece of the skinny man's babble backward. The voice was strange, high-pitched, but it was English.

As we listened to the excerpt I stared at the suspect through the glass.

"*. . . I killed them all and took their skin to my house on Moorpark right at the corner of Ponca. Tell me if you like what I did. I worked very hard. . . .*"

That was it. The same strange phrase over and over. Why he had blurted out my name was anybody's guess, but my guess was he was a fan. That's what I called the freaks who came after me since I'd become better known for doing what I do.

I had become so notorious for hunting monsters that every freak from Los Angeles to Romania thought they could take me out. They were wrong, of course, but it didn't keep them from constantly picking me as a target. Screw them. Screw all of them. Let them come. It's easier than tracking them down.

I drove to the corner of Moorpark and Ponca. It was located in a posh little pocket of homes near Warner Bros. Studios. Brueger wanted to come but I told her to stay and keep an eye on the skinny man. Instead I dropped a line to my partner and creepy-ass ghoul, Mo'Lock. If things got weird, I wanted him around for backup.

There were four houses to choose from at that corner. Two had families I could see washing cars, playing in the yard, and shit like that. The third was for sale and had an open house going. The fourth, a little Tudor-style number, had no activity, no car in the driveway, and made my hair stand on end when I looked at it.

Mo'Lock arrived as I was heading across the Tudor's lawn. A cab dropped him off. The driver was also a ghoul. L.A. was worse than D.C. Ghouls were fucking everywhere.

"What have we got?" he asked as I checked the front door for anything odd.

"Dunno," I said and kicked the door in. "Hey, look. It's open."

From the outside, the house looked pretty normal. The inside was the same except for some ugly-ass carpet. But there was a vibe hanging in the air like poison gas. There was something definitely wrong inside the skinny man's house. But did it have anything to do with bodies, like he said, or was it just a ruse to lure me in? Those were a couple of the thoughts racing through my mind.

In my pocket, my cell rang, and I jumped. Worse, the ghoul saw me and smiled. I glared at him and pointed. "Tell anyone and I'll bury you in ten feet of cement."

I answered. It was Brueger, checking on me.

"I'm in the house now," I said. "So far I don't see anything."

"I just wanted you to know," she said, "the suspect just stopped talking."

"What's he doing?"

"Just sitting and staring."

"Tell me if anything changes." I shoved the cell back in my pocket.

The ghoul had moved ahead of me, now in the living room, and he was so close to the wall it looked like he was sniffing the wallpaper. He ran his big, dead hands over the surface, slowly feeling for something, any kind of abnormality.

"You got something, Mo'?"

"Possibly," he groaned. "There is a strange smell coming from behind this wall."

I walked over and joined in the wall-feel and I picked up slight traces of a sharp odor. It reminded me of shoe polish. As I ran my hands over a smooth spot, my fingers felt an inconsistency in the texture.

"Here." I said.

I gave the wall a push. There was a click and the panel opened. Classic hidden door bullshit. I glanced at Mo'Lock. He was looking at my hand on the wall.

"Cal . . . your hand."

There were spots on the back of my hand, freckles, like the skinny man's hands. A sinking nausea swelled in my throat and felt like a stone to my belly. Something had me. I didn't know what, but I knew, somehow, and I also knew it was too late to do anything about it so I pushed through the hidden door. The ghoul followed. I was pissed.

I should have waited. I should have taken a step back and looked at the situation, but I didn't and I walked right into the skinny man's trap. On the floor of the hidden room was a symbol like a pentagram, but more complex, with smaller signs inside each triangle. The pentagram was burned into the wood floor and I was inside it.

The ghoul had been smart enough to move slow. He was outside the burned circle, looking around at the walls of the claustrophobic room. I looked up slowly and saw one of the worst sights I'd ever laid my eyes on.

The walls were covered with faces.

The skinny man had told the truth. He had taken his victims home. He'd skinned them and nailed their faces to the walls, their empty mouths stuck in permanent howls of pain, their eyes stretched wide and empty.

From the doorway I heard the ghoul. "You better get out of there, Cal."

But his warning was just for show. He had to warn me, but he knew by my expression I couldn't. He saw the spots growing on my now tightening skin.

I was stuck right where I stood. The symbol had me and held me in place with an invisible death grip and I was being drained of life.

I watched spots grow and spread up my arms. My skin turned sickly and transparent. Blue veins rose to the surface through the diminishing pigment. I could see small flecks of my flesh rising off me, like wisps of dandruff. They floated in the air around me, swirling, as if teasing me and then they whisked off, sucked into the eyes of the dead faces on the wall.

I didn't have a clue what to do and I was losing strength fast. I reached for the phone and dialed. Brueger picked up after half a ring.

"I was just calling you," she said. She sounded excited.

"Where's the—"

She cut me off.

"The suspect . . . he escaped."

I couldn't believe it.

"I don't fucking believe it! What happened? How?"

"H-he grew . . . or something and snapped his cuffs," she said. "By the time anybody realized what was happening, he'd smashed the glass with the table."

I looked down. My body was shriveling.

"How did he get out of a police station?!"

I could hear her frustration. "I don't know," she said. "He just ran and before we knew it, he was gone."

"And he was bigger?"

There was a long pause. "Yeah."

"Is Norris there?" I asked. I needed a ghoul's perspective and help. I waited.

"Norris here. What can I do for you, Mr. McDonald?"

"I know you can't talk in front of the humans, but I need you to spread word among the ghouls about this guy. I don't want him stopped or even touched."

At the door Mo'Lock looked as confused as Norris sounded.

I went on. "Just do it," I said. "If I know these bastards like I think I know them, he's heading straight over here to finish me off. Let him. It's the only chance I have."

Norris agreed. I hung up.

I could tell by the look on Mo'Lock's face I wasn't doing too well. I looked at my arms. I was so drained I could see my joints and my skin had begun to wrinkle and sag in between the gaps of bone. But what appeared to be aging, I feared, was much worse. My skin took on a gray hue and a smell rose from it like death. I wasn't aging, or just being drained. I was rotting away, right where I stood.

I didn't have to understand the exact hex to know I'd be dead in less than an hour if I didn't do anything, but I couldn't move my feet. It was like they were cemented to the floor.

"Mo'Lock," I barked. "Go into the garage and see if you can find me some kind of tool like a rake or a hoe!"

Mo'Lock nodded twice quickly and then ran back through the hidden door leaving me alone in the room with the circle and the faces. I was hardly aware of the flecks on my skin being pulled by a gentle current into the sockets and mouths. I scanned the faces, stretched and tacked, looking for anything common among them, but there was nothing. They were the faces of men and women and of varying races. The only thing they shared was a horrible death.

I twisted and turned, scanning the massive burned-in symbol that held me. It was a basic magic circle. Any asshole with a library card can learn how to make one, like a bomb from fertilizer or a nativity with Popsicle sticks. It was easy to obtain the info, but unlike those other items, a circle had to have a sequence of elements; the materials, the know-how, and the will to bring it to life. Any one of those things could be the key, but figuring out which is like guessing which wire to cut on a bomb. Snip the wrong one and the whole thing could blow up in your face.

Only with this hoodie-voodie bullshit, you could wind up taking the whole fucking planet with you by unleashing god-knows-what.

Mo'Lock came running back to the room. If he breathed, he would have been breathing hard. His deep sunken eyes were wide and wild. In his arms he had a rake, an ax, a hoe, and a Weed Whacker with the long orange cord dangling behind.

"Don't break the circle," I said, "Just place them down where you are."

Mo'Lock placed the lawn tools down on the floor where I could reach them, then he looked up at me.

"He's coming."

I knew who he meant, but I asked anyway.

The ghoul nodded. "He's walking down the street calm as can be, with police trailing right behind him," he said. "And he's big . . . very big."

"Great."

I looked at the tools and began to reach for the hoe, but then the Weed Whacker caught my eye. I grabbed it and chucked the cord to the ghoul. He plugged it in.

"Are you sure this is wise?" Mo'Lock said. "I suspect it will take more than that to stop this gentleman."

I grinned. My face felt tight and bony. I was glad I couldn't see myself.

"This isn't for him," I said.

By the looks of my hands holding the bright orange grass cutter, I could see I was little more than a skeleton with a thin layer of transparent veiny flesh holding me together. Even the lightweight tool felt heavy in my hands.

By now I could hear a ruckus outside. I heard sirens and voices speaking through bullhorns telling the suspect to stop. I could tell by the repeated order he wasn't listening.

I revved up the Whacker and it sputtered. I yelled for the ghoul to clear the room and to stay out of the skinny man's way. I wanted him to come after me. I wanted *him* to break the circle, and I was pretty sure when he saw my indoor gardening he'd do it.

The Whacker purring in my hands, I began running the business end over dead faces nailed to the wall. If that was the conduit of my flesh, then I had to destroy them. As the spinning cord touched the first face, an empty-eyed male with a mustache, the flesh blew apart like gelatin and made a sickening sound as chunks of face began to fly from the wall.

I swept the wall with the Whacker and soon it was raining fleshy debris. Outside I heard slamming and banging as the skinny man made his way into the house. He was yelling my name. There was anger and panic in his voice. I knew I was on the right track. I'd disturbed the hex.

I quickly worked my way around the walls of the confined room, slashing and mowing the faces of the skinny man's victims. Chunks and dust flew, blinding me as I saw a shape appear in the doorway. It was the skinny man, but he wasn't skinny anymore. He filled the doorway with his new stolen body.

When he saw what I was doing he charged at me. I was defenseless except for the Weed Whacker so I spun at my hips and connected with the side of his face as he barreled in. His face tore open and howled. He also broke the circle. My feet snapped free and I fell backward against the wall with only the lawn tool between my withered body and the skinny man.

"You think you're so fucking great!" he yelled.

I had no idea what he was talking about.

I clocked him right across his nose with the whirling plastic blade and split his face open. He grabbed at his face, but it was too late. The dried flesh flecks clouding the room began to stick to the wound, and soon the gash was a vacuum sucking in the dust.

I could feel my strength returning, but not fast enough. The killer let go of his face and grabbed me by my jacket. He lifted me off the ground and pounded me back and forth against one wall, then the other. I tried to hit him with the blade again. I was too close. He yanked it from my hands and smashed it onto the floor.

I tried my best to resist, to get a few choice punches in, but I was still weak. On his face the two gashes I'd made were bloated with murdered flesh particles crawling inside the killer's body. I planted my palm into the bridge of his nose and made another bloody opening. The particles leapt from the air into his face, attacking the opening.

My strength was returning, and the skinny man was shrinking. I saw fear in his eyes. I saw him for the coward he was and he knew it. He let me go and tried to back away, swiping at his face like a man attacked by a swarm of bees. But these weren't insects. He was under attack by the fragmented spirits of those he'd murdered to create destructive black magic.

I stood and balled my fist. I was almost back to normal. I walked toward him and laid one right on the side of his face, leaning in with all my returning weight. I connected and the skinny man spun. Blood sprayed the wall. I kneed him in the groin. When he buckled I used the other knee to his face and stood him upright again.

One last ball of knuckles knocked him out.

I stood over the skinny man as the particles invaded his body, a last desperate attempt to have revenge on their killer.

By the time Brueger and her buddies stormed in yelling cop warnings, it was over. The dust had settled.

Later, after the skinny man was dragged away, he was identified as Karl Doll, a single accountant for one of the studios. In one of the rooms we found a box of news clippings. They were all about me. Evidently Karl fancied himself a junior monster hunter but he was jealous of me and thought if he could take my energy, he could do what I do.

Fuck that wimp. If you can't do it with what you have, you can't do it.

Thinking about what he did, killing people to get something from me made me glad I didn't kill him like I wanted to. Let him go to trial and look at the faces of the families of those poor people he killed. Let him go to jail. With any luck he'd wind up in a cell with a belt thief, the way I had.

The whole horrible thing showed me just how vulnerable I had made myself, allowing magazines like the *Speculator* write about me.

Then it hit me.

I'd never called Sabrina. As far as she knew she'd bailed me out of jail and then blew her off. There would be no sweet-talking my way out of this one.

Fuck.

From one shit-storm to the next.

SOUL SUCKER

Tuesday, the fifth of September, began like any other day; I woke up, threw up, and went back to bed. It was five-thirty in the evening. Cases were few. I was, and had been, completely flat fucking broke the better part of a long and shitty L.A. summer.

By the time I got showered and dressed it was almost six-thirty and dark. There was a hot, dry breeze blowing through the house. Within seconds of getting out of the shower my skin dried up and scabs were falling off me like dead flies. I'd had a run-in with a gang of fiends a few days before. Those fucks have some nasty unkempt fingernails and they scratched the crap out of me. I beat their skulls in with a hammer.

To help get the blood flowing, I swigged down some coffee spiked with whiskey and a Vicodin chaser to achieve the proper balance for the night. Unfortunately the only bottle I thought I had was as empty as my wallet. I had to down the pill dry.

The phone rang as I began gathering all my empties—empty liquor bottles—until I had about twenty or thirty. I was interrupted, of course.

"Yeah?"

"It's me." The voice sounded like dry bones. Fucking ghoul.

"Mo'Lock, what the hell are you doing? Where are you?"

He took a deep, slow breath. "I am right outside," he groaned, "I just walked from Ventura Boulevard. There is an interesting street fair happening and—"

"Quit fucking around. Get your dead butt in here," I spat, and slammed the receiver down.

While I waited for the ghoul I began turning the bottles upside down in glasses around my office/house. Well, technically it was my old friend Sam Burnett's house, but since the whole *losing his head* incident, he left it to me and left the country. I think getting duped by a teenage burnout really took it out of the old guy.

The bottom of a dirty glass filled drop by drop with alcohol, but I'd get a fucking shot one way or another. Just as I turned over about the fifteenth or so, Mo'Lock came lumbering in, looking pale and disoriented, which was fine 'cause that's how he always looks. He's a ghoul after all. They're not known for their color or grace. Lumbering's about as good as it gets.

"Hey," I said, continuing to turn the bottles.

"Hello," said Mo'lock, and he crossed the room to the window behind my desk. "What are you doing?"

"Trying to get a drink," I said. "Where you been? Ain't seen you in weeks."

He looked out the window and said, "I fell asleep."

I nodded, telling myself not to ask. I'd only get more confused. Ghouls sleep? You learn something new every fucking day, I guess.

Finally I got to the last bottle and I was pleased to see I had more than a shot. I took the glass and kicked bottles aside as I went to my desk.

Mo'Lock turned his head. "Any cases?"

"Zero, zilch, not a one."

"Broke?"

"Completely." I sipped my whiskey. Ahhh.

The ghoul made a noise similar to a cat sneeze and said, "If you want I could loan you some money."

I choked a little. "What the f—"

Before I could finish he had produced a wad of cash you could kill a man with. And from where I was sitting I could see that it was all in twenties and hundreds.

I swigged the last drops from the glass and stood. "Where the hell did you get that?!" I yelled.

"From my fellow ghouls," he droned. "All monies made by ghouls are thrown into a collective slush fund for everybody to enjoy."

"What are you, dead or a hippie?!"

"What is a hippie?"

I waved him off. "Never mind." I rubbed my eyes. "I don't mean no disrespect, but what the fuck do you need money for?"

"Cabs."

I held back my laughter. "Could you loan me a few bucks so . . . I . . . ah . . . can get a few things?"

There was a short pause. "Sure, here's forty."

"Thanks," I said laughing a bit as I took the bills from his big white hand. "You suppose you could watch over the place while I pop to the store for a few necessities?"

He agreed. I put on a jacket and grabbed a baseball cap I'd grown out of about ten years ago. But I liked it, so I stuck it on the back of my head and left the office.

I walked out the door of my house, and, as if on cue, it started raining. Just a drizzle, but enough to piss me off, and it was that shitty L.A. rain. Hot and wet. It might sound good in a porno movie, but in real life it sucked ass.

I walked fast down Laurel Canyon to Ventura and as I moved closer to the liquor store I saw a guy leaning against a wall ahead of me. I could see he was trouble. Long, lanky, and greasy with a wide smirk on his face as he watched me approach. At first I thought he might have been a ghoul, maybe a fiend, or even a goon, but as I got closer I saw he was just human.

When I was within several feet of him, he looked right at me and his smirk widened. "Nice hat," he said.

I smashed my fist across the side of his nose and felt it snap beneath my knuckles. "Nice nose," I said, and kept going without losing a step. Fucking loser.

As much as I wanted to, I didn't look back, but I could hear the guy "Oh my god!"-ing, and "Jesus Christ!"-ing. I felt pretty good. Might be a good night after all.

I bought a big, jug-sized bottle of whiskey, a case of good cheap beer and a carton of cigarettes. I had enough left over so I grabbed a lighter and a large bag of chips for dinner.

I was disappointed to see that Mr. Smart-mouth was gone but there was a decent puddle of blood and a trail of drops that led across the street. They were big and wide apart so I knew the guy had run like a sissy. I laughed a little and headed back to the pad, not minding the steaming drizzle a bit.

I was already on the porch of the house when I heard muttering voices coming from inside. They didn't sound threatening, but just to be sure I slowly placed my armload down next to the door and drew my gun.

There were two voices. One kept interrupting the other and both spoke quickly. Then when I heard what I thought was Mo'Lock's voice, I eased the door open with my left hand and fixed the gun, cocked, in my right. The door clicked and slid. Inside the office all eyes turned on me. Three sets of 'em.

Mo'Lock was sitting at my desk, his feet up, entertaining two suits. I put my gun away, glancing at the two assholes, then slowly up at the ghoul, nodding my head. "What's goin' on here?" I said.

Mo'Lock took his feet down. "I was just briefing these two potential clients—"

I shook my head.

Mo'Lock stood and walked away. "Damn."

I grabbed the packages, dragged them inside the door, and slammed it shut. Then I eyeballed the two geeks in suits. I saw that one of them had a ponytail. I hate that shit.

We were off to a bad start, I thought as I snagged a beer, then went around the back of my desk and sat.

I was right on one count. These two were major geekoids. The one on the right, Mr. Fuckin' Ponytail, had on the fattest, ugliest tie in the universe and it was stained with all manner of scum. The suit itself was the color of vomit after a frozen dinner, and believe me, I know that color. His face was that of a true dullard; long and thin with half-closed eyes and a slobbery hanging lower lip.

Basically he looked like a half-hearted hippie in a bad suit. I wanted to point out what a hippie looked like to the ghoul, but I let it ride instead of immediately alienating some potential cash.

The other guy was different, but a geek just the same. He had on a black suit, bowtie, white socks, and brown shoes. He had thin greasy black hair, big-ass horn-rimmed glasses, and a face that only a mother could love, if she were blind and retarded.

They both screamed to be beaten up.

"So, gentlemen—" I belched. "What can I do for you today?"

The guy with the glasses got nervous and sat forward, pushing back his glasses with his finger. "Um, ah, my name is Sinclair Walters, Mr. McDonald, and this is my partner, Alex Daniels," he said, gesturing to the ponytail.

"How nice. What d'you want?" I said as I swigged my beer and glanced over at Mo'Lock.

"I . . . I mean we . . . are—" Horn-rimmed stuttered.

Ponytail Daniels broke in with a cocky snort. "What Dr. Walters is trying to say, is that we need to ask you for a favor, Mr. McDonald."

"I don't do favors."

Ponytail rolled his eyes in a way that told me this kid was used to getting his way, which really pissed me off. A geek is one thing, but a pushy geek demanded a severe beating. I was about to inform him of this when he broke in.

"Maybe we should start with a question," he said, "Do you believe in the soul, Mr. McDonald?"

I slammed down my beer can. "What kind of goddamn question is that?! Do I believe in souls?"

I acted extra angry to watch them jump. Mo'Lock tried his best not to smile.

Horn-rimmed was sweating like a dorky pig and I could see Mr. Ponytail was getting annoyed. Good. Fuck 'em. Then he took a breath.

"It's a fairly basic question. Do you believe in the human soul?"

I shrugged. "I believe in filet of sole, soul food, and I believe that the sole of my boot is about to become the biggest fucking suppository in the world if you don't get to the goddamn point," I said, and stood.

They were stunned, so I used the time to throw Mo'Lock a wink and grab the bottle from the bag. By the time I swigged a few and returned to my desk the schmuck brothers were ready to talk biz.

Horn-rimmed talked first. "We've heard about you for a long time, read about your exploits in *Speculator Magazine*, and we know that you have a sort of expertise in a particular area of work. We know that you have had encounters with . . . eh . . ."

"A lot of weird shit," I cut in.

Ponytail nodded and took over. "We are in the process of some very 'weird' research, Mr. McDonald, and we would like to hire you to act as an advisor."

I looked over at Mo'Lock, then back to the boys. "What exactly are you guys doing? What sort of 'research'?"

They looked at each other. Ponytail nodded as if telling Horn-rimmed that it was okay to tell.

Horn-rimmed looked at me sheepishly. "I'll have to ask you one more time, Mr. McDonald. Do you believe in the soul?"

I groaned. "God almighty. If it'll get you to the fucking point, *yes*, I believe, I believe!" I moaned.

To my side Mo'Lock giggled. It wasn't some girlish giggle, but a raspy dead man's convulsion.

Ponytail seemed relieved by my sudden surge of belief and dropped the bomb. "My partner and I have devised a method by which we can capture the essence of a human being, the soul."

Mo'Lock stepped over to the desk. "What do you mean when you say *capture*?" he said.

The ghoul sounded suddenly on edge. I raised my hand. He nodded and went back to the window.

Horn-rimmed took over. "Not really capture, but we believe we can bring a human soul into the physical world."

I swigged out of the bottle, nodding, and then I threw my hands up. "So, the million dollar question stands. What the hell do you need me for?"

"We just need you to be there with us during the procedure," said Ponytail.

I looked at Mo'Lock, then back at them. "What, as a fuckin' good luck charm, a goddamn cheerleader?!"

Horn-rimmed pushed back his rims. "Well . . . yes, in a sense."

I thought about it.

"What's the pay?"

"A thousand for the day. In advance."

"Whoa, for that I'll bring my pom-poms."

Everyone nodded and smiled. That is, except for Mo'Lock. He seemed none too pleased about the whole deal, but he knew enough not to say anything in front of the clients. He knew I needed that grand bad, so he just stood at the window while I made all the arrangements. The day was set for the day after tomorrow at a warehouse in South Central L.A. They gave me the cash and that was that.

Mo'Lock was quiet for awhile. I ignored him and concentrated on my drinking. He stood at the window, sighing heavily every minute or so, trying to get me to ask him what was wrong, but I wasn't gonna. No way. If the fucking ghoul had something to say, come out and say it. I don't play counselor. Besides, it was fun watching him pout.

After about an hour of hearing the ghoul breathe like a bulldog I was drunk and sick of the game. I slammed down the half-empty bottle of whiskey. "Okay, okay. What the hell's wrong, Mo'? I give up. Tell me what's wrong."

Mo'Lock turned to me slowly like he was trying to play up the drama. "If they can do what they say they can do, the ramifications could be disastrous."

"*Ramifications*?! Hoo, boy! You been reading the dictionary, dead boy, or what?"

"Cal, I'm serious."

I nodded. He was serious. I curbed my dickheadedness. "Okay, but let's say they can't do what they say. That's what I think's most likely the case. I think I'm gonna pull a cool grand watching these jerks toot their horn."

"But what if they can?

I shrugged. "What real harm could it do?"

Mo'Lock started to say something, but stopped himself and just shook his head, turning back to his window. I waited and watched him. Nothing.

Then he turned to me. "They're messing with dangerous territory, even if they don't get results this time," he said.

I wanted to agree, I did agree, but all I could see was a thousand bucks. "Well, that's the chance I'm gonna have to take," I said. "It has nothing to do with you. Besides, I've dealt with weirder shit before. Don't worry."

The ghoul turned back to the window. "You've never had your soul taken from you, have you, Cal?" he asked, and that was all he said for the rest of the evening.

The day arrived as most do with me: late and in a pool of vomit. I'd passed out at my desk the night before after being thrown out of a few bars, kicked around by some cops and generally harassed by the planet. I felt like shit and was in no mood to deal with those science geeks, let alone their lame-o experiment.

I wiped the vomit off my desk and was surprised to see I'd had a pretty decent dinner. Looked like steak. Too bad I couldn't remember.

I took a big swig as I glanced at the clock. It was almost five. I had an hour to get my shit together and get over there. I didn't have time to waste so I took the bottle with me and got into the shower. I killed the bottle, washed, hocked up some bile, and before I knew it I felt like I might not kill somebody.

Mo'Lock was waiting for me outside the house. I had gotten the idea that he wasn't tagging along so I figured he was just gonna give me a hard time. "Hey, gruesome, you coming?"

He nodded. "What else have I got to do," he said. "Besides, knowing you, there's bound to be trouble."

I laughed. "Let's hope you're wrong," I said as I got into my car.

We pulled up in front of a big gray warehouse just as the sun set. I got out and lit a smoke, surveying the big building hidden in the shadow of some other abandoned houses. The warehouse was half stone and half steel. The kind they use for airport hangars and army barracks. Very dull, very cold, and so plain I doubted I would have ever seen it if I hadn't been looking for it.

There was a single door stuck on its front like a pig snout. No windows, just a few vent ribbings above the doorway where the stone turned to steel. Next to the door there was an unmarked buzzer button. I pressed it as Mo'Lock came up behind me.

I turned to him. "Look, about the other night," I said.

Mo'Lock shook his head. "Do not worry about it. Let's just get this over with."

I was about to tell him again that I doubted the experiment would even work when the door opened and there peeking around the corner was Ponytail. He was wearing a lab coat.

"You're late," he said.

We pushed past him. "Yeah, I know," I said. "So let's get to it."

Ponytail led us along a dark white stone corridor for what seemed like the length of the warehouse, then turned and took us about another twenty feet to a double steel door. I looked around. The door, as well as the stone walls, were new. It looked like the junior science corps had done some expensive renovating.

Outside the door was a combo lock. Ponytail slid a card through a slot, then punched some numbers on a tiny keyboard. There was a buzz, a beep, and then finally a click followed by the hiss of the door pushing open. He signaled for us to follow, which we did.

Inside was something out of either a really cheap or really expensive science fiction movie. I couldn't decide. The room was huge and had a massively high ceiling. Everywhere you looked lights were flashing, machines beeped, liquid ran through tubes, and computers cranked. They even had one of those arc-light deals buzzing above a huge glass tank in the center of the room.

Inside the tank was a slab, and on the slab was a naked man hooked to wires from every part of his body. A machine outside the tank beeped along, telling us he was alive. And as if that wasn't enough, pointing at the tank was a syringe the size of a Chevy. Its huge needle, a fuckin' tube really, stuck into the tank.

Even Mo'Lock was impressed. I looked over at him and we both did that wide-eyed thing.

Ponytail was nodding his head beside me waiting for me to ooh and ahh. "Well, what do you think?"

I bobbed my head. "Quite a chemistry set you got here, kid. Where do you want us?"

"Over there," he said, pointing to a couple of chairs to the left of the tank.

As he said this, Horn-rimmed came in from another door and jumped when he saw us. Skittish fuck.

I ignored him and we went over to the chair and sat. "You boys run along and do your thing. I'll be over here cheering," I said, and sat.

Mo'Lock sat down next to me and crossed his big legs. As I took out my flask, he leaned over to me and whispered, "Creepy, isn't it?"

I took a swig, offered some to the ghoul. He shook his head. "Fucking stupid, if you ask me."

For the next hour we watched the two geeks scramble around the room pushing this, turning that, and being science types. For all I knew they were doing nothing. It was all a bunch of knobs and tubes to me. I was getting pissed because I'd emptied the flask in the first fifteen minutes.

At one point Horn-rimmed got close to us. I belched really loud and he jumped. "Hey Einstein," I said pointing to the tank, "Who's the stiff?"

"Oh, ahh, that . . . that is . . . ahhh, Mr. Andrew Thomas Blue," he blubbered.

I nodded. "And what's his deal?"

Horn-rimmed pushed his glasses back. "Well, he uh, has been kept alive by machines for a year now and . . . well, his family finally signed the papers to have him cut off."

I looked at Mo', then laughed, looking back at the geek. "Bet they didn't know he'd wind up in Frankenstein's lab, did they?"

"Well, ahh . . . no. We had to shuffle a few papers."

"I bet you did."

Finally they were ready. Horn-rimmed sat at a panel behind the tank while Ponytail took position at the machine attached to Mr. Blue.

"Hey doctor, where's the popcorn?" I shouted.

Ponytail turned and shushed me. "Mr. McDonald, please. You are being paid well."

He had me there. I shut my trap. They began working feverishly. Ponytail had one hand on what I assumed was the cut-off button and one finger in the air that Horn-rimmed was staring at. Slowly Ponytail turned a switch and then signaled his partner by lowering his finger.

"Now," he whispered.

Suddenly the tank was filling with a smoky blue mist that came from the giant syringe. It filled quickly and as it did Ponytail completed turning off his machine and backed away, staring intensely into the mist.

I realized that both Mo'Lock and I were standing and staring too. At first I couldn't see a thing, but then gradually something began to form in the thick mist above the body inside. I moved closer.

There was something solid in there but I couldn't make it out. The shifting mist made it hard to see what was going on inside the tank.

Then Ponytail signaled Horn-rimmed again and the syringe began sucking out the smoke. It was gone in seconds.

Behind me I heard the ghoul let out a gasp.

They'd done it. I was stunned.

There, floating above the body was another body, naked and as blue as a summer sky. It floated, facing the corpse as though studying it. It was the dead man's soul. A motherfucking human soul. I couldn't believe it, but there it was. It was odd it didn't really look like the dead man. The corpse was old and flabby, but the spirit was smooth and muscular, almost featureless. It was staring at the corpse below it.

Then slowly it began to rise away from the corpse and was only a few feet short of the top of the tank.

Everybody was standing around the tank, silent, in awe. I hate to say shit like this, but it was as if we were all sharing the same dream. We just watched the soul rise, floating as gentle as a feather.

Then it hit the top of the tank.

The spirit jolted and bumped the top. It shook, it spun, it shuddered, and suddenly the blue mist form began to take on a greasy, solid form. It tried to rise again, but nothing; it hit the roof again. For a moment it just stayed there, suspended. Then it seemed to decide something and began to descend to the body again. It was trying to get out, but it would find no way there either.

The spirit just bumped against the body as it had the roof. Then it began to panic. It began flying around the tank, trying every direction. It hit the glass and the sound of it made us all jump.

Mo'Lock stepped toward it. "It's trying to get out."

But no one said a word. We just watched the soul swim in its cage. The expression on its smooth blue face was one of agony, fear, confusion. I suddenly felt terrible. This is what Mo'Lock had been afraid of. I understood. Souls are supposed to pass on to some other place or form, not get trapped in a big fish tank.

I looked over at Ponytail. He was grinning at me. "Well, Mr. McDonald. Do you believe in souls now?"

I glared at him. I almost attacked him, but where the fuck would that get me? I walked toward the door instead and signaled the ghoul to follow.

As we passed by Ponytail I shot him one last glare.

"You suck," I said and left.

Behind me I could hear the soul pounding against the glass.

Back at my office I got good and drunk but it didn't help. I felt like shit. I couldn't believe I was a part of that horror. Mo'Lock was standing at the window staring out and didn't say a word for hours.

Then, "It's not your fault, Cal," he said. "You didn't know."

I looked at him. I was slobbering drunk and could hardly speak. "You told me. I didn't listen."

"Now you know."

I shrugged a drunken shrug. "Shit."

I was about to whine some more when there was a crash outside in the yard. I sprang to my feet and pulled my gun. I was drunk but not *that* drunk. Mo'Lock came over to me as I came around the desk. There was another crash, then a thud and with each noise whatever was out there got closer to my door. Then it hit the door. The ghoul stepped over to it while I fixed my gun on it.

I nodded. He opened the door.

There at the door was Horn-rimmed, sans specs. He was covered with blood, beaten to a pulp, his lab coat torn apart. The top right side of his head had been chopped away and I could see skull and brains. The kid should have been dead.

He had time to say two words: "Mr. Blue," he said and fell to the floor, smashing his skull completely open on the floor.

I stared down at the brains.

I looked at Mo'Lock. "Shit," I said.

The ghoul nodded slowly. "Shit indeed."

I shook my head, then walked over to the doorway and helped Mo' drag the body inside so we could shut the door. I knew what was coming and I didn't like it a bit.

Mo'Lock beat me to the punch. "We better get over there."

This time I did the nodding.

We got to the warehouse a little after one in the morning. The front door was ajar as we walked up to it. All was quiet. I had my gun drawn. We made our way inside. The corridor was dark. The walls and floor were smeared and spattered with blood. We moved along, taking quiet steps and avoiding the blood.

At the end of the hall we peeked around the corner. There was light coming from where the double steel doors had been. They had been ripped out of the wall.

I listened. Nothing. Then suddenly a noise like shifting feet. I edged around the corner, my gun out in front. Then I stopped. Inside someone spoke.

"I hear you out there." It was a woman's voice. "You can't hide. Get in here," she said.

I looked at Mo'Lock. He shrugged. I bobbed my head and we turned the corner.

The lab was painted red with blood. Everything in the place was destroyed. There was a woman there, bright blue and naked. She was changing even as we stepped through the door, changing into something else, a man, a child. I couldn't tell. It was as if it was trying to figure out what it was.

Then finally it settled on the form I'd seen in the tank and it stood there looking at us. At its feet was a corpse I could only guess had been Ponytail. The blue man had ripped his flesh completely from his body. All that was left was a skeleton covered with glistening fat and muscle tissue.

His skin was lying in a pile nearby like a wad of dirty laundry.

The soul took a step toward us. "You were part of this. You took me away," it said angrily, and then just as fast, slumped sadly. "Now I'll never know where I was going."

I pointed at the pile of skin on the floor. "I'd say after this the answer's pretty clear."

I immediately regretted saying anything.

The soul came right at me. It was mad. It shape-shifted as it took strides toward me, each step triggering a new form. Man, woman, child, big, small, short. All blue, all mad, and all coming right at me. I fired the gun but it had no effect. The bullets didn't bounce. The soul just absorbed them.

I tried to jump out of its way but it got a grip on me and the next thing I knew I was flying through the air. I hit the wall. I felt ribs snap. I looked up.

Mo'Lock was going after the thing, but it wouldn't fight him. It just kept coming after me. The ghoul grabbed onto it and tried to stop it and the thing lashed out and turned to him.

"I have no quarrel with you. You are soulless. Get off me!" it screamed, and threw the ghoul clear to the other side of the room.

It swung at me. I dodged and leapt out of the way, just missing a fist that smashed stone. But it kept after me. I saw it coming, still shifting and this time it was getting bigger and bigger until it had turned into the biggest fucker I had ever seen in my life.

I was frozen.

It lifted me off the floor and pulled me close to its face.

"Do you have any more wisecracks before I kill you?! Any last words?! Do you? Do you!?" it screamed.

I was done for. I looked him right in the face. His hot odd breath went right up my nostrils. "You know, dead or not, a Tic Tac would go a long way," I said.

BAM!

It felt like a bowling ball smashed against my head and I was flying through the air again. My nose was definitely broken, maybe my jaw, maybe my entire head was broken.

I hit the floor, moaned, and rolled. But the damn thing had me by my legs and was spinning me. I started barfing and all I could think was poor Mo'Lock, having to get sprayed by my puke.

Then it got worse. The blue soul-thing let me go. Wheee! I was beyond pain. I was a meat-bag flying through the air.

I hit brick, wood, plastic, and finally glass. I was pulp. And it was still after me. I could see it through bloodied eyes. I was doomed.

But Mo'Lock was there too. I'd forgotten. He was running to get in between me and the beast, but Mr. Blue just kept coming at me. There was nothing I could do. I couldn't even feel my arms or legs, let alone move.

Mo'Lock didn't fight. He didn't even raise a fist. The ghoul did the one thing I didn't expect.

He inhaled.

He faced the blue beast and sucked in a lungful. The soul stopped in its tracks. Mo'Lock sucked again and this time I swear to God the side of the blue man's face was pulled outward toward the ghoul. He sucked again, and harder, and suddenly the entire side of the monster was being stretched, sucked toward Mo'Lock.

Now Mr. Blueman was the one screaming. It was trying to get away, but old Mo' just kept sucking and sucking, breathing in and out as hard as he could get his dead lungs pumping, until he was at last actually drawing the "flesh" of the blue man into his mouth. Sucking and sucking and sucking.

It was unbelievable. I got to my feet, dripping blood and watched awestruck as inch by inch, Mr. Blue disappeared into the ghoul. And after a minute it was done. No more Mr. Blueman. It was just me and the ghoul.

I shook my head and stepped over to him. I think everything was broken, but I was too happy and stunned to pay attention.

"Are there any other things you can do you'd like to tell me about?" I laughed.

Mo'Lock seemed disoriented. He turned like he was lost and then looked at me with utter surprise. "Where am I?" he asked.

I laughed. "You're here . . . in the lab . . . with me. Hey, Mo'Lock, you okay?"

The ghoul's face twisted. "And who are you, sir?" he said, and it wasn't Mo'Lock's voice. It was higher pitched, and kind of snooty.

"It's me, Cal. What's the matter, Mo'Lock?" I said.

I reached out for his arm.

He jerked it away. "Unhand me! And what is this "Mo'Lock"? My name is Michael Thomas Locke! And I want you to tell me where I am. And where are my wife and children?"

Oh god, no.

"Don't you know who I am, Mo'?"

"No, I should say not."

I felt a ball growing in my throat as I began to understand what was happening. "What year is it, Mr. Locke?" I asked, barely whispering.

He was indignant. "What kind of question is that? It's 1919!"

I walked away. I didn't know what else to do. I thought about shooting him, maybe freeing the soul from his body, but what if it just killed him? I couldn't take that chance.

Behind me, Michael Thomas Locke was yelling. I didn't listen. I didn't care. Mo'Lock was gone. He got a soul back and now he was his former self again. I walked out of the place and tears kept coming.

What'd he have to go and do a thing like that for? Crazy fucking ghoul.

To save my lame-ass life, that's why.

I didn't go to the hospital. Fuck that. I went back to the house and drank until I could barely see, let alone stand or speak. I tried not to think about Mo'Lock, and the fact that he was gone forever. Christ, he was a fuckin' ghoul, a spook. I'm supposed to be killing them. Not forming close personal bonds, right? I mean, he wasn't even human. Well, now he was. I wondered if he liked it.

The night passed and before I knew it I was waking up slumped over my desk. The sun was blaring in through the cracks in the blinds. My head pounded as I looked around the room and for the first time in my life a feeling hit me. I felt alone and somehow that was worse than my injuries and the hangover combined.

I swigged from my whiskey until it overflowed from the corners of my mouth, until my mind and body numbed, but the feeling stayed. The phone rang. I ignored it. Whoever it was could go fuck themselves.

Then there were footsteps outside. It was the landlord, most likely. I dug into the top drawer of the desk and pulled out a wad of bills and stood. When he came through the door I was going to throw the bills into his face. Maybe that would feel good. The steps stopped outside the door and there was a quiet rapping.

"Come in," I said

The door opened. I dropped the bills.

It was Mo'Lock.

I squinted. "Mo'?" I said, "Is that you?"

The ghoul stepped in nodding. "Yes, it's me."

I could have hugged the big dead freak. I didn't though. I just stood there looking stupid. "What happened to Mr. Blue?"

Mo'Lock shrugged. "I let him go," he said and smiled. "I didn't like being me again."

Now I smiled. "You were kind of uptight. You didn't like me, that's for sure," I said.

I looked down at myself and realized I was covered with blood.

Mo'Lock put his hand on my shoulder and began pulling me out the door. "You look like you could use a few thousand stitches. Let's get you to the hospital."

I followed the ghoul out of the house and to my car.

"Don't read into this too much," I said, "but I'm glad you came back."

"Me too," he said. "Besides, you owe me forty bucks."

STITCH

Have you ever had that déjà vu feeling and then realized that your life *was* repeating itself, that the same horrible things kept happening over, and over, and over? If you have, then you might have some small smidge of an idea what it's like to be me.

My name is Cal McDonald. I hunt monsters. If you wanted to be all dramatic and shit, you could say that monsters are my business.

I was visiting the hospital to have a few hundred stitches removed after a particularly nasty incident with a rogue soul. I'd gotten pretty fucked up. Who am I kidding; I got bitch-slapped around like a rag doll. The only reason I'm still alive is because Mo'Lock stepped in and saved my life.

At one point during the suture removal process, the doctor pointed out that I kept grabbing my gut. He asked me if I had stomach problems.

"I throw up a lot," I said. "Hurry up with the stitches."

The doctor bobbed his head and ran his fat tongue along the inside of his mouth. "Mr. McDonald," he said, "let's check it. Better safe than sorry, riiiiight?"

I hated him for no other reason than the way he rolled out the word "right." What a freak, and I couldn't for the life of me determine what the hell accent he had. It was either Armenian or Turkish. I couldn't decide.

I allowed him to run a few tests and poke around my gut. Every time he checked some part of me he'd shake his head. Finally after an hour he'd finished and said my stomach lining looked like Swiss cheese. I had a bleeding ulcer, acid reflux disease, and possibly a problem with my "digestive tract" or something equally disgusting. It was a polite way of saying my ass was falling apart.

"You have to take care of yourself, Mr. McDonald. You are not a young man anymore."

"Hey, fuck you!" I said, and meant it.

"Fuck me? Okay, everybody fuck me, but you have to stop drinking alcohol."

I glared at him. "Say what?"

The doctor said I had to stop eating spicy foods, quit drinking, and start taking down at least a quart of milk a day. Milk. Can you believe it? I hate fucking milk. It's liquid mucus as far as I'm concerned. Just to get the asshole off my back, I agreed and left the hospital. On the way back to my house, I stopped at a corner store and picked up some milk, cigarettes, and a twelve-pack of some shit beer that was on sale. There was whiskey waiting for me on my desk.

At home, I sat at my desk and sorted through my mail while I killed one six-pack. It was nothing but a bunch of collection notices from bill collectors as usual. I took a swig, and I swear, because that dickhead doctor had put the idea in my head, it hurt like shit, right in the bottom of my gut. Shit. I took a bigger swig of the whiskey and now, it hurt again.

Finally, I got sick of playing tough guy with my stomach, so I got the milk I'd bought, and started alternating shots of whiskey and milk. After about fifteen shots, I was feeling pretty normal, and then the phone rang.

I stared at the phone as it rang a couple times and debated letting it ring, but in the end I buckled and lifted the receiver.

"Yeah, hello."

It was Detective Lieutenant Gretchen Brueger. She was my LAPD contact. "I got something on the slab that I want you to look at."

"What's the job pay?"

"A big fat zero," she said.

"Well, since you put it that way," I started to hang up.

"There's a reward on the case."

"I'll be there in, say, twenty minutes."

I immediately grabbed for the bottle wondering what the hell they had down there for me. Cops spook easily, so I was willing to bet that it wasn't anything too strange.

I downed another beer or two, a couple shots of whiskey, chased it all with milk, and then headed down to the precinct to see what there was to see. It was early evening and the heat of the daytime sun had cooled along with the dimming light.

Inside the precinct building, I gave my name to a guy in uniform at a desk. He said Lieutenant Brueger was waiting for me in the morgue, and then pointed in that general direction. I knew where it was. I'd been there before. I walked a ways down a hall and then followed signs pointing down a short flight of stairs. At the bottom of the stairs there were some double doors. On the other side was the morgue.

Brueger was there waiting. She was small, but tough as nails. You might even say she was pretty, but something about the way she carried herself made the description sound all wrong. There was this thing about her that said *I have a gun and I'll shoot you if you fuck with me.* So I guess, what I'm trying to say is she's pretty, but in a homicidal sort of way.

We didn't shake hands. We just gave each other the nod. Brueger gestured with her head for me to follow as she pushed open another door with her shoulder. I followed. The room we entered was a huge rectangle, plain walls, each covered with either cabinets or bunks stacked four and five high.

On the bunks were dead bodies, most in steamy bags, but several wore only their toe-tags. I wandered around the room, checking out the bodies with minimal interest. I could feel Brueger's eyes following me as I strolled. I waited a moment, stopping in front of a John Doe, and then turned toward her.

"So, where's this mess you want me to look at?"

She bobbed her head sideways. "This way," she said. "In the next room."

I followed her to a door marked "Private" and we entered. The room was dim, only light from one fluorescent tube flickered on the ceiling. In the center of the room there were five bodies. All of them were covered but I could see by the size of the lumps they were small, which meant young. I could also tell by two protrusions, breasts and heads, that they were all female. Male corpses have two lumps as well, but the placement is distinctly different.

The fifth pile was short one lump. It had no head.

Brueger strolled by each body and removed the tarps that covered them. I hate to admit it, but my heart jumped a little when I saw the bodies. Or maybe a better way to describe it would be: my heart *sunk*.

They were dead all right, young women, but they were a bunch of parts sewn together into bodies. As in each one's head, arms, hands, torsos, legs, and feet were sewn on. Most of the limbs were sewn at the joint with thick black cord and pulled tight so the skin ruffled at the bond. The folds of skin and cord sent a chill straight up the back of my neck.

I had a bad feeling about this. Not just because these poor women had been hacked up and reassembled, but because I'd seen it before. It was the specialty of a twisted fuck named Dr. Polynice.

But I'd put him away twice after he'd made one too many Franken-teens and sold them as personal sex slaves.

What is up with people reanimating dead bodies? I don't get it.

These bodies were different though. First of all there was no clear sign that any attempt had been made to reanimate the bodies. At this point, they were just chopped up and reassembled. And I'm not saying that's not strange. It's sick as fuck, but I wasn't so sure this case required my particular area of expertise.

I turned to Brueger. "The bodies are scrambled. Maybe it's just a way to cover the evidence or make it hard to identify the victims."

"You tell me," she said, pointing to one of the bodies. "This one's got that one's arm. This one's got that one's hands. The medical examiner drew up a complete map if you want to see it."

"What about that one?" I gestured to the headless one. "Where's her head?"

"Look at this." Brueger moved over to a table against the far wall.

She flicked on a desk light and there on top of the table were two boxes.

"Two," I said.

She nodded, chewing the inside of her mouth nervously. "Honestly, McDonald, we don't know what to think."

I nodded at the heads. "I guarantee there's another patchwork body out there somewhere," I said.

"Right. The ME arranged the limbs on the computer. Unscrambled, they all come together as five complete bodies, except," she held up a finger, "each one has a missing part—some internal as well. We thought another body like these would turn up, but instead, we got these two heads."

I rubbed my head. "I don't see why you called me on this one. This is weird, but not my kind of weird. Not yet."

Brueger looked annoyed. "Don't start that crap."

"I'm just saying," I said, "murder's bad and all but until one of these dead ladies gets up and does something, it's just a sick, twisted homicide."

Brueger seemed a tad more stressed than she normally did. She leaned against one of the examination tables and sighed heavily. She was collecting herself.

"Look, the Feds are moving in and taking us off the case as of seven in the morning. They're taking the bodies. I won't be able to do a thing without risking my badge."

"Well, the Feds are good at this sort of thing. They have the resources," I said, pulling out a cigarette. "Can I smoke?"

"No you can't," she barked.

I lit it anyway just to see how far I could push her. I hadn't known her all that long. I met her after I was pulled out of the drunk tank a few months after coming to Los Angeles. She seemed cool, but you can never tell with these law enforcement types. They're as strange a lot as any. You gotta keep an eye on them. They can turn on you.

Brueger slumped. For a moment she looked like she wanted to give up. "The Feds will drag it out for years. They always do. These are local girls, Valley residents. I don't want to see any more of this. I want it stopped. The Feds are good, but they have different motives."

Her eyes were wide; all the coldness was gone.

"My hands are tied, Cal. I need you. You can do things I can't. And besides, I don't think this is a straightforward serial case. I think . . ."

I moved closer. "You think what?"

She shrugged. "I don't know. I just got a feeling . . . a really bad feeling."

"Well, leave the bad feeling for me. That's my specialty."

I nodded, turned, and scanned the bodies. They were all women, white and similar to each other in their overall appearance, each with a variation of dirty-blond hair and an athletic build. They had clearly been murdered, but for what reason, I didn't know. It didn't look like a monster case, but then again human monsters are sometimes the worst. They are certainly the most unpredictable.

I looked at Brueger, who was waiting for me to say something.

"All right, you got me. I'm in," I said, "and you better not be lying about that reward."

She looked sideways and down. Total guilt.

"There's no reward."

She shook her head. "Sorry."

"Well, you got twenty bucks I can borrow?"

I returned to the house about an hour later with the case and a promise from Brueger to leave me to my work. She said I could use their computers if I needed them. I told her I probably wouldn't need them. Computers gave me a rash. But I might need her to make some calls for me. She agreed, but only if I kept her up to date on any progress. Whatever.

I made a gallon of coffee and downed some speed to get in the studying mood. It was some low-grade meth, probably made in some redneck's basement in West Virginia. I swore to myself, speed was next on the quit list. I was getting too old to be doing hard stuff. One of these days my heart was just going to explode.

Once my scalp started to itch like it was covered with ants, I began combing through the files. The bodies had all been found on or near a jogging/walking path that ran through Runyon Park. They had all been killed the same way, and this was strange.

They had been drowned.

Runyon Park was as dry as a bone.

The medical examiner guessed they had been held under in a small pool of water such as a bathtub or even a large pan. Bruises found on three of the victims were on the backs of their necks from being forced into the water. The killer was strong. Either that or the victims trusted the killer.

There were no signs of sexual assault on any of them, no signs of robbery. If anything, the bodies were treated with extreme care. They were killed for whatever dark reason the killer had in mind, but something told me it wasn't motivated by rage or hate. There was an odd sense of caring surrounding these jigsaw women.

Brueger's report was good. It was solid. Everything seemed to be there. I doubted the Feds could do any better. I kept reading.

The victims had been cut apart and sewn together with surprising expertise, and this is where the case took the leap into weirdness that I needed: on all but one of the bodies, autopsy results showed that not only had the flesh of the bodies been put back together, but the bones and nerves had been, or attempted to be, fused together.

This was pretty advanced, sophisticated stuff. The killer was not only sewing, but doing considerably difficult surgery. I've had plenty of cases where some twisted fuck tried to make his own love doll out of dead bodies. Usually the flesh was bonded, but not much else. These women had everything mended; nerves, veins, bones. The works. They were being built to work.

I didn't want to admit it; it looked like I had a mad genius on my hands, and what I call a *Franken-Case*.

People have always tried to defeat death, but there's always a nut in the bunch who tries to create life out of death. *Frankenstein*, the book, was a story based on this concept and I'm sure Mary Shelley borrowed from something true she had heard or experienced. In the novel, Dr. Frankenstein waited for death to come and for body parts to become available, but I was afraid this killer wasn't waiting. He was killing to harvest limbs and organs. What didn't make sense was why would he dump them all.

I started to shake. Not from fear. The speed had kicked in with a vengeance. I put down the report and lit a cigarette. The room was quiet and a layer of smoke drifted around just short of eye level in the dim light. As I smoked, each drag long and deep, I sifted the facts of the case through my head.

Brueger mentioned the ME had determined that if the bodies were rearranged back to their proper order, each one would still be missing one part. Then there were the two heads in the boxes. Again, two white females. One I assumed belonged to the headless body. The other one, most likely, belonged to the jigsaw body they hadn't found, or that hadn't been dumped yet.

I was just feeling around in the dark.

I turned back to the file to investigate the victims themselves. All five, or six counting the head, were from the ages of twenty to twenty-two. They were all in college. They all disappeared on their way home from school, a week apart. The last one, the head, disappeared a week before yesterday. All the women lived within a ten-mile radius of each other, but it was not yet known if any of them knew each other.

I leaned over and picked up the phone. I dialed Brueger's private line. It rang twice, and then she answered. "Lieutenant Brueger."

"It's McDonald. I need to ask you some questions. Can we talk?"

"Not on the phone," she said quietly.

"Meet me at the Black Cat."

"That dump again?"

"They let me run a tab," I said. "See you in fifteen."

I slammed down the phone. I was jittery. I needed a counter-dose. I checked the desk drawer. I was dry; no drink, no weed. I'd have to wait and grab some drinks at the Black Cat Club. I packed up my cigarettes and gun. I left the file on my desk.

Lieutenant Brueger was there waiting for me when I arrived at the club. She had a drink in front of her and shockingly a cigarette burning between her fingers. She watched me come in and make my way toward her without ever blinking or moving. I sat down, lit a cigarette, and looked at her.

"Well?" she said.

"I might ask you the same question. Why are we meeting here?" I asked. "And why couldn't you talk on the phone?"

"The Feds showed up early. They took the bodies, the files, and I'm pretty sure they've got taps on the phones."

I raised an eyebrow. That was alarming. I hadn't heard about the Feds moving that fast since JFK got his head blown out.

Brueger let out a billowing cloud of smoke followed by a hacking cough, then traded the smoke for her drink. She was trying to play it hard, but she was out of her element. Like I said earlier, she was tough, but she was suit-tough, office-tough. Out on the streets, in a hellhole like the Black Cat, the drinks with the little pink umbrellas just didn't fly.

I thought about the file I left back at my place. "Then I have the only copy of the file. Great. You think they're on to me?"

She winced. "If they're not yet, they will be. Take care of that file. Copy it when you get a chance." She took a sip from her drink. The umbrella rolled around the edge of the glass and smacked her nose. "Now, what are these couple of things you wanted to ask?"

"Well, to start with, what tips did you guys follow up on? There wasn't much in the file about the actual investigation," I said.

A waitress with a chain through her nose came over to us and I ordered coffee. Brueger seemed shocked. I ignored her. I was determined to stay wired. It's the only way to work these types of cases.

"What do you mean? Be specific," she asked.

"Did you do a search on other cases where decapitations were involved?"

Brueger took a final gulp of her drink. "Of course. There are no criminal cases involving decapitations on file in this area. And we went back more than twenty years."

I stewed on that a second, then said, "What about accidents?"

"I doubt there are many accidental beheadings," she laughed.

"Brueger," I said, "we only need *one*. Plus if you narrow the search down to women around the age of twenty, I'm sure something will pop up."

That got her attention. "Decapitations, huh?"

"Check all kinds of accidents: cars, construction. I'm willing to gamble something comes up."

The waitress brought our drinks. My coffee smelled like old shoe. Suddenly the little umbrella drink wasn't looking so bad.

"I can't promise you anything. Records aren't filed by type of injury. What else you got?" Brueger asked, after the waitress was gone.

"This guy we're looking for definitely has some medical background. Those kids were put back together by a pro. They used methods for bonding bones that are only now being tested by surgeons. Have you run checks on medical supply houses and shit like that?"

"Yeah, but that got us nowhere. Most of those supply houses do mail order. There's no way to trace that crap. Orders vary from small town practices to major urban hospitals."

"Couldn't you narrow it down to just local small practices?" I asked. "You know, maybe they flag orders that come from homes instead of hospitals."

"Maybe," she said, shaking her head, "But records like that just aren't tracked."

"Christ, they flag teenagers for checking books of witchcraft and communism out at the library, but any jack-hole can mail-order a bone-saw and formaldehyde," I said. "Have you checked hospitals for any surgeons that have been booted for . . . uh, strange practices?"

"I'm with you. Yeah, we did. A big fat zero is all we got."

"What about the military, Red Cross, and the like?" I asked, a little desperate.

She shook her head. "Can't get at the files. It would take months and besides, the Feds are probably checking it already."

I threw up my hands. "Well shit, I'm licked." I stood up. "Let me know what you find with those accident files. Thanks for the coffee," I said, and left.

Outside, the night air was cool. I looked forward to the walk home. Evidently, so did two guys who were following me. They were Feds. They had that stiff, cardboard I've-got-a-big-pole in-my-ass walk. Only FBI walks like that. I think it's in their training. Evidently, the art of tailing someone isn't. They were close enough behind me that I could hear the heels of their dress shoes clicking.

I decided to take a little detour, and headed left at Coldwater instead of walking straight to my house. I came up with a little plan and I needed to find a buddy of mine, Mo'Lock.

He's a ghoul, but a hell of a nice one. When he wasn't hanging around my place he could usually be found lurking around Studio City. It had all these narrow dark alleyways. He liked that. Perfect for lurking.

Sure enough, I found him sitting outside a Starbucks talking to a few other ghouls. Mo'Lock had on his usual funeral director black suit, white shirt, and black tie. The two ghouls were each wearing orange vests. They were road workers.

I made sure not to glance over my shoulder as I approached the chatting ghouls. I stopped once to light a cigarette, and behind me, I heard that their heels had stopped clicking. Jesus, these guys were dumb. Dumb or cocky. Those are the only types of Fed agents.

Mo'Lock saw me coming. He stepped up and stuck out his big bony white hand to shake mine.

"Cal. How are you? Is there trouble?" he said. "Did you know you are being followed?"

"Yeah, that's why I came here. Feel like running a little errand for me?"

"For you Cal, anything, any time."

"Okay, then, I need you to meet me in front of my house in around five minutes." I threw down my butt and ground it out with my heel.

The ghoul nodded. "I'll be there."

"Cool."

I started walking back toward my place. The ghoul followed me for about half a block and then disappeared into an alley.

I arrived before the ghoul did, as I'd hoped. The Feds were still on my tail, but they dropped back when I reached my place. I guess they were going to stake me out. No problem. That's what I wanted.

I went up to my house and grabbed a file out of the cabinet, then went back outside. Mo'Lock was there, waiting. He smiled when he saw me. A ghoul smiling is even creepier than one frowning. It just isn't right.

I walked up to him, holding the fake file out in the open, and handed it to him.

"I want you to take this and walk to the freeway overpass. Walk to the middle of bridge, stop, pretend to scan the papers in the file, and then *throw* the whole thing over the edge. That should fuck with them."

Mo'Lock looked a little confused, but he nodded. "Whatever you say, Cal," he said and walked off.

I went back inside and ran to the back window. I climbed out then crept along the wall back to the front of the house. The Feds were gone. They fell for it. They were following Mo'Lock now.

I strolled back inside. I took the file and hid it by separating the sheets of paper, rolling them and stuffing them into the shower curtain rod in the bathroom. That would do it. Stupid Feds.

I was feeling pretty damn pleased with myself despite having done zilch on the case.

Then there was a knock at my door.

I grabbed my revolver.

"Who's there?" I said, pointing the gun at the wood just where a chest would be.

"It's me, Brueger. Open the fucking door." She was whispering.

I opened the door as she pushed past. She was out of breath, but wasted no time. She turned to me, panting and waving her finger at me.

I looked her over. "You okay?"

"I'll tell you, I thought I was nuts bringing you onto this case but look at this." She held up a crumpled fax printout. "The computer came up with three accident-related decapitations. Three!"

"I thought it would," I said. I was lying. It was a shot in the dark. Most detective work is, despite what people claim.

"Yeah, well pat your fuckin' back later. Listen, the first one is as recent as two months ago, and guess what?" She eyed me, grinning.

"Ooo, I'm breathless."

"You were involved."

"Wha—?"

"You know when you caused all that havoc when you first got here? Caused that pileup down near Staples Center? In the report, witnesses say they saw you running from some kind of dog . . ."

"It was a werewolf."

"Whatever . . . this wolf threw the hood of a car through the windshield of a car belonging to a Mr. Tom Davis and a Ms. Nancy Wright. Both dead. Both decapitated."

I shook my head. "They're not the ones. Next."

Brueger laughed. "You are one cocky son of a bitch."

"I know my beheadings. What about the other two?"

She fumbled with the paper. "Okay, next we got a case that happened on Mulholland."

"That's pretty close to Runyon Park," I said.

"That's right. Mulholland has one of the jogger entrances, but listen to this. . . . About three years ago, a single father that goes by the name, now get this, Admiral Walter Bennington. He used to command one of the largest fleets in the Navy. He retired four years ago. It says in the report that three years ago he was on an outing with his daughter, Jenny, age twenty, and several other fathers and daughters. Evidently they had been white-water rafting. The admiral's daughter was in the front of the raft. . . . Well, some local kids thought it would be humorous to tie a line of rope across the path of the rafters. It didn't work that way. The rope was too strong. Jenny Bennington was decapitated."

"And they never found the head," I said. "That sucks."

"You got it, but there's more. Admiral Bennington spent time during Vietnam working in the ship's hospital."

"Lots of amputations, I'm sure," I said. Brueger nodded. "And there's that drowning/water connection, too."

"You're just smart as the dickens, aren't you?" said Brueger. "That, and the medical background puts Bennington in the prime suspect column."

"What about number three?"

"A little more cut and dried. Divorced father, Tom Burns, is driving on the 101 with his nineteen-year-old daughter, Trisha. There's some kind of confusion, and the car loses control. The top of the car is ripped clean off and the kid's head goes with it. The father suffers minor injuries, but—"

I cut in, "They never found the head."

"Right."

"A highway accident and they can't find a girl's head?"

"Evidently."

"This stinks like all hell. What's this Burns's record like? What'd he do for a living?"

"You ready for this? He's a bio-engineer. Still is. He's one of those fucks trying to genetically alter vegetables and fish. He was supposed to retire last year, but after his kid got killed, he decided to stay on."

Both men sounded suspicious as fuck, but what were the odds? The Valley is a big place and Los Angeles is fucking huge. Was it possible that two men who lost their daughters could meet?

It was going to be a matter of checking each of them out and seeing how they ticked. The Feds were bound to run a check on accidental decapitations sooner or later, so I wanted to beat them to it.

I looked at Brueger.

"If we're going to do anything, we have to move tonight," I said. "I say we split up. Bennington has all this medical experience and, this Burns guy . . . it really bugs me they didn't find the daughter's head. I mean, Christ, how do you lose a head on a highway?"

"Okay, let's say we flip a coin. See who gets who." She already had a coin in her hand. "Heads the Admiral, tails the bio-engineer. You call it." She threw the coin into the air.

"Tails."

The coin landed. She flipped it onto her forearm. "Heads. You lose. You get Burns."

Perfect. He would have access to all kinds of lab and medical equipment and I just couldn't shake the idea of them not finding his kid's head. It was just a little weird. I stood up and put on my gun. I noticed as I did this Brueger was picking up the phone receiver.

"What are you doing?"

"Call into the station. I want to see if the sixth body has turned up yet. Don't worry; I worked out a code with the desk sergeant. The Feds won't know what the hell we're talking about."

"Don't bother. There isn't going to be a sixth body," I said.

Brueger stared at me for a second, hesitated, and then hung up the phone.

She walked over toward me, ripping the fax sheet in half. "Here's Burns's address. No matter what happens, we meet back here." She glanced at her watch. "In two hours. That'll be about three-thirty."

"Right," I said and we left the building.

Brueger went to her car, while I walked to the curb and hopped into mine. Burns lived in North Hollywood. It was just down the street, and smack in the middle between the accident and Runyon Canyon.

I wasn't surprised to see the house when I pulled up. It was a big detached deal, two stories with yard and pool. I guess bio-engineers make a pretty penny. Who knew there was money in making giant mutant food?

I got out of the car and stood, staring at the house. The entire second floor was dark, but there were several lights lit on the first floor. There were two cars in the driveway. Both had California tags. I made my way up the drive.

As I passed the first car, I stopped and stared down at a sticker on the back window. I was glad I lost the flip.

I made my way around to the back of the house with my gun out. I was willing to bet the place had a basement and that was where the action would be. I found a back door, scanned the glass for alarm tape, and then picked the lock with a phone card. It opened easily.

I stood silently in the open doorway, waiting to hear if there was a dog in the house. Nothing lunged and ripped my throat out so I moved in, sliding the door closed behind me. I was in the kitchen and not less than six feet from me, there was a door with light coming from under it.

I edged quietly over to it and pressed my ear to the wood. There were voices. Two of them and they were having one hell of an argument.

"... *you have to be patient. Memory is tricky. It's going to take a while!*"

"*I'm not paying you to be patient. I want results and I want them now!*"

It was worse and weirder than I thought. I had to make a move. I only hoped they weren't armed. I began to reach for the doorknob when I heard the sound of feet on the stairs. Someone was coming.

I moved as fast as I could into the house, glanced around, and saw stairs. I tiptoed up as fast as I could without making a sound and stood, listening.

Someone opened the basement door. I couldn't tell where they were or what they were doing. Then I saw someone appear at the bottom of the stairs.

And he saw me.

Shit, shit, shit.

It was a balding man. He looked stunned, and when he saw my gun he went from stunned to shaking.

I pointed it at him. "Don't move! Police!" I yelled.

But he didn't listen. They never do. He bolted off back toward the basement. I had a clear shot at him for a good couple seconds, but curiosity wouldn't let me pull the trigger.

"Bennington!" he yelled.

I fucked up. I looked around. There was a dim light coming from beneath a door down the hall. I ran toward it and went in, slamming the door shut behind me. I heard feet, four of them, running up the basement stairs. They were rushing, confident, which meant they were armed. This was not what I planned. After a lifetime of fighting monsters I was going to get shot by My Two Dads. Fuck!

I looked around the room I was in. It was a girl's room. I say this not because it was pink or anything like that. It was clean. Boys' rooms are *never* clean, and this room was pristine. It looked like it hadn't been touched in years.

Then I saw the half-empty glass of milk. I wasn't alone in the room.

I lowered my gun. The closet was partially open. Hearing the voices coming closer, I moved and pushed the closet open.

Crumpled naked on the floor and shivering was the sixth body. She was alive, all balled up in a fetal position.

I knelt down. The kid looked up at me. She didn't seem afraid. Her face was stark white with blue lips and yellowed eyes.

They hadn't preserved the head very well.

"Are you Jenny?" I whispered.

The patchwork woman shook her head. "Jenny's dead. I'm Trisha. Are you here to help me?"

I nodded, glancing quickly over her body; a web of thick cord holding patches of flesh in place. "I'm going to try," I said.

Outside the door, I could hear that they were right there, whispering a plan to each other.

I looked at the kid. "Don't worry about what I'm about to say, okay? Understand?"

Jigsaw Trisha nodded.

I turned toward the door. "All right Bennington, Burns! I've got a gun and I've got the girl!"

There was no reply. I put my hand out to Trisha. She took it and I helped her to her feet. Each part had a slightly different tint to it. I grabbed a robe out of the closet and wrapped her in it. She nodded and looked at me doe-eyed, like a suffering animal waiting to die.

"Come on, we're going to get out of here," I whispered.

And I meant it.

The door flew open. The crazy fucks bum-rushed me, and it worked! They caught me completely off-guard. I was helping the kid, the room was small, and they crashed into me, both of them, and dragged me to the floor. My gun dropped out of my hand. The bald guy, Burns, pummeled my face while the other man, Bennington I assumed, kicked me in the stomach.

I was down for the count. I had no air and the speed only made it worse.

They had me pinned and each of them had guns. They were old men, but the guy I guessed was Bennington was big and burly. He leaned into my face.

"Who are you? Who sent you?" he spat.

I didn't say a word. I just looked at them. God I fucking wanted to kill them.

He repeated his question. I stayed quiet.

Bennington pounded his fist into the side of my face. It felt like a hammer.

I dug a hunk of torn cheek out of my bleeding mouth and spit the glob right into Bennington's face. It stuck on his forehead like a spitball until he wiped it away.

Behind them, Trisha was bending down.

The other guy, Burns, slugged me across the face with the butt of his gun and was about to do it again when his head sort of exploded. One second he had a face, the next it was a red pile of goop.

I didn't wait to see what happened.

The woman had my gun and was staring down at the gory mess that was on top of me. I pushed it aside. I was covered with blood and brains. I was watching the admiral. He had the gun on Trisha.

"I'm gonna kill the girl! I'm gonna kill the little monster, do you hear me!!"

I got to my feet and raised my hands. I was the only one alive in the room who didn't have a gun.

"Trisha," I said, "Just stay calm and I'll get us out of here, okay?"

The patchwork woman looked at me and tilted her head. "I'm Jenny. Trisha died in an accident."

Uh oh.

Bennington, the fucking admiral started to cry. "I can't kill Jenny! I can't!"

I leaned in. "How about everybody lower their weapons."

I held out my hands and waited for one of them to hand me their gun.

Bennington shuddered and bawled like a baby. Snot streamed over his mouth. He aimed the gun on the young dead woman. "I don't want to kill you."

And then Trisha, Jenny, and the others spoke.

"We don't care what you do. We want to die. You already killed us once," they said.

Bennington's eyes were as wide as mine and he responded as I would have. "We?" he said. His gun hand was shaking violently and sweat gathered on his forehead.

The girl took a step toward him. "You're not my father. You're my killer," she said.

"I didn't kill you, baby," he whined. "It was an accident."

She pointed to her hip where the flesh appeared tanner than the rest. "You killed Stephanie and Sally and Beth . . . killed all of us."

They didn't even know I was there. It was the jigsaw girl's moment and I let her have it, or more to the point I let *them* have their moment with their killer. I believed Bennington hadn't killed his daughter, but he'd lost her and the grief drove him to murder other girls for parts.

Maybe he met Burns by accident, maybe they sought each other out. It didn't matter. Two fathers had lost their daughters. Both heads had never been found. I looked at the girl and saw the stitching around the back of her head and guessed that the head was one daughter's and the brain the other.

The patchwork woman raised the gun and clenched her teeth. "We're going to kill you now."

Bennington pissed himself and sobbed. He let the gun slip from his hands. It was finally too much. He surrendered.

But this seemed to upset the girl all the more. As I reached for Bennington's dropped weapon I felt a stinging pain shoot through the back of my head. I knew what it was. I'd been there a thousand times before. The jigsaw girl had knocked me out.

I woke later in a pool of meat and blood.

My heart jumped. I sat up and pulled myself off the floor and out of the gore. My head pounded, and my tongue throbbed metallic. When my eyes finally focused I saw the blood.

Spattered on the ground below was Bennington, his head smashed open, his body bent like a rag-doll. Scratch marks and bullet holes covered what wasn't torn.

But no jigsaw girl, Trisha, Jenny, Sally; whoever she was, was gone.

Behind me, I heard someone suck air.

"Hi, Brueger. What took you so long?"

Brueger came over and helped me to my feet. It was the first time she had touched me, and it felt pretty good. It felt real and alive.

"You did it."

I glared at her. "I didn't do anything but get my ass kicked."

"I looked in the basement. There's proof: photos, plans, everything."

I turned and faced her. There were about ten thousand wise-cracks I could have thrown out, but I felt sick. I just nodded and started walking out of the house.

Brueger seemed confused at my lack of excitement. Then she looked around the room.

"Any luck finding the sixth body? It wasn't in the basement."

I saw the bloody footprints in the hallway, seeping into the plush white carpet, and leading to the stairs.

"Brueger, trust me on this one. You *don't* want to know."

EATER

I think it was a Tuesday. It didn't really matter. I don't exactly keep a nine-to-five schedule. I was lying face down on the floor, fully dressed, about three feet from my door when the phone woke me up. Each ring ripped through my spongy skull and drilled straight through to my brain like an electric charge.

Next to me was a puddle of vomit I didn't even remember throwing up. At the moment I was just glad I wasn't lying in it. I've been there before and it's a nasty way to wake up.

I didn't remember how I got home. I had been drinking at a bar; I'm not sure which bar it was. It was probably the Black Cat Club. It had become my favorite drinking hole for a couple reasons. One, it had the same name as the club I hung out at in D.C. Two, they let my tab run for six months without once asking me to pay. God bless the Black Cat Club.

After I crawled to my feet, nimbly avoiding the circle of puke, I looked out the window. The Catalina was safe and parked at the curb. It was parked straight and there weren't any trees, signs, or bodies smashed in the grill, so wherever I went, I must have walked home afterward. There are about thirty dive bars in Studio City. For all I know, I hit every one. It wouldn't be the first time. I tended to stick to the BC, but I liked to go to other bars to scan for freaks.

I touched my face and it stung like a motherfucker. It felt swollen and suddenly it all started coming back to me in slow, stomach-turning flashbacks. I remember popping some pills. Then I had a few shots. From there—and I was still home at this point—things get a little fuzzy.

I know I got into a fistfight with just about everyone in the place. They threw me out. I went to another bar, and started another fight with some Zeppo Marx–haired L.A. slickster in a red satin pirate shirt who bumped into me. He gave me some attitude so I dragged him into the bathroom and slammed his head into the urinal until I was tackled from behind and thrown out.

The phone rang and rang, louder than I ever recall hearing it. It sounded like a cathedral bell was right next to my head with a little hunchback swinging and yelling. My head was about to split open, and it wouldn't stop. I took out my revolver, gave the phone one warning, and then shot it.

The bang hurt even worse. I'm a fucking retard.

Besides, the phone wasn't dead, even with a slug through its mechanical body. It still rang. I had to stop it. I was Baretta. The living room was the hood of a car. I lunged across the room, almost slipping in the puke, and reached for the cradle before it could squeeze off another brain-crippling ring.

"What in god's name do you want?" I said.

There was a long silence. Whatever dickhead was on the other end knew they were playing with their lives.

"Cal, it's me, Mo'Lock."

It was the ghoul. He had a knack for calling at exactly the wrong time. But he had done me right too many times for me to blow him off. He'd pretty much set himself as my partner when he followed me from the East Coast out to Los Angeles. That was one dedicated dead guy. You hadda love him.

Well, at least tolerate his weird ass.

"Where are you?" I said, glancing around the house looking for clues, still trying to figure out how I got home. All I had was; drinking, drugs, fight . . . blank.

The ghoul said, "I'm right around the corner." He sounded excited, which, coming from a creepy-ass ghoul, was kind of scary.

I could feel a volcano of bile and beer rumbling in my stomach.

"Um, uh, give me a few minutes. I gotta throw up," I said, and then followed with, "Did you see me last night?"

"No. I was at the reservoir."

I started to ask why, but thought better of it and slammed the phone back into the cradle.

I bolted for the bathroom like an all-star sprinter. I almost crossed the finish line too, but just as I ran through the bathroom doorway, I projectile-vomited, sending a sickening (and strangely perfect) arcing fountain through the air. I must've looked like one of those water spouts people put in their yards to tell the world they're rich and have bad taste.

Funny thing was, most of the puke actually landed in the toilet. Years of throwing up perfects one's aim, I guess.

Half-dead, I climbed into the shower and let hot water pummel my aching head until I got my eyes most of the way open. I felt like hell, but I'd felt a lot worse. At least I wasn't suffering from any major injuries for once. Things had been pretty quiet lately. There had been a vampire skulking around Silverlake a couple weeks back, but I tracked him down and killed him in the same night. Jack-hole.

Most of my free time I spent with Sabrina Lynch. I guess you could say the two of us were going out. She runs a little rag about unexplained phenomena called *Speculator Magazine*. She used to trash me all the time, calling me some kind of fraud, but now that we're sleeping together she's backed off.

She was off somewhere for the past week, thank god. I recall her mentioning some crop circles or a Chupacabra sighting in Mexico she wanted to cover for the magazine. She did everything for the magazine pretty much herself. It was damned impressive.

Just as I finished dressing, there was a knock. I walked over and pulled open the door. It was Mo'Lock. In his arms he had something bundled up in a blanket.

The bundle was moving.

I was in no mood for surprises or moving bundles.

"Come on in," I said in my best fake-happy voice. "What's that you got there?"

"That's why I came. I don't know what it is." The ghoul lumbered past me into the office.

I didn't pay much attention. I didn't even look at the bundle. I was still asleep. "I'm making coffee. You want some?"

"No," he said, but he wasn't looking at me, he was staring down at the pool of vomit on the floor. "What's this?"

"Chicken and dumplings. Help yourself." I got my coffee; actually I just grabbed the pot, and sat at my desk. "So, let's see what you got."

Mo'Lock stepped up to the desk with his bundle and laid it on the desktop. It was pretty big, for a small bundle, about the size of two soccer balls stacked, inside a canvas sack. The sack was tied off with some thick cord.

Then the ghoul untied it and revealed the contents.

I shot up from my desk.

"AAAAAGGHH, what is that thing? Get it the fuck off my desk!"

Mo'Lock held up his hand. "Relax. It's only a baby."

"A baby *what?!*"

The ghoul explained in calm detail how he had come to possess the creature. The story was strange, but it made sense and I believed him. I'd heard stranger.

The way the ghoul told it, he was crawling around in the sewers with some of his ghoul buddies doing god knows what and they came across this big brown humanoid hippo-looking creature that had been injured. Turned out the creature's wounds were fatal, and after giving birth to the thing on my desk, the big creature died. Mo'Lock took the baby.

"We couldn't just leave it there," the ghoul said, wrapping up his story.

I looked at the thing on my desk. "Sure you could've. You just didn't."

I studied the small creature on my desk while I drank from the pot of coffee. It was around three and a half feet long, dark brown in spots, but mostly a light gray-green. It was bulky looking and its hide looked pretty tough, like rhino skin or maybe crocodile. Its mouth was wide and when it opened, I could see double rows of tiny but sharp-as-shit teeth. Its nose was nothing more than two punctures above wide lips and the eyes were the same except bigger and completely red with small black pin-sized pupils.

Mo'Lock told me how big the dead mother had been and I could only imagine how large this little shit was going to be.

"It's grown since this morning," Mo'Lock said.

Great.

I stared at the thing a little more. It kept moving its mouth over and over. Open close, open close. I looked at Mo'Lock. "I think it's hungry."

"What do you think it eats?" he asked.

"I don't even know what it is. How the fuck am I supposed to know what it eats?"

I was a bit frazzled. It had been peaceful lately and I wasn't really in the mood for anything like this. I'm not the goddamn Humane Society, for Christ's sake. What was I supposed to do? Then again, I thought, it was probably better that I deal with the creature before it got bigger.

Knowing my luck, it would probably come after me when it was as big as a house.

"I think I have a plan," I said.

Mo'Lock lit up. "Yeah?"

"Let's kill it."

"Cal!" exclaimed the ghoul. He looked really upset at the suggestion.

"Okay, okay, it was just an idea." I looked down at the thing. It was kind of cute in an ugly sort of way. "What do you think we should feed it?"

I put my finger a little too close to its mouth.

It chomped down. I screamed, stiffened, and slapped its head until it let go. By the time I got my finger free, the little fuck had gotten away with at least a half-inch of my left-hand index finger. Blood got all over the place until Mo'Lock handed me a cloth and I wrapped it up. But it still hurt.

Mo'Lock smiled sheepishly. "Well, at least we know what it eats."

I glared at him and told him there was some ground beef in the fridge that was only a little moldy. He went and got it while I studied the creature and tried to figure out what the hell we were going to do with it. My first plan was still sounding pretty good.

The ghoul came back from the kitchen area with the beef and the creature proceeded to eat it. It took the mound out of his hand and then, I swear, it sat up and devoured the entire hunk in a single swallow.

Mo'Lock and I stood there staring and, as if that wasn't enough, it grew. Right there in front of our eyes, it grew. It just sort of expanded. It licked its lips, rubbed its face, and then looked up at me, then Mo'Lock, as though asking for more.

I glanced over at the ghoul who was looking less confident than usual. Good. I was pissed. Fucking stupid, do-gooding ghoul.

"This is really fucked up, Mo'," I said. "Why don't we call someone who can tell us what we're dealing with here?"

His sheepish expression changed into a more cocky version. "Like who, Cal? Rod Serling is dead."

I actually started laughing. Where the hell did a ghoul hear about *The Twilight Zone*? They probably showed episodes at undead training seminars. Who the fuck knows?

I started pacing around the office, occasionally looking at the thing on my desk. It had grown when we fed it. That really freaked me out. Time was a factor. The mother was the size of a hippo and she was female. Chances were males grew even bigger, and the little bastard had a set of balls and a hole that probably housed a little gray dick.

My brain was just too cluttered. I was hungover as all hell and trying to think of what to do with the little creep was just making it worse. I needed a drink, but the apartment was dry.

I told Mo'Lock to stay with the thing while I ran to the liquor store. Hair of the dog that bit me. That would do the trick.

I ran a bit late getting back to Mo'Lock and the creature. I wound up drinking half the bottle I'd purchased while I drove home, so I turned back around and bought another one. The clerk at the store said he'd give me a discount on cases. I sneered at him. I should've clocked him. Fucking dick.

It really pissed me off when some asshole butt-fuck thought it was his right to get into my shit. I mean, I'd never consider walking up to someone on the street and telling them what I thought. Oh well, screw it. Most people don't know half the shit that's going on around them anyway. If they did, they'd have a heart attack.

I made my way back to my house about forty-five minutes after I'd left. I ambled my way up the stairs, sensing something almost instantly. There was something very wrong ahead of me. I got to my floor when the scent rolled beneath my nostrils. Blood and lots of it . . . coming from my house.

I shifted my parcel into my left arm and took out my revolver. I slid along the outside of the house, moving quietly so that I could hear any noise that might be coming from inside. The sounds I heard were strange and unnatural. There was a sort of sloshing, followed by a wet slap, then more sloshing.

I got right outside my door and made my move. I hate putting things like this off. I kicked in the door. It flew open and the smell of blood grew thicker. My office was covered with it, and I mean fuckin' everywhere. The walls and floor were smeared sticky red.

And there in the middle of the room was Mo'Lock, with a mop.

He looked up at me. There was a hint of fear in his hollow eyes, but beneath them, a slack-jawed guilty mouth.

"I can explain," he said.

I almost dropped my bag, but instead put it on the floor, slowly, as I kicked the door shut. I kept my gun in hand. I could feel my body shaking, but I couldn't tell whether I was scared or mad. I made a sort of side-swipe gesture with my head telling the ghoul to get on with the explaining.

He stood there holding the mop, covered in blood the way a spastic kid gets covered with mud. "Well, you had a client stop by. A new one, I think, and well, she came to the door . . ."

That was all I needed to hear. I was looking around the room. "Where's that little fuck?"

"It's in the bathroom," said Mo'Lock. "It was a woman and I managed to lock the thing in the bathroom before she saw it . . . and well . . . while I was explaining that you were running an errand . . . the thing got out of the bathroom . . ."

I ran my tongue against the inside of my mouth. "It locks from the inside."

". . . the creature ran right at her. I tried to get it off, but before I knew what was happening it had ripped her head off and blood was spraying everywhere. It was horrible, Cal. Her body was flopping around while the thing practically swallowed her head whole."

I just stood there staring, stunned, at the ghoul.

"I didn't know what to do, Cal. Honest. So when the thing started eating the rest of the body, I figured, you know—what is that phrase you use? What the hell, at least it gets rid of the body, right? Right, Cal? Why are you looking at me like that?"

I tried very hard to maintain control, but I was going to explode. I held one finger up in the air. "Now, let me get this straight. I may have gotten the first paying client I've had in months and that little mystery pig ate her?"

Mo'Lock nodded. "Yeah, that's pretty much the story."

That did it. I pulled the hammer back on my gun and headed toward the bathroom. "Okay, okay, here we go. The mystery is solved! You want to know what that thing is . . . it's soon to be deceased! How's that!?"

Mo'Lock jumped in front of me. "No, Cal! Don't!" He had his arms spread out, blocking my path. "I can see why you're upset, but killing that baby won't solve anything."

"It'll solve EVERYTHING, you idiot!"

The ghoul wouldn't let me past and he knew I wasn't going to fight him. "Come on, calm down. Have a drink. Take a pill. Smoke something." He smiled a strained, dead man's smile.

He knew me too well.

I nodded and put my gun away. "Any idea who this woman was?"

Mo'Lock pointed to my desk. "I've been trying to clean the blood. Her purse is over there."

I grabbed one of the bottles from the bag on the floor, locked the front door, and went to my desk. The purse was red Prada, ultra-shiny leather and had a diamond-studded clasp. Great. She was rich too, or rather, used to be rich.

She had probably come to me so she could pay me out the nose to follow her husband. He was most likely cheating on her and she wanted the upper hand in the divorce. All I would have had to do was get some pictures of an old fat-ass porking some eighteen-year-old and I'd be set for a year. Just my luck she got herself eaten.

I opened the bottle first and chugged it down a good inch. It burned the shit out of my ulcer, but felt perfect flowing into my brain. I could feel my heart rate steady. I grabbed the purse, unclasped it, and then dumped the contents onto my desk blotter. Contents as follows: a handkerchief with the initials AMN embroidered in the corner, a Prada wallet of matching red leather, a keychain with one sort of bulky key on it, some scattered change, and some lint.

I picked up the wallet. It folded open long-ways. First, I found her ID and saw her picture. She was gorgeous. Dark hair, full lipped and eyes that said; *"I'm really rich and beautiful so forget I am a loser."*

Her name was Annette Miles Newman, which meant nothing to me. The ID was new, only about two weeks old. There were a ton of credit cards and a little cash. I took it. I took everything out and as I pulled out the last plastic card, a bus ticket stub fell onto the blotter. It said Arizona.

Now, that was strange. What would a woman with as much dough as she obviously had be doing with a bus ticket? And from Arizona, no less. Who the fuck would live in Arizona?

I looked at everything in front of me. It all, except for the stub, looked pretty straight. Then I noticed the key. I picked it up. It was plastic, not flexible toy plastic, but hard and smooth. That was strange, but it was probably some rich-people thing. I wouldn't know. I've never been rich. I put the plastic key in my pocket just in case. Then I gathered all the stuff and threw it into a plastic bag.

Mo'Lock was mopping away, but didn't really seem to be making much progress. "Hey, why don't you just let the little fuck lick it up?"

I was joking, but the ghoul didn't get the joke. He nodded, impressed with the idea and went to the bathroom and opened the door. The thing came waddling out. It was bigger, almost a foot bigger, and its body had a lot more bulk. It looked at me. I gave it the finger.

Mo'Lock gave its head a little push toward the floor. It fought at first, but then after sniffing the pools, began lapping them up. It was disgusting watching the thing go at it, but it was doing the trick.

Mo'Lock smiled at me. "Good idea, Cal."

I wanted to throw up again. Let the little fuck lick *that* up.

It took a few hours but eventually, with the help of the mystery beast, the place got cleaned up (and it even ate my vomit from the night before). I kept a close eye on the thing, knowing that sooner or later it was going to try to escape or take a swipe at me. Every once in a while it would sniff at me, then look away when I flipped it off. It was nearly twice the size it had been this morning.

Mo'Lock kept pacing around the room while I drank and smoked myself into a nifty stupor. I had no idea what to do about the creature but my concern was nowhere near as great as the ghoul's.

"We've got to think of something," he said. "We've gotten nowhere."

I was drunk. "I stand by plan A. Let's put the little bastard on a spit and roast him."

The ghoul got pissy and ignored me for the next hour.

I didn't really care. Fuck him. He's the one who got us into the mess in the first place.

Mo'Lock was sitting and pouting at the window when the limousine pulled up to the curb outside the building. I had started going to work on the second bottle and I was riding a pretty hard buzz.

He turned to me. "Cal, come here and look at this."

I got up, fell back into the chair, tried again. Once I got my footing, I went to the window. The back door of a huge, shiny black limo was being held open by an equally huge bald guy at the curb in front of the house.

I sobered a bit and turned to the ghoul. "Get into my room with that thing and keep it quiet while I deal with this," I said.

I immediately began scanning the room for blood or anything else that might give us away. Outside, I heard footsteps clicking up the walkway. I fast tiptoed over to the door and gently unlocked it. Behind me, Mo'Lock, with the creature in hand, shut the bedroom door. I fast tiptoed back to my desk and kicked over my trash can by accident. It made a tremendous noise, but I was sitting by the time the knock came at the door.

"Come in!" I yelled.

And in they came; three of them. I first noticed the two gigantic, oddly identical-looking thugs. They were the twin towers of goons. In front of them was a little crotchety old man, their boss, I assumed, who looked like he soaked in salt water for a month, then rolled in a ball and was pounded with a mallet until every inch of his flesh wrinkled.

The thugs were scanning the room with a secret-police arrogance that set my temper off quick. It didn't help matters that I was inebriated. Fortunately, the old man spoke before I let my anger show or pulled out my gun and started shooting.

The old man's voice was just plain creepy; somewhere between Boris Karloff and Mr. Rogers. "Are you Mr. McDonald?"

"That's what it says on the audit."

"I am looking for my wife. She said she was coming to see you today."

I shook my head and shrugged. "Well, I wouldn't know anything about that. I was out all day," I lied. "Maybe there's something else I could help you with?"

The old man hobbled forward, narrowing his eyes. "You are a very bad liar, Mr. McDonald. A child could see through your charade."

I stood up. "Hey! Fuck you! Who the hell do you—"

The goons began to step toward me. I whipped out my gun and raised it. That didn't stop the giants so I pulled back the hammer.

"Okay, you old fuck," I said, "tell your bookends to back off!"

The old guy raised his hand. The goons stopped in their tracks like humungous wind-up toys. "There's no need for violence," he said, "yet."

I waved the gun in their faces. "Fun's over. I hate you all. I see no future in this relationship." I pointed the gun right at the old man. I had to close one eye to focus. "Now get the fuck out of my office!"

There was a moment of frozen, tense silence. I was breathing so hard I could smell my own liquor breath. I thought they might actually attack me or something. But instead the old wrinkly guy just sort of shrugged, though it looked more like a hiccup, and waved his hand at the goons. Without a word the trio walked out of the house and slammed the door behind them.

I waited a couple beats, then . . . "They're gone. You can come out now."

Mo'Lock lumbered out with the creature at his side. His hand was on its shoulder. "That was weird," the ghoul said.

I nodded and looked at him. "Yeah, a little too weird."

I didn't want to alarm the ghoul, but that little old man and his twin freaks set off every inner alarm I relied on. There was something unnatural about all three of them, but it wasn't anything I'd ever dealt with before.

It was something new.

I pointed at the ghoul. "You want to stay or run recon?"

Mo'Lock looked at the creature standing against his leg. "I'd better stay here."

"Right," I said and went to the front door.

I eased the door open. The street was clear . . . until I stepped onto the porch. The limo had only moved a few yards down the street. I ducked quick and made like a spy, edging along the fence, crawling over the neighbor's fence, and then skulking along that yard until I was within earshot of the limo.

Then all three got out of the car. They scanned the area. They didn't see me.

The two goons stood side by side in the shadows in front of the old man.

One of the thugs spoke first. "The animal was there."

"Yes, I know," the old man said. "And *she* was there as well, or had been at one time. That disgusting detective was lying about more than just the animal."

Disgusting? Screw that fuck. I hoped his diapers broke.

The other goon spoke. He had the same exact voice as goon number one. "Why didn't we just take it, then?" he asked.

"Because, idiot, if the detective knows anything about Annette's whereabouts, we don't want him dead yet. Annette has the key."

The goons nodded their bald heads in unison.

The old man grumbled for a second or two, then made a decisive grunt. "I want you to spy on the detective."

"Now?" both asked.

"Yes, now. Shift into Spy Mode."

Spy Mode? What the fuck? I couldn't resist. I slowly peered up through the chain-link fence. There were shrubs obscuring my view, but I could see the goons facing their boss.

Both goons went rigid and closed their eyes. Each exhaled long and controlled breaths. On about the third breath, their bodies just froze. It was so sudden and so stiff I thought I was seeing things. They were absolutely still, like a machine turned off.

If only it had stopped there.

Then the tops of their heads began to part and the fronts of their eyelids went soft as the heads lost their contents. The heads parted smoothly in two parts; first the skin split and opened, exposing the skulls beneath, and in turn, the skulls did the same.

Their brains were visible.

I think I almost pissed myself. I didn't need to see any more. I looked away and turned and crawled back the same way I'd come until I reached my house. Inside Mo'Lock sat on the couch with the ugly little creature next to him.

"We've got big trouble," I said.

Mo'Lock tilted his head, "How do you mean?"

"I have no idea."

When I get scared or freaked out, it turns to anger pretty fucking fast. I was really pissed. I mean, first this orphan flesh-eater devours a potential client, now threats from a thousand-year-old man and his thugs.

I had sobered up, so I tried to finish off the bottle. It wasn't working. My stomach was raging and every shot I took felt like a fire in my gut. I didn't really have a plan for the evening, but all of this was not it.

Mo'Lock was pacing around the room and the little thing watched his every move. Finally, after a couple hundred laps around the office, he stopped and turned to me. The ghoul opened his mouth to talk, but instead, he just sort of froze. His eyes weren't on me, but the window behind me.

I turned around.

"Oh, give me a fucking break," I said.

There, floating outside, were two sets of prying eyes dangling from two flying brains. I assumed the brains had come from the skulls of the old man's goons.

That was it. I'd seen everything.

I jumped to my feet and my gun was in hand in an instant. I fired right through the window. Glass shattered, mixing with smoke from the blasts. The little creature behind me started squealing like a pig.

"Shut that little bastard up!" I yelled.

I couldn't tell if I'd hit anything at all, and it didn't matter. Before I knew it, the client-eating creature ran past me and jumped out the window. Mo'Lock yelled after it, but it was gone, as were the flying brains.

The office was quiet.

I looked at Mo'Lock. His mouth was still open.

"Can we stop now?" I asked. "Any more of this shit and my head's going to explode."

"We can't leave it out there. It will kill everything it comes across."

The big dead freak was right. I jammed my gun back under my shoulder and, with me leading, we left the house. We didn't get very far. Outside we found out I was a better shot than I thought. One of the brains was on the sidewalk. I'd blown a decent chunk out of it. It wasn't moving.

"Check it out. I killed the brain."

Mo'Lock looked at the dead brain. "I have never seen anything like this before, have you?"

"Nope."

I was about to bend over for a closer look at the brain when all of a sudden, there was the sound of screeching wheels and people screaming nearby.

I shot a look at the ghoul. "The thing?!"

He nodded and we both bolted toward the commotion. We were running up my street, headed toward Laurel Canyon Boulevard. I could see up ahead that there had been an accident. I prayed the thing had been mowed down.

As we ran, I turned and glanced over my shoulder. The other brain was following us. I yelled for Mo'Lock to keep going. I swung around, pulled my gun in a single motion, and fired at the spy brain. It swooped left, then right, dodging the shots perfectly. That brain really knew how to fly. I took a couple more shots at it, but didn't aim too carefully. The brain avoided those as well. I was wasting my time.

I reached the street just as the ghoul was passing through it. He stopped and turned to me, pointing ahead.

There was the little thing, only about a block ahead of us. We ran on and I caught up with the ghoul.

I looked over at him as we ran. "You run ahead. It trusts you. See if you can get it in the park."

I glanced over my shoulder. The brain was hot on my tail, and not only that, but I saw the old man's black limo moving past the intersection toward us. I just kept running but I cut to a slower pace.

Within seconds, I could feel the brain on my neck. That's what I wanted and I kept moving. The Hugh Beaumont Memorial Park was just ahead. Mo'Lock was already there. I kept up the deliberately slow pace until I was right at the edge of the park grounds. Then I made my move. I swung around, snatched the brain in midair, and pulled it down. It fought me but I was stronger. I tucked the brain under my arm like a football, turned back, and sprinted into the park for what I hoped would be the winning score.

Mo'Lock was there waiting with the creature next to him. I ran up to them.

We heard a car door slam. I went up to the ghoul, then turned and waited. I had my gun on the brain.

It was a standoff.

Of course the old man took his sweet-ass time. I yawned at least once waiting for him to hobble within sight. The old man was smiling. He saw I had the gun on the brain, but didn't seem too concerned.

"Don't move!" I yelled. "Or the brain gets it."

The old man stepped forward. "Oh come now, Mr. McDonald. There's no reason for theatrics. Just give me the animal and I'll be off."

Huh? The animal? Did he mean our miniature flesh-eater? I looked at Mo'Lock, who was glancing sideways at me. He looked just as confused. We had no idea what was going on.

The old guy took another step. "Please, there's very little time," he said. "And, I wonder if you might tell me what happened to Annette?"

"Pig-Baby ate her," I said.

"Oh dear," the old man said, rubbing his chin. "That does present a problem."

"Yeah, how's that?"

The old fart looked at me with a static stare. "I suppose it's time we all come clean. I assume you have the key, then? Am I right?"

Fuck it, I thought. This guy knew what was happening. I didn't. Part of wading through the murk of the macabre is knowing when to throw in the towel. I pulled the key out of my pocket, letting the brain go. It flew back to the old man. I threw him the key.

"This was part of the deal I had with Annette," he said. "She knew I couldn't leave without the key."

As he spoke he worked the key under his collar until we heard a loud cracking sound. Then he turned it and the skin of his head split open. He grabbed it with both hands and tore it back and off. It all became a little clearer when I saw his real face.

He was a greenish-gray, with no nose or ears. He had huge eyes that blinked slowly and smoothly. Just like those stupid UFO drawings you see in the tabloids. The head was a lot smaller than you'd think, but I guess compared to the skinny body it was a pretty large melon.

All I could think about was Sabrina off in Mexico taking pictures of crop circles, and I had the real deal right in front of me. She was gonna shit.

The old man alien-thing reached into his pocket without moving his big blinking eyes from us. He pulled out a device that was about the size and shape of a television remote, and pointed it at us.

I jumped a bit. Mo'Lock, beside me, stepped forward just a touch. It was his way of saying he had my back.

A misty ray of sorts came from the object. A thin light-like line appeared like a flashlight in fog. It didn't touch either the ghoul or me, but connected with the little beast and grew slowly around it like a spreading stain on cloth. Then, as if it couldn't resist, the creature was pulled by the light that surrounded it to the alien's side.

We all stood there for a moment in the quiet of the park just sort of studying each other: me, the ghoul, one alien, one alien animal, and a flying brain. The little monster looked agitated, but could do nothing to free itself from the grip of the light.

The old guy gestured at us. "I'm sorry to have acted the way I did, but we behaved the way to which we thought you would respond best," he said, placing his hand on the light bubble around the creature. "This little fellow is the last of his kind.

They used to flourish on our planet, but as things will happen, they died off one by one. We only recently discovered that they were here on Earth also, but again, very few. Their appetite tends to lead them to death."

Mo'Lock straightened up, rigid. "Then he's not one of your people?" he asked.

The alien laughed. "Oh my, no. He's an animal. He will be kept in a zoo, and seen and enjoyed by millions every year. He's quite an exceptional specimen."

I glanced at the ghoul. He was pissed.

"You mean to tell me you're going to lock this . . . this baby up in a cage?" Mo'Lock said. I could hear the anger building in him.

I put my hand on the ghoul's arm. "It's not worth it," I said to him, and then to the alien, "I think you should go. We don't want any more trouble. Just leave."

"Let's fuck 'em up, Cal," Mo'Lock said in a low, serious tone.

The alien laughed again, the cocky little fuck. I was almost tempted to do what the ghoul asked. In fact I realized I was still holding my gun and instinctively raised it.

The alien looked at the weapon without emotion. "You act as though your people do not have zoos. They do, don't they?"

I shrugged. "We're not our people. So why don't you fuck off before I shoot your ass."

"That would be most stupid of you," said the alien as he pointed the remote thing up toward the night sky.

There was a click and then a pop-like noise and above our heads, the sky became gray steel. It was the alien's ship and it covered the sky for as far as I could see. Mo'Lock and I stared up at it in awe. I let my hand holding the gun fall to my side.

Then, as if I needed to see more of a show in one night, a beam of light came down and surrounded the alien and the little creature, but not the flying brain.

The alien gestured toward it. "I leave you this as a token of friendship."

"What?!"

"The lobe-tracker. It is a gift from our world to yours."

"I don't want your fuckin' brain,"

I was too late. The light was drawing them up and in seconds the alien, the beast and the ship were gone.

It was just me, the ghoul, and a flying brain.

It hovered over to us and floated in front of my face. I shuddered and backed away, but the stupid thing followed and probed at me with its tentacle eyes. I couldn't get away from it. It was like a giant slimy bee.

Mo'Lock laughed. "I think it likes you, Cal."

I backed away. It glided after me.

"Fucking great," I whined. "What the hell am I going to do with a brain?"

Mo'Lock laughed. "No comment."

No matter where I ran, the brain was right on me, so finally I stopped and sat down on the edge of a fountain. The brain hovered next to my head. I sighed and once he'd collected himself, the ghoul came over and sat next to me.

I looked over at him, exasperated. "I don't suppose you'd mind if I shot it, would you?"

Mo'Lock smiled. "Don't you dare!"

It was June or thereabouts. I'm never really sure any more. The longer I'm in Los Angeles, the harder it is for me to differentiate between the months. There are no seasons, unless you count rain and fire as seasons. I don't. I'm from back East, where you tell the seasons by the murder rate.

On this particular day, I had been dragged into the woods against my will. I was also showered, clean, and sober. I hadn't had a pill, drink, or smoke for almost an entire day. I was completely off my game.

It was Sabrina's idea. She'd finally put the summer issue of *Speculator Magazine* to bed, I'd just come off a series of bizarre cases, Mo'Lock had gone off to Death Valley with some ghoul friends, and overall things were looking pretty quiet for once. Basically I ran out of excuses and Ms. Lynch took the opportunity to rent a cabin in the woods for us.

She didn't tell me about the no-drink-or-drugs catch until we pulled into the park. Believe me, I never would have agreed to such madness had I known.

My name's Cal McDonald. Usually I'm a detective, hunting and killing freaks, and trying to ride a steady, mind-numbing buzz.

On this particular stretch of summer I was clean, straight, sober, and staring down the barrel of a long, long weekend in a cabin made out of Lincoln Logs. Only two words came to mind: *fuck that*.

"What you're not understanding is that humankind has spent thousands of years working toward *not* camping," I said as we walked up a dirt path.

Sabrina glanced over her shoulder, leading the way. "I have never heard a man whine like you, you know that?"

"Wait until we're in bed later."

I was trying to have a good attitude, but my head was throbbing and rattling and my stomach felt like a ball of cement. I knew she meant well, but you can't just tear a guy away from everything he knows and loves and not expect some bitching. Shit, this was more than anyone had ever convinced me to do outside of working. I had to give her credit for that. Still, my body had other ideas.

Sabrina walked and I followed until the path all but disappeared. Suddenly I was surrounded by tree branches, pine cones, and dirt. Bugs were swarming and for a heavily wooded area, it was fucking bright. All I wanted was a case of beer, something to smoke, and my dark house to hide in. This was bullshit.

Sabrina finally came to a stop up ahead of me. I couldn't see a cabin through the foliage, but anything indoors was going to be a welcome change. At the end of the trail Sabrina was standing in a clearing. She was taking off her backpack. I looked around.

"Where's the cabin?"

She looked at me puzzled. "What cabin?"

"You said there was a cabin."

Sabrina shook her head and let her pack fall to the ground.

"You said *come to the cabin in the woods with me*."

"I said *come camping in the woods with me*."

I could see she was trying to hide her face from me as she started undoing the button on her pack. She was laughing.

"You lied to me," I smirked. "You unbelievable bitch."

"Consider it payback for bailing you out." She put her hand to her chin. "Gee, I've lost track. How many times?"

She had me. I unfastened the belt to loosen the backpack, but the weight caught me off-balance and dragged me backward to the ground. I rolled on the backpack like a tortured turtle. Sabrina started laughing until I bashed my skull on a rock and split my head open. It was totally humiliating. Even Mother Nature wanted to kick my ass.

"Poor baby. Are you okay?"

Sabrina pulled off my pack and started picking through my head like some kind of she-ape. I had a cut from the fall, but there was only a little blood. Once she saw I was okay, she launched back into laughing. I just sat there in the dirt like a discarded puppet and wished like hell I didn't like her so much. If she were anybody else I would have pistol-whipped her by now.

It took a while to get the camp set up; one big tent and a fire pit with folding chairs. By the time we'd finished the sun was already down. And when the sun went down in the woods, it was gone. It was pitch black. And when I say black I mean like no light whatsoever. Damn woods.

We built a little fire and roasted some hot dogs and it was about this time I started getting the shakes. My body was demanding to be fed, but I'd given my word, so I rode out the pain. Unfortunately Sabrina had a different kind of pain up her sleeve.

"Can we talk?"

I felt my heart sink as sweat gathered at my brow. "About what?"

"About us."

De-tox and a relationship chat. If there were a cliff around, I would have run and jumped off it.

"Can I have a drink?"

"We didn't bring any."

"Anything to smoke?"

She shook her head.

"How about a pill?"

Sabrina looked me hard in the eyes. "No."

I wiped the beads of sweat from my face and looked at the fire. "You know, I hear there are some plants in the woods with hallucinogenic properties. We could go on a nature walk."

She looked at me, at the sweat on my face and my shaking hands. "Is it that bad?"

"It's been four hours. That's the longest I've ever gone without something since I was sixteen."

She shook her head.

"Don't shake your head at me," I said. "I'm fine."

"Then can we talk?"

I sighed. "Sure."

Sabrina leaned close to me and took my hand. I tried to smile, but I felt my stomach balling up tight.

"There's no simple way to say this," she said. "Cal . . . Honey, you're a mess."

I went from sick to mad in half a second. "What're you talking about?"

"We've been seeing each other for almost six months and I don't think you've been sober once the whole time."

"Define sober."

"Nothing in your system."

She squeezed my hand. "I never said anything before because I didn't think we had anything, but now, I think we do."

"Yeah?" I smiled.

"Yeah," she returned. "But I don't know if I can be with someone who's so self-destructive."

I rolled my tongue inside my cheek. "In case you haven't noticed, more than just my habits are trying to kill me. I have a lot of enemies and they'll be your enemies too if you keep hanging around me."

I got up and walked away. I didn't want to hear another word of her bullshit. I got all of five feet away before I walked out of the firelight's range and smacked into a tree. She didn't laugh, but I could tell she wanted to. That made me really mad. I swung around.

"Look, you knew what I was when you met me!" I said. "Now you decide you like this and don't like that?"

She was shocked and just stared at me like a wounded puppy.

I wasn't done.

"I'm not going to stand here and make excuses. I do what I do because I LIKE IT! Why is that so hard to understand?"

She stared at me. I forced myself to calm down and walked toward her.

"I'm not a fixer-upper, Sabrina," I said. "I come *as is*."

She just sat at the fire and looked down. I couldn't figure out if she heard me or if she was disappointed. I looked down at the ground and saw something. It looked like a white stick. I leaned down and cursed my luck, my strange, strange luck.

On the ground, undamaged and lying there waiting for me to pick it up, was a perfectly rolled joint.

I leaned over and picked it up. Sabrina was looking at me.

"I swear to you," I said smiling, "I didn't bring it."

Sabrina shook her head and laughed a light breathy laugh. Then she patted the space next to her with her hand. I walked over and sat down.

I held up the joint. "I think it's a sign."

Sabrina laughed. "From who, Cheech and Chong?"

She looked at me until I began to feel nervous and added, "I'm just worried about you."

I stuck the joint between my lips and said, "I appreciate that, but I've been taking care of myself for a long time. I'm fine."

I lit the joint, took a long smooth hit, and then offered it to Sabrina. "Come to my side, little girl," I coughed. "Join us!"

She grabbed it and took several short puffs. A second later she hacked and a huge plume of smoke rose from her like exhaust from a locomotive. It was a monster hit.

"Damn," I said and took the smoke for myself while she hacked and coughed.

She had one or two more hits after that, but I smoked most of it and it felt damn good. The shakes calmed and the sweating stopped. Now all I needed was a ride back to civilization and I'd be fine. But that wasn't in the plan. Evidently we were still going to sit around the fire and chat. I did my best to play along, but human relationships are not my strong point.

It didn't help that Sabrina was a casual weed smoker. She acted like a cartoon drunk, wavering from serious to clown-like giddy in the span of two seconds.

Then she had an idea.

"Let's read the bear safety pamphlet they gave us!"

I didn't even get a chance to answer. She was up and rummaging through the tent, giggling like a damn fool. A second later she crawled out of the tent and kept on crawling until she was hanging on my legs. In her hand was the crumpled safety sheet the park ranger gave to us earlier. It was a small handout with basic tips on how to avoid bears stealing your food, and what to do if one comes into your camp. Shit like that.

Here's a little tip about bear pamphlets: never read one stoned.

Sabrina thought it would be funny, and some of it was, like the chapter that told you to bang pots together if a bear advances on you. But then she got to the part about bears being meat eaters who like fish and *small* mammals.

Sabrina looked down at her five-foot-five-inch frame and frowned. "Small mammals? *I'm* a small mammal!"

Suddenly she looked scared. Her eyes went wide, her face pale beneath the flickering firelight.

But it wasn't the pamphlet.

It was the moaning sound coming from the woods.

"What was that?"

I shook my head. "Dunno. It sounded like somebody let the air out of a cow."

"Maybe a wolf?" she said, almost wishful.

"I doubt it," I replied. "Maybe a bear."

Sabrina shot me a look. I had forgotten all about the small-mammal thing.

Then there was another sound, almost the same: a long, painful drone of a wail. This time it came from behind us. The first had been from the front.

Sabrina was scared and all I could think was what an asshole I was, thinking I'd get a day's peace. There was something out there in the woods, and I don't know much about the wild, but whatever it was wasn't human.

I pulled my .45 out of my pant leg, and a small .38 custom from the other. I handed the .38 to Sabrina. She took it, bobbled it, then gripped it firmly in her hand and smiled.

"You got me high and holding a gun in no time, didn't you?"

I nodded. "I do my best."

Suddenly the moaning sounds came from all around, and they sounded closer than before. It was dark and we were sitting ducks standing near the fire, so I led Sabrina outside the light and deep into the woods. When I'd put some distance between us and the camp I silently signaled for her to stop.

From this vantage point we could see the camp and the creatures that now stood in the glow of the firelight.

There were three of them. They were humanoid in shape, but completely covered with hair and about seven feet tall.

Beside me, Sabrina whispered, "Ohmygod. Do you know what they are?"

"If they spot us, they're gonna be carpets, that's all I know."

We watched as the hairy creatures tore through our camp. They shredded our bags, our clothes, and ate all the food. It took them less than a couple minutes to destroy and devour everything. It looked like we would be able to wait them out until I watched one of them, the tallest of the three, pick up Sabrina's camera and fiddle with it. Just when the beast had the flash pointed at its face, it went off.

The creatures freaked out.

I burst out laughing.

Bad move.

The two that weren't blinded by the flash spun, spotted us hiding in the woods, and started running toward us. They had faces like gorillas with sharp teeth and flat, leathery, black faces. I'd always wondered how these creatures had maintained their legendary status and avoided being photographed or captured. Watching them run at us I began to understand . . . everybody who ever saw one had died.

I wasn't planning on becoming their next victim and I sure as shit wasn't gonna let them get Sabrina. I stood my ground and aimed at the charging wild men, screaming for Sabrina to do the same as I fired.

I hit one in the shoulder and the other in the leg. They both stumbled and slowed, but they didn't stop. Sabrina emptied the .38, but didn't hit a thing. I evaluated our options, then grabbed her and ran like hell into the darkness with those things roaring at our heels.

It was a crapshoot. Either we'd smack into a tree or those things would get us. We needed time to hide. I turned, without giving Sabrina warning, and fired. One of the creatures' ears exploded.

The other flailed and fell because of the flash. I could have finished them, but I wasn't alone. Time was more valuable than a kill. Lucky for the Bigfeets.

By now, my eyes had adjusted to the dark enough for me to make out where the trees were and where they weren't. I steered us through the forest as fast as we could move, but within seconds we could hear the creatures again. From the sounds of their growling I could tell the third had joined them in the hunt. I could also tell they'd fanned out. Sounds came from behind, right, and left. They were going to surround us. They were as smart as they were ugly.

Then up ahead I saw something. It looked like a tower of some sort. I pointed it out to Sabrina, and we ran toward it as fast as we could. As we got closer I could see there was more to the structure, that most of it was obscured by ivy and other overgrown foliage. As we came up on what was a short guard tower, we also saw a long stretch of rotted chain-link fence and beyond that, a bunker-like structure embedded and abandoned in the woods.

"There!" I whispered, and she followed me.

Sabrina paused for a moment as we approached the rusted box of a building almost completely devoured by the woods.

"What is this place?"

I ushered her along. I could hear our wilderness friends crashing through the woods behind us. They were back in the chase. Besides, I didn't have a clue what the place was. Whatever had been in the building had been stripped away. It was hard to tell what it had been but I recall thinking of a classroom or a lab of some sort. It reeked of secrecy and had clearly been unused for a very long time. Not to sound like a ten-year-old, but it felt like a *bad place*. Some places just have that feeling. It sticks to them like an odor that never fades.

Bad or not, it was shelter from the creatures pursuing us. We ran through a doorway and into a small flat room made of steel that had long ago lost its paint and surrendered to rust and growth. The space inside was wide open. There were no other rooms and no obvious place to hide.

I glanced through one of the windows, the glass crystallized with moisture and mold and age. The three creatures were standing near the tower sniffing at the air, debating, I think, whether or not to go any further. I couldn't see their faces in the darkness, but their body language spelled caution. This was a bad place to them, too.

By the time I turned back to Sabrina she had wandered to the very back of the short, flat bunker. The back of the room had been overrun by a massive tree root and part of the metal wall was twisted and mangled right into the bark like the tree was eating the structure and taking its time about it.

Feeling like we might be safe, I edged over to Sabrina and tapped her shoulder. I pointed to a hole in the wall near the tree root damage. It would be a tight squeeze, but it looked like we could fit through and maybe lose the creatures by disappearing out the other side. She nodded and glanced over at the creatures.

"They're scared of this place," I whispered.

Sabrina nuzzled against me. "So am I."

I went through the hole first. It was a squeeze, and I ripped my shirt and pants on the jagged metal edges, but I got through. I immediately looked back through and started helping Sabrina through, but as I did I saw the creatures at the door just a few yards behind her. They were coming in and all three of them had their fierce black eyes fixed firmly on her.

"Hurry!" I said. "Don't look behind you, just hurry!"

She did good. She listened and came through the hole without hesitation. She even resisted the urge to look back. Trust me, I know from experience that those looks back can be deadly.

I stood and looked around as I helped her to her feet. We weren't on the other side of the building as I thought. We were still inside the place, but in a small enclosure. I looked closer and saw that the hole we'd crawled in through had been some sort of entry. The overgrown tree roots had both sealed *and* ripped apart what had once been a door. The rip was the hole we'd come through. It was the only way in, or out.

"Oh god," Sabrina whispered, piecing together what I already had.

We were trapped.

Outside in the main area, we could hear the creatures cautiously moving around, but they were getting braver by the second. I looked at the hole, no bigger than a basketball, but the edges were shredded steel. There was a chance they could reach inside and grab us. There was also a chance, if they were as strong as I feared, they could peel back the tears and come in after us.

I stumbled back away from the hole and my feet kicked a pile of what I wished were sticks and debris, but I knew that hollow sound. Only one thing makes that sound: bones.

I took out my lighter and sparked it for only a second; long enough for Sabrina and I to see the chamber we were in. It was a cell, steel, cold gray with no windows, just the sealed door. There were bones on the floor, whole skeletons. At first glance they appeared human, but the skulls were larger, and the limbs were longer and thicker. It didn't take a genius to see they were the bones of creatures like the ones outside the chamber. But why were they here, and how?

Listening to the nervous snorts and grunts outside the hole gave me some possible insight. If the creatures had put the remains in the hole, I doubted they would be afraid, but if this place had been a laboratory where they were captured, or raised, or grown, or whatever the fuck crazy people do with monsters in labs, then that would explain their fear.

I didn't care at that moment, but the idea that these legendary creatures of the woods were created in a lab, or at one time captured for study intrigued me. Sabrina must have been having a stroke. For *Speculator Magazine*, her magazine, something like this was like finding the Holy fucking Grail.

Sabrina had moved to the corner farthest from the hole, and she was looking at a skull in the pile of bones, a particular skull.

I leaned down to her. "What is it?"

"Look."

I followed her finger to the side of the skull. It was smaller than the rest and right at the temple was a hole. All of the skulls had them. They had all been shot in the head.

"What happened here?" Sabrina asked.

I glanced around the cell. "If I had to guess," I said. "It looks like somebody tried to study these creatures and when the money ran out, they killed them."

"That's a harsh guess."

"Yes it is."

Just when I was thinking warm and fuzzy thoughts about my fellow man, a face appeared in the hole and roared. I jumped and aimed my gun at the face and started to pull back the trigger. At the last second Sabrina slapped my hand. The gun went off. The bang was deafening inside the steel cell. It scared off the creature from the hole, but it also rattled Sabrina and me.

"What the fuck?!" I yelled at her.

She looked more upset than angry. "Don't kill them."

I just sort of convulsed in confusion. "If I don't they're going to kill us, and *eat* us, I might add."

"I know, but . . ."

She didn't finish her thought and she didn't have to. I knew.

I touched my hand to her cheek and smiled. I had me an idea.

"I lied to you," I said.

"You lied? About what?"

Outside the creatures grunted and stomped their giant feet.

"When you asked me not to bring any drugs on the trip."

She tilted her head in that *I don't understand what you are saying to me* sort of way that only a woman can pull off without looking fake. It worked. I felt like a complete heel.

I tried to look her in the eyes as I pulled the baggie out of my sock. It was full of pills, painkillers mostly. "I'm sorry."

She looked disappointed, then confused. "Why are you telling me now?"

The guilt was gone. I wasn't that whipped yet. I smiled and pulled a bag of beef jerky out of my pocket and proceeded to empty the meat on the floor, then I did the same with the pills. I placed four or five of the stronger pills onto a slab of the dried meat and then folded and rolled the whole thing into a jerky/painkiller burrito.

By now Sabrina had figured out what I was up to and was busy making the second one.

"Think it'll work?" she asked.

"One of these can knock *me* out."

She just nodded.

When we were done we had three large meat-and-sedative burritos ready for use. I tossed some of the extra meat out to whet their appetites and they went for it. I saw a huge hand grab the first bit, then heard the sound of chomping and what might have been Bigfoot yummy noises.

Then I tossed one of the burritos out. It sat there for a *loooong* moment, then a face came down and gave it a sniff. For a second I thought it was a failure, but then it chomped down on the meat and ran off. I threw the second. This time a hand grabbed it fast.

One to go. I waited, then gently placed it on the edge of the hole in the cell door. A moment passed and two fingers—index and thumb, black and covered with hair—plucked the snack and disappeared.

We sat in the cell waiting and listening. The creatures munched and barked at one another, protecting their food, I assumed, and for a while it looked like the drugs weren't going to work. Then, slowly the sounds faded and turned to grumbling. Finally we heard a gentle thud or two and some heavy breathing.

I looked at Sabrina. "It's now or never, sister."

She nodded as I crawled for the hole, but she didn't follow right away. Instead I watched as she removed her jacket and loaded the bones, skulls and all, onto the spread-out clothes. Then she zipped it and tied the sleeves, creating a makeshift bag. I was a bit surprised, but if I published a magazine specializing in UFOs and strange phenomena, I guess I'd do the same.

Still, it didn't seem right.

I didn't say anything. I went out through the hole, easing as quietly as I could. At first I didn't see anything, then as I pulled my legs clear I saw the three creatures sprawled on the floor like a gang of drunks. They were out cold.

Sabrina followed, carrying the bag of bones. I pointed to the exit and signaled to be as quiet as possible, then began tiptoeing around the massive creatures snoring on the floor. I cleared one, then the second, and finally the last and was at the doorway when I turned and saw that Sabrina had stopped.

She was placing the bag of bones down next to the creatures. She even placed the makeshift sleeve-handle into the palm of one of their hands.

I just stood there and watched her standing fearlessly over the legendary monster and a rush of emotion came over me. I think I really fell for her then.

It was the scariest thing I'd ever felt.

We made it back to camp with relative ease because the fire was still burning. We packed what hadn't been shredded and headed out fast. On the drive out of the park we gave the ranger back his bear pamphlet and laughed as we drove away.

Later that week, I received a card from Sabrina. Inside was a note saying how much she enjoyed the camping trip, and there was a picture attached.

It was closeup of the creature who'd held the camera to its face.

A PROPER MONSTER

Anyone who knows me knows I shoot first, ask questions at the funeral when it comes to werewolves—or any other monster for that matter.

The first time I met Grimshaw was through a letter I received. It wasn't sent by mail, someone slid it under the door of my Studio City house. The note was handwritten with what looked like an old quill pen, there was no return address, and the envelope smelled like lilacs and musk.

The note was short and to the point. Under normal circumstances the content would have meant someone, namely the sender, wanted me to kill them. But this was different.

The note went like this:

> *Detective McDonald—*
> *My name is Paul Grimshaw.*
> *I am a werewolf and it is*
> *imperative that we speak about*
> *a grave matter that concerns the*
> *lives of many thousands.*
> *Sincerely*
> *—Grimshaw*

The fact that he told me he was a dog-boy before showing up proved he wasn't a complete retard. As a rule werewolves are the least civilized of all monsters, so Grimshaw intrigued me.

I'd let him talk before I smeared him all over the lawn.

It was "winter" in Los Angeles so it rained and there was a little wind. Sometimes it dropped to fifty degrees at night. The way the locals reacted to it you'd think the fucking state was sliding into the ocean, but it wasn't so bad. I liked it. The rain reminded me of back east.

The day after the smelly note slid under my door, a car pulled up in front of my house. This wasn't some Honda Civic, this was one of those block-long vintage Rolls-Royce deals with a canopy and a hood ornament the size of a midget.

I opened the front door and stood on the porch while a chauffeur, dressed like some sort of gay Nazi, jumped out and ran around to open the door for the passenger.

I knew it was Grimshaw before the door opened. When I saw him I was only a little surprised. I hadn't seen anybody that fancy-pants this side of a classic forties film. He was a tall, husky guy wearing a fine tailored suit, close-trimmed hair and get this, a fucking monocle over his right eye.

I stood on the porch as the regal man approached. He looked completely out of place, out of the past, strolling all elegant and shit down my cracked, white asphalt walkway dividing two plots of grassless yard.

As he reached the foot of the porch, he stopped, clicked his heels, and extended his hand. "Cal McDonald. I'm Paul Grimshaw."

"Yeah, I got your note." I gave him the once-over, then stepped aside. "Come on in. Sorry about the place. It's the maid's day off."

Grimshaw smiled slightly and stepped across the porch and through the open front door. He was good. He looked a hundred percent human, but he glided like an un-natural. To the normal eye, he seemed to walk like anyone else, but if you looked very close you could see he was hyper-aware of his every movement.

I stepped inside after Grimshaw. He had his back to me and he was scanning the living room. I didn't have to see his face to see he was disgusted. I imagined his office had carpet and red velvet chairs. Fuck that. I like my squalor.

I waited for him to take in the mess and get over it.

"Take a seat anywhere you like," I said knowing fancy-pants would be appalled at the prospect.

But he surprised me and brushed aside a stack of magazines and sat on the edge of the arm of the couch, his ass covering years of unmentionable stains. I took a seat behind my desk.

"So," I said eager to get things rolling. "What can I do for you?"

Grimshaw adjusted his monocle. "Well, it's not so much what you can do for me, as what you can do for your country, really."

"And I have nothing to fear but fear itself. Your turn."

Grimshaw gave me that one and then got serious. "In 1939 I was sixteen years old. I was born in London, but my father worked as an engineer and we moved around, eventually winding up in Germany, where my father worked for the military until he was killed when I was fifteen. A year later my mother passed away as well. I was alone. They were my only family."

"Until the Nazis took you in."

Grimshaw sort of nodded/bowed. "Exactly. Thank you for keeping up with my story."

"I look a lot dumber than I am."

"As you probably know the Ger . . . the Nazis experimented with the supernatural, the occult as well as unnatural science."

"Unnatural science?"

"The study of the supernatural from a scientific viewpoint," Grimshaw said. As he spoke he allowed his index nail to extend to a razor point. He scratched carefully under his eye. The monocle was bugging him.

"Yeah, yeah, I'm familiar with the concept . . . vampires have a virus and werewolves are a mutation of that same virus," I said. "I just never heard it called unnatural science before."

"It was a fairly unpopular term, coined by Dr. Joseph Mengele himself."

"He was really a renaissance man, wasn't he? Just loved to dabble."

I knew all about the Nazis and their brief experiments with the supernatural. I knew they fucked around with a lot of weird shit and I knew they didn't get much in the way of results. I also knew that they *did* achieve some results, but nothing ever made public. Well, until Victor Von Fleabag walked in.

Grimshaw went on to tell a pretty tragic story. Evidently the Nazis took him in when he was a teen, but they hardly took care of the boy. They kept him locked up. They beat the shit out of him, and when they weren't kicking his ass, they were making him exercise and build his body up. After a while, when his strength was up and his spirits were as low as they could get, they exposed him to a regimen of strange experiments.

"Most of these experiments were sheer nonsense," he said. "These Nazi doctors tried putting spells on me and had me perform my own ceremonies trying to raise demons and the like."

I lit a smoke. "And nothing worked?"

"Nothing," Grimshaw shook his head, "until they captured an unusual specimen in the forest near Kaiserslautern."

"Bless you."

"What?"

"Nothing. I'm an idiot," I said. "Please go on."

Grimshaw gave me a head tilt of confusion and then went on to tell me that the *specimen* the Germans captured was a werewolf, which had been preying on local farms and villages for years. But the Nazis didn't capture the lycanthrope to help the town, they captured it to use for their own mad purposes.

"You see," Grimshaw commented, "they wanted to see if they could harness the power of the werewolf. They wanted to see if there was a way to transfer what gave the wolf its deadly power into the bodies of Nazi soldiers."

"An army of Nazi werewolves. That *is* scary."

Of course the Nazi doctors tried everything to discover what made a werewolf a werewolf, but there was one problem; even though they had successfully captured the creature, there was no taming it and not even the strongest sedatives would put the thing to sleep. At least thirteen doctors were killed trying to run tests on the wolf.

I nodded. "So they'd have to kill it to get inside it and see what made it tick?"

"Basically, but the Nazis weren't about to exterminate such a marvelously rare find without exhausting every possible scenario. They may have been mad, but the Nazis were always thorough."

Grimshaw removed his monocle, breathed on it, and wiped it on his jacket lapel. He had a very proper manner about him. He reminded me of the English butler stereotype; very stiff, overly polite and probably the one who committed the murder. I liked him, but I didn't trust him. Not entirely. Not yet.

He went on to tell me what they did to him. In some kind of sound stage or air hangar they created a false wooded environment, a fake forest in a contained area. Both young Grimshaw *and* the captured werewolf were placed into the environment so an attack would occur as it happened in the villages and farms. The idea was to recreate a werewolf attack in its natural environment and see what the results were.

"You must've been shitting," I said.

"Yes, I *was* quite afraid. I thought I would die," he said. "I had no weapons of any kind, and I was alone against an unnatural predator of extraordinary skill."

"And then what?"

"I was hunted . . . and attacked by the werewolf."

There was a long silence as Grimshaw remembered what must have been his death. It must have been horrible remembering when and how you died. I know Mo'Lock rarely speaks of his death and when he did, he would usually skip the details.

For the gentleman monster sitting in front of me it must have been painful beyond belief. Werewolves primarily hunt for food, and they like it hot. They like the blood flowing and the flesh as warm as possible. To do this they will literally rip a person apart piece by piece, skillfully avoiding major arteries or any major organs, and stave off death as long as possible. People who fall prey to werewolves are usually alive through the worst of it.

"I thought I would die in that awful, fabricated forest, but the doctors had other plans for me," Grimshaw went on. "At the moment I thought I would breathe my last, a Nazi sniper shot the head off the werewolf and freed me from its grasp."

Grimshaw went on to explain that the Nazi doctors rescued him and nursed him back to health. They didn't want a dead man; they wanted a fresh werewolf attack victim to nurture, to bring to full health and then train.

"And you were a werewolf?" I asked.

"Yes."

"How did they control you when you were transformed?"

"Torture," he said. "They tortured me as a man and they tortured me as a wolf with one goal: to join the two, to create a monster with a man's mind, a soldier's mind."

I shook my head. "Christ. Did it work?"

When I looked up, Grimshaw had not only transformed into a werewolf, he had done it without so much as wrinkling his clothes. He removed his monocle and stared at me as he changed his face into a perfect blend of man and monster. He had the eyes and hair of a gray wolf, but not the extended snout. Instead he had a fairly wide but normal nose and mouth. Then he smiled and I saw two rows of the sharpest teeth I'd ever seen.

"What do you think, Mr. McDonald?"

"Looks like it worked."

Suddenly, Grimshaw jerked in his chair. His eye twitched and a sound damn close to a growl rose from his throat. He reversed the transformation quickly and when he was almost all human again he replaced his monocle and looked at me like he was embarrassed.

"I apologize," he said. "That is *one* of the reasons I contacted you."

I pulled open the desk drawer and looked for something to swallow. I found a couple of painkillers in the pen rack and threw them back. I was feeling twitchy myself.

"After all of these years of controlling my . . . my state, I have suddenly begun to lose control. I can feel a wildness returning to me. Sometimes I cannot even control when I change"

"That's fucked up," I said. "But what can I do about it? If you go wolfman on me, I'm going to have to kill you."

"Good," Grimshaw nodded. "That is why I came."

"You want me to kill you?" I said, trying to hide how surprised I was.

"That and more."

I nodded and looked right into Grimshaw's eyes. If he was taking me for a ride, it was the best damn job of slapping on the bullshit I'd ever seen. I don't know why, but I trusted him.

He explained to me that if he lost control, he would want me to kill him before he hurt anyone. I didn't say it again, but he didn't have to worry about that.

But then he went on to the next chapter, as if planning his own death was one thing on a macabre checklist he'd completed. He told me how once the Nazi doctors had tortured his wild side into submission, they turned him over to the SS who in turn began exhaustively training Grimshaw for soldiering. They trained him as man and as werewolf, honing skills from stealth kills to all out-slaughter, from using weapons and setting bombs to disarming attackers.

It was a long, brutal time period in Grimshaw's life. When it was all over, almost a year had passed, and Grimshaw was a perfect Nazi monster killing machine.

"But soon I would discover that I was not the only one of my kind," he said. "The good doctors had created a small army of other soldiers like me. I thought I was the only one because they had killed the werewolf which attacked me, but they had others."

"Werewolves on the battlefield," I shook my head. "That certainly would have changed the war."

"It was not on the battlefield they planned for our use. Our use was for right here, in America."

That got my attention.

"We were trained to do many things. One of them was to hibernate inside specially designed *capsules* or *pods* made of the strongest metals available at the time," Grimshaw said and twitched.

"You okay? How about a drink?"

"Do you have a beer? I rather enjoy American beer."

I smirked at him. "Do I have beer? Are bears Catholic?"

The joke flopped like a bag of whale blubber. I skulked out of the room and loaded us up with drinks and a bag of tortilla chips. I was kind of starting to enjoy storytime at the McDonald homestead.

As Grimshaw went on the yarn got crazier and closer to home. He saw things in the days before his hibernation that chill him to this day. He saw hundreds of capsules loaded with Nazi werewolves and hundreds more filled with undead SS soldiers called the *scheintod soldat* which meant something like *soldiers who appeared dead* or some crap like that.

These capsules were then smuggled into the United States one at a time thanks to the help of some rich and influential Hollywood players, namely an actress named Helga Freed. She played some big roles during the war and evidently used the money to buy "antiques" from all over the world. She would receive all manner of furniture and artifacts, and every single one of them was a Nazi monster capsule in disguise.

"I remember Helga Freed," I said. "She was in that famous picture with what's-iz-face . . . what a bitch."

"Yes, quite."

I started pacing around the room, alternating gestures between the hand holding the beer and the hand holding the smoke.

"So they smuggle hundreds of these capsules loaded with Nazi monsters into the country," I deduced. "The purpose being to release the creatures all over the States, creating enough murder and mayhem to give the German fucks—*no offense*—the edge in the war."

Grimshaw nodded. "Very good, Mr. McDonald. I am impressed. That was, more or less, the plan."

"But then what happened? How did you get here? Why didn't they use the capsules?"

Grimshaw smiled. "The war ended and Ms. Freed killed herself, fearing she would be exposed."

"That doesn't explain how you got out of the capsule."

"I was never inside one of them," Grimshaw said, watching my reaction carefully. "I escaped from the training facility the night before I was due to be packed away like some sort of fish in a can."

I sat down. I had to think. There were too many factors to shuffle. It didn't help matters I'd downed the better part of a twelve-pack and I was feeling pretty sloshed. Grimshaw was still sipping his first. Some German.

"Okay," I said, holding up my fist and one finger. "We have you losing control of your ability to control being a werewolf, right?"

"Correct."

"And we have a couple hundred capsules filled with similar Nazi aberrations somewhere in Los Angeles."

"Very good."

"So my question to you is . . . why now, unless this is just about you and the whole control thing?"

With this Grimshaw placed down his beer, adjusted his monocle, and stood. "I have something to show you."

We took Paul's car. It was the size of a tugboat and about as fast. Luckily we were only driving from Studio City to the Hollywood Hills so it was a pretty quick trip. In the driver's seat, the chauffeur kept glancing at me through the rearview mirror. He had a huge head and sunken, black-circled eyes.

Next to me Grimshaw twitched.

"Where'd you get the wheels?" I asked. It was as much to break the silence as to distract him from his inner struggle. The last thing I needed was him losing control inside the car. Werewolves and closed areas are always a bad mix.

Paul looked at the driver then me. "It is a rental."

As the tugboat lurched around the winding, narrow roads up into the hills I caught the driver glancing at me more than once. I studied the back of his large head. The palette of his skin was like sick death.

Next time he looked at me I was ready. I caught his eye and leaned forward. "Ghoul?" I asked.

The driver took a wide turn and shook his head. "No sir," the driver said in a deep hollow voice. "I believe the term used is 'fiend.'"

I looked at Grimshaw. "Really?"

Grimshaw shrugged. It was a rental. He didn't care.

I cared. Fiends are the crazy cousin of the ghoul. They do everything ghouls are thought to do: stalk children, eat human flesh, dead bodies. You know the whole Boogeyman thing. They aren't exactly known for being a part of the work force.

Great, I thought. Here I am on a narrow winding road at night, in a car with a twitching werewolf and a driving fiend.

"Kind of unusual for a fiend to be working a job," I said.

The fiend in the front seat nodded. "I am trying to adapt."

"Still eat people?"

"Not for two hundred years."

"No shit." I nodded at Grimshaw.

He nodded back. He was impressed too.

"What's your name?" I asked.

"Lon."

I pulled a card out of my wallet. It wasn't much of a card, just my name, address, and phone number with a little graphic of a monster with a target over it. Sabrina made them for me. Because she did *Speculator Magazine*, she had access to all this kind of shit.

I handed the card over the seat to the fiend. "Give me a call sometime, Lon," I said. "I can hook you up with the local ghoul scene if you like."

The fiend smiled wide as he took my card and slid it into his blazer pocket. "I would like that very much. It would make me very happy. Thank you."

"Well, you keeping your nose clean makes me happy."

When I glanced back at Grimshaw I was feeling pretty damn pleased with myself, but the werewolf was not looking good. He was holding his arms against his body, sweating profusely and shaking.

"Grimshaw . . . you okay?"

"I'll be fine," he stammered. "It will pass. I . . . it is always hardest during the night."

That was comforting.

Finally we reached the top of the hill. Grimshaw instructed the driver to pull over alongside a tall cement wall that surrounded a gigantic property. There were hundreds like these all over the Hollywood Hills; huge sprawling mansions owned by actors, directors, producers, and other people with way too much cash.

"Where's the gate?" I asked.

"We will enter over the wall," Grimshaw said and then turned to Lon standing by the car. "I have no further need of your services. Thank you very much."

Lon clicked his heels and marched back to the driver's side. I watched him as he looked at us one last time, and then drove off, further up the hill. I assumed the road circled the top, then went down the other side. That's the way most of the hills were laid out.

Grimshaw waited for me by the wall.

I surveyed it and knew I wasn't going to be able to climb it, even with a boost. Along the top there were shards of glass embedded in the plaster, so even if I could climb fifteen feet up, I'd get shredded. But Paul already had it figured. He transformed his legs and arms and came at me. I didn't even have a chance to resist. Grimshaw grabbed me, tucked me under his arm, and jumped the wall.

We landed hard on the other side. I shoved Grimshaw away. I didn't like the feel of his paws on me. We were in a yard. Ahead was a huge Spanish-style mansion. It was pitch dark.

Grimshaw, now transformed back to all human, walked toward the house. "Are you armed, Mr. McDonald?"

"Always."

"I wouldn't think there would be reason for any violence, but I want to be sure you come out of this safely."

I didn't respond. What a strange fucking thing to say. I had the feeling he was half talking about outside threats, but mostly he was referring to himself. In an odd way, by asking earlier and now this, Grimshaw had given me permission to kill him.

I didn't give a shit one way or the other. I had entered that hour-since-my-last-drink stage. The painkillers I took had absolutely failed. I was getting edgy, and I didn't like being led around like some kind of rented mule. Buddy time was over. I wanted some action or I wanted to get back to my place, call Sabrina, and get some fucking drugs into my system.

Grimshaw led me up to the back of the house. His manner was pretty casual for breaking and entering. He either knew the place or knew what was inside.

I was sick of being out of the loop. I stopped. "How about you tell me where we are and why we're here."

Grimshaw cocked his head. "The lair of the beast."

"Seriously," I shot back. "Whose house is this?"

"Inside, Mr. McDonald," the werewolf said, leading on, "inside you will learn everything!"

I followed Grimshaw begrudgingly up a short flight of dark marble stairs and to a row of patio doors, one of which was open. I took out my gun as I followed the leader inside. If it was some kind of trap I wanted to at least get off a round before I got mauled.

As I stepped over the threshold of the door and pushed aside a curtain, I saw a gigantic room. It was some sort of library; dark wood shelves lined three of the four walls and went up two stories. At floor level there were statues of demons and devils of all kinds scattered about in between large decorative plants. The focus of the room was split between a grand piano to the right and a huge oak desk to the left.

There was a strange contraption built on top of the oak desk: a shotgun mounted on wood braces with a pulley and wire rigged so that the person sitting in the chair could blow their head off while sitting comfortably.

Above the desk was a large, elaborately framed oil painting.

It was a portrait of Paul Grimshaw.

I turned and lowered my gun on the subject of the portrait and said, "I'm not a big fan of being lied to."

Grimshaw showed me his hands. "I'm sorry, but I had to have you here. I told you everything. I told you the truth."

"Why the break-in routine?" I asked.

"I couldn't risk you running off. I had to get you in here to show you—"

"The Nazi capsules."

Grimshaw nodded slowly.

I gestured toward the shotgun suicide rig on the desk. "Explain that."

Paul twitched and for an instant his eyes flashed wolf. "I was going to end it all, but I cannot do it by my own hand. I cannot die in such disgrace."

I kept my gun on him. "Where are they?"

Keeping his hands in plain sight, Grimshaw began leading me out of the room. While we strolled I played with the facts. "So this was Helga Freed's mansion, right?"

"Correct, Mr. McDonald."

"And you were inside one of the canisters after all."

"Correct again."

"But you woke up and broke out and have been occupying the house ever since."

Grimshaw stopped and turned. I took a step back.

"You almost have it right," the werewolf said, "but I woke from the capsule while Ms. Freed was still alive."

"You were lovers?"

Grimshaw laughed, "Dear God, no. She was a hideous woman!" he said. "I removed myself from the capsule—".

"Then you killed the hag, made it look like suicide, and took possession of the house, right?"

"Correct yet again."

It made sense, I guess. Despite the fact that Paul Grimshaw was a werewolf, a Nazi, and a murderer, I still trusted him.

Grimshaw continued walking ahead of me until we came to a small bookshelf against a wall in the short hall between the library and the foyer. On either side of the shelf were large black iron candle sconces.

As Grimshaw began to reach for the sconce on the left, I laughed and said, "You gotta be kidding me."

But he wasn't. Grimshaw pulled the sconces and a secret passage was revealed. I was impressed. Of all the weird shit I'd seen, this was the first secret passage door. I was kind of excited.

I followed Grimshaw down a winding cement stairwell until we hit a really short corridor leading to a large wooden door with a second door made of thick black iron covering the wood. There were three locks: a huge steel padlock and two huge bolts. It was clear that these weren't locks to keep anyone from getting in; any half-assed lock-pick could bust it open in ten seconds. These locks were to keep someone or something from getting *out*.

As Grimshaw popped the locks, I noticed that his twitching was getting worse by the minute and thick black hairs were sprouting on the nape of his neck. He was trying his damnedest to hide it, maybe even fight it, but the lycanthrope virus was strong. From the looks of him, he might fall apart any time.

Great, I thought, I'm heading into a locked dungeon with a werewolf on the verge of a complete breakdown. Good plan.

Grimshaw unlocked the lock and unbolted the bolts and pulled back the iron gate, then used a large skeleton key to unlock the door itself. After a loud click the thick wood door squeaked open and I could see a huge, low-ceilinged room beyond.

Grimshaw stepped inside. I followed. The room was a long cement bunker lined with shelves on either side. On the shelves, stacked five high, were unusually long wooden barrels. They were big enough to hold a man inside them.

Only one barrel, the closest to the door, was open and emptied. This must have been the one Grimshaw emerged from.

"I have been watching over these capsules for many years," Grimshaw said as he twitched. "Now, with my losing control, I wanted to hand off the duty to someone else."

"What if that someone else doesn't want the job?"

Grimshaw smiled and I could see his teeth were turning to fangs as he spoke. "I had nowhere else to turn."

"They should be destroyed," I said bluntly.

Grimshaw was covered with hair, his hands were clawed. "I realize that now but—"

I shook my head. "You weren't sure it was such a bad idea."

The werewolf looked sheepish for an instant. "They are marvelous creatures . . . it is hard to destroy such beauty."

By this time, Grimshaw was a full-blown werewolf. So much so that his shirt and jacket had burst open and his eyes had turned wild. His breathing was erratic and drool began gathering at his gum line.

I kept my gun on him. Any trust I had for him was blown to bits.

"I want," Grimshaw growled, "you . . . to . . . kill me."

"And then what? Baby-sit two hundred Nazi freak jobs? No-fucking-thank you. I got enough problems already!"

I could see the dilemma though. The house rested on top of the Hollywood Hills, home of the mudslide and the quickly spreading fire. The place was nothing but soft earth, dried brush, and ritzy homes. If we tried to burn or blow up the barrels, the risk of taking down half of Hollywood with them was a distinct possibility.

But it seemed Grimshaw was sticking to his plan: death by detective and let the poor fuck (the poor fuck being me) deal with the mess.

He started coming at me, teeth gnashing, his huge clawed hands poised to gut me. I was ready. He was close. I took careful aim and fired. The bullet ripped the tip of his pointy left ear and Grimshaw screamed. I removed my blackjack from my boot and smashed him over the head.

He hit the floor hard, but he was far from down for the count. I couldn't take the chance he'd get up. I didn't stand a chance against those claws in a closed space. I hammered down on him one more time with the blackjack and then jumped onto his back. He growled and squirmed, but I got him in a nasty-ass full nelson, and yanked back until his growls turned to yelps.

The werewolf tried to struggle, but I had him.

"Now listen to me, Grimshaw," I said, "I want you to shift back to human."

Grimshaw replied with a growl and a lame attempt to break the pin hold I had on him. I tightened my grip, lifted his head, and smashed him face-down into the pavement. I heard a crack and a single fang slid across the cold floor followed by a small geyser of blood.

"Shift," I said lifting his head. "Back!" I completed as I hammered his snout into the floor.

He tightened up again, but he didn't fight. Instead there was this feeling in my arms like a balloon deflating. Grimshaw was letting go. He was shifting back.

I waited until he was all human before I released him from my grip. I stood. Grimshaw stayed on his knees, holding his bleeding mouth.

"If you were losing control," I said, "you would've lost it and torn me to shreds."

Grimshaw nodded and stood holding his jaw. He had a bloody nose and mouth. I looked down and saw his monocle lying near my feet. I stooped and picked it up. I stayed down for a second, completely vulnerable, and nothing happened.

When I stood back up I smiled and handed Paul Grimshaw his monocle. "Here. You dropped this."

"Thank you, "he said, "But why the smile?"

"You don't want to die. You're just sick of being the caretaker of all this death."

"Perhaps."

"When was the last time you ate a human?"

Grimshaw placed his hand on his chest and opened his mouth. "Human flesh?! Never! I have killed in self-defense, but I have never eaten a person!" He was missing a tooth.

I nodded. "That's what I thought. Otherwise I'd have killed you back at my place."

Grimshaw lowered his head. I was right and it embarrassed him.

"The twitching was a nice touch though. The shotgun rig too," I said. "In fact the whole thing was a pretty nice production."

Grimshaw shrugged. "Thank you."

I turned away from him and turned my attention the barrels. "Have you ever opened one of these?"

"Good Lord no!"

I approached one of the barrels and surveyed the round cover. There was a latch on four sides. "I think the wood barrel is just a cover," I said, and reached for the first latch.

"I wouldn't do that if—"

I ignored Grimshaw, popped the latches, and removed the wooden cover. Inside there was a steel container with a thickly glassed portal window. Most of the glass was fogged from years of steam and condensation. I couldn't make out what was inside. I used my lighter to shed some light and what I saw inside was just about the most disgusting thing I'd ever seen.

But it made me smile.

I turned to Grimshaw. "So, you never looked inside *any* of these."

"No . . . uh . . . why?"

"Look for yourself."

I held the lighter to the glass so Grimshaw could see the skeleton inside, virtually covered with fossilized maggots and mold. Whatever the fuck was in this canister was long dead. I suspected the same of the others.

I pulled the lighter away just as it started to burn my hand.

Grimshaw looked like a man who'd just been told he was going to live, but in a very reserved, proper manner. "Well, this changes everything, does it not?"

"Yes, it does, but I suggest you get rid of these things just in case."

The werewolf shrugged. "How? Believe me I would have done so decades ago if I'd had an idea."

I slapped his shoulder. "You're going to feel very stupid when I tell you my plan."

"Oh dear."

I told Paul Grimshaw my idea and he admitted he felt pretty stupid considering he'd been living in Los Angeles since the end of World War II. But once he'd slapped his forehead, he moved into action, eager to remove the canisters from his house for good.

We needed a couple big trucks and some help. I called Lon, the driving fiend, for the trucks, and a couple ghouls I knew who lurked in the Hills. We had all of the canisters loaded by

three in the morning. By three-thirty we arrived at the La Brea
Tar Pits located in the middle of downtown Los Angeles, along
Wilshire Boulevard.

The tar pits had devoured countless dinosaurs over the
centuries. I figured a few hundred Nazi monster capsules
wouldn't hurt.

One by one we unloaded the barrels and threw them into the
pits. They bobbled on top of the steaming, bubbling tar for a
second and then slowly sunk into oblivion beneath the city.

Grimshaw was officially the sole survivor of this particular
Nazi atrocity.

Lon drove Grimshaw home first. We said our good-bye and
I told him to stop by whenever he got the chance. A guy like
Grimshaw was good to know. He showed me that a man can be a
monster but not act like one, and that was a good thing to know.

ALL MY BLOODY THINGS

By the time I came to, fuck-head El Beardo De Psycho was already trying to take a chunk out of my leg with a rusty scalpel. He had my pant leg ripped and my juicy thigh exposed.

The scalpel was pressed right into my flesh when he paused and saw my eyes were open.

He was SO fucking dead.

Stupid cannibals.

It all began a couple days ago when I got a call from a guy who talked to a guy who knew this lady who mentioned her brother's family went missing on a lonely stretch of California highway.

I heard about it because the guy, the first guy, got attacked by some weird vampire freak-thing. I saved his ass, and he was calling me to thank me for shooting the beast before it shredded him.

"I still can't believe it happened." He had a high whiny voice that made me want to pop his skull with a hammer.

"Well, believe it," I said trying to get off the phone. I wasn't much for follow-up friendships. I save you. Thank you and fuck you. We're done.

"Well, Mr. McDonald, I can't thank you enough for saving me."

"Glad I could help," I went silent. If this conversation was continuing I wasn't going to be the one keeping it alive. I had shit do to. I had a bag of painkillers just waiting to enter my bloodstream.

"There's something else . . ."

Fuck. Here it comes.

"I have a friend who's dating this lady and she mentioned that her brother's family never showed up driving from Vegas to Los Angeles."

I put my head face-down on the desk blotter. "Call the police. That's missing persons. I only do weird shit."

"The way the lady tells it, it might be . . . weird shit."

I just wanted to get rid of him. "What's this lady's name and number?"

"Um . . . let me see here,"

His squealing whine of a voice was shredding my last good nerve.

"Kelly Hughes. She's in Glendale."

He gave me her number, thanked me again. I told him to have a good life and hung up the phone. What a dink.

Ninety percent of what I do is gut feeling. That's why I took the whiny man's lead. People have an inner sense of the strange and supernatural. They tend to believe subconsciously what their conscious minds won't allow them to comprehend.

People always ask me why I'm the only one who sees the freaks and monsters crawling in the dark corners of the world and I tell them it's because I trust my gut. My gut and the fact that I've had my ass smeared across the city by some freak or another enough times to know there's shit out there that just defies logic, plain and simple.

I arrived at Kelly Hughes's house in Glendale. It was one of those Spanish pillbox numbers like I had, but hers was painted and clean, the fence was white picket, and there were flowers planted in window boxes. The whole thing made me sick.

The woman was pleasant enough. She told me how she'd never heard from her brother, Andre and his wife, Debra and kid, an eight -year-old boy named Doug, after they were supposed to have arrived a couple days ago. They were driving a 2004 Volvo wagon, silver. Calls have gone unanswered. She tried the police, but they turned up a big donut, and frankly, she told me, she thought the worst.

I had nothing to go by but my aforementioned gut, and it told me something was wrong. Families just don't disappear off highways in the middle of the night. I asked her for all the info I'd need; phone numbers, descriptions. All that crap. I figured I'd start by tracing the cell calls and credit card charges to figure out where they disappeared.

The police are retarded. The last credit card charge by Andre Hughes was made from a remote spot on Highway 15 between Los Angeles and Las Vegas. What makes the charge interesting is that the amount, some forty bucks, was posted but never charged. Either something happened during the exchange or the merchant decided they didn't want the money. I smelled trouble.

I drove the Nova out that way the same night. I didn't bring Mo'Lock with me because he was meeting with some ghouls who had recently moved from Europe to L.A. In the last few months there had been a large influx of the friendly undead to L.A. It had something to do with me, but frankly, I didn't give a rat's ass as long as they didn't eat anybody.

The drive was long and boring. There were few other cars on the road. It was late and mid-week, not the busiest time for Vegas traffic. I popped a few blues to keep sharp, and some codeine to take the edge off, then I put the finishing touches on my buzz with a joint and whiskey pint chaser.

The barb cocktail made my head tingle and the desert night, the hills in the distance, the wide flat of nothing near, began to trail brilliant colors until I came up on a small shock of a business next to a rundown gas station with old fashioned gas pumps straight out of the *Grapes of Wrath*.

There was a silver Volvo station wagon parked around back. It was partially hidden by a wreck of a pickup, but I could see the California plates and luggage still secured to the roof rack.

Follow my gut. Connect the dots. That's what I do that the cops can't seem to. It takes them days to even track leads, while people die. It's really a shame.

I parked the car right in front of the place. There was a poorly painted sign that read JUNIORS PULLED MEAT BBQ in crooked red and white letters. Beneath that, in chilly type it said AIR CONDITIONED.

I entered through a screen door and immediately the smell of blood and BBQ sauce hit my nostrils. There was a counter, old, stained, and disgusting. There were a few tables just as stained with broken rusty chairs. It was dead quiet. I looked toward the counter. Behind the stained Formica I saw a door to the kitchen.

I walked forward. I also removed my gun. All I could smell was blood and all I could hear was the buzz of flies.

I saw two things as I entered; two people, a young boy and an older woman, the Hughes family I assumed, bound to a gas pipe. The other was what was left of the father, Andre Hughes, naked and tied to a table. He had been stripped of skin from the chest down to his feet and several large sections of meat from the buttocks and thigh were cut away.

But worst of all, he was being kept alive. Tubes ran air to his exposed lungs through his nose and IVs numbed him to the pain.

That's what I saw. What felt as I walked deeper into the room was a burning pain across the back of my skull. I'd felt it before. It was probably a wrench being hammered against my head. I reeled forward. The gun fell from my hand, and I managed to half-turn my head and see a large man with long blond hair, a mustache, and a Hawaiian print shirt. He had the wrench.

I remember thinking *my God I'm going to die at the hands of Jimmy Buffet*, and then the wrench came down again and caught my brow. I hit the floor and fell into a buzzing pool of total darkness.

Which brings us back to the beginning.

I don't know how long I was out cold, but when I started to come back, my pant leg had been ripped up and the big guy in the Hawaiian print shirt was making ready to cut into my thigh. He only stopped because he noticed I was awake.

My hands were bound behind my back. I was tied on the pipe about four feet from momma Hughes and son. Dad was passed out or dead on the bleeding table.

"What the hell do you think you're doing?" I grunted.

El Beardo looked up. His eyes were yellow; his teeth were rotten and brown, black along the gum line.

"You didn't stay out long," he commented, almost too relaxed.

He paused the cutting, but kept the blade pressed to my leg. If I struggled, he would only cut me. I decided to play it out.

"So . . . how long you been eating people?"

He seemed taken aback by the question like nobody had ever asked.

He pulled the blade back slightly. I felt a wave of relief and dizziness. I'd taken way too much shit in the car. I could hardly see straight.

"All my life," he said softly. He had a speech impediment, a sloppy lisp. "My Paw taught me how to cook."

When he spoke the grizzled cannibal looked like a stupid five-year-old not sure what he was supposed to do. He stared off sadly then seemed to come back around and looked me in the eyes.

"Eating peoples makes me strong. Eating peoples gives me their soul. That's what Paw said. He ate Maw and said her soul loved me forever inside him."

"No shit?"

The cannibal in the Hawaiian print shirt nodded shyly. I glanced over at the captives. Mom was out cold. She'd probably fainted watching her husband get skinned alive. The kid was awake and aware. His eyes were wide and staring not at his dying father, but at the killer. The kid was staring at him, memorizing him, planning vengeance he may never have.

"Why not let the family go," I suggested. "You can feast on me. I got enough meat on me to keep you in meat for a month."

He didn't like the idea. The killer shook his head furiously and squeezed the scalpel in his hand. "No, no, no, no, no, no."

I nodded. "You sure?"

"I SAID NO!"

Okay, I needed a new approach. This nut-bag was teetering. I had to play my cards right. I had to keep him talking.

"Okay, sorry," I said quietly. "I just never met a guy who sold human meat sandwiches."

El Beardo had been squatting. He had this round body with no discernable distinction between his upper and lower torso like a squishy melon with arms and legs wearing a pineapple print shirt. As he sat down crossing his legs, I saw his sandals and socks were caked with dried blood, dirt, and hair.

He wanted to talk. I wished I wasn't so fucking wasted. On top of the serious concussion I probably suffered, the pills and whiskey didn't mix very friendly-like, and I was feeling beyond screwy.

"I don't sell the people meat."

He spoke very matter-of-factly. His blond hair was thick and wavy, knotted with clots of congealed blood and grease. He had that beach bum look, the leathery, tanned skin, and light facial hair.

His hands were like mitts with thick, overworked sausages for fingers. I tried not to think what those hands had done.

"What ya mean you don't *sell* it?" I asked buying time.

Psycho Beardo shook his head. "People meats for personal use," he said proudly. "Customers get pork and beef BBQ."

"Why is that? People meat too special for customers? They might like it too, you know?"

"Paw said people meat's for just us, just us special folks who know the truth."

He didn't sound so sure about that last part. He spoke like a parakeet repeating a hard-learned phrase.

My head was spinning. I could barely stay awake. I didn't have a clue what to say to the cannibal. I just wanted to bash his head in with a hammer. Hand out a little payback for the bleeding knots on my head.

While I kept him talking I tried to work a small piece of wire into the cuff lock, but I couldn't get leverage. Behind the killer, Mrs. Hughes had begun to come to. Her eyes were fluttering. The boy, however, still stared wide-eyed, blank. He was in shock. If he didn't get help soon, he'd crack for good.

The killer was slumped, sitting right in front of me on the filthy floor of the backroom slaughterhouse and all of a sudden, despite the blood, he looked like a big-ass baby sitting there. He was even poking at his knee with the scalpel like a pouting child.

"What's the matter, Margaritaville?" I asked. "You got a hunk of that kid's dad caught in your throat?"

"Nobody never talked to me before," he said with a straight face. "All they ever do is scream."

"Well, maybe that's because you're killing them."

"Yeah, I guess."

I gestured toward papa Hughes on the table. "You done with that one?"

El Beardo looked over his shoulder at the half skinless man, then quickly back at me.

"You interrupted me," he said. "Now he's spoiled. I should start on the lady or the kid. Kid meat's the best if they haven't been fed processed sugar their whole lives. Even with it, they're a better eat than adults."

The killer looked back over his right shoulder, this time at the woman and child. The woman, Debra Hughes, was fully cognizant of her surroundings now. She stared at the bloody, still breathing body of her husband. Her breathing was hard and fast. She was crying and even though gagged she still made a lot of noise. Too much noise I was afraid. The killer kept looking back at them. I had to do something or he'd start hacking them to bits as well.

I looked around the room. My vision was blurred, my teeth were numb. I was in bad shape. What was I thinking mixing blues, painkillers, and whiskey? I mean, I did it all the time, but it wasn't mixing too well with the massive head injury. I was screwed.

I watched the sloppy killer in the Hawaiian pineapple shirt weigh his choices. He looked from me, to the woman to the kid, then back to me. I wasn't sure I was even in the running for the feast, and it was that thought that gave me an idea. A bad one, but an idea none the less.

"Hey, Margaritaville, you got a name?"

He looked at me dumbly. "It's on the front. Can't you read, mister?"

"I can read."

"Says my name on the sign. My paw put it up there right before he passed the business on to me."

I tried to picture the sign out front. I wasn't doing too well, and then it came to me. "Junior?"

The killer smiled a big, wide smile and I saw the inside of his mouth. It was a cave of rotten teeth, a fetid tongue, and rancid meat. There were black spots on his tongue and odd sores around the inside of his lips.

"That's my name," he said, scratched his face, then added, "Me, my Paw, and my grandfather was all Juniors."

"You don't say? Was your grampy a people eater too?

Junior smiled. "Uh huh."

All of a sudden, Baby Huey got up and walked out of the room. Just like that I was alone with the Hugheses.

I shot a look at Debra Hughes. "Are you okay? Are you hurt?"

She immediately came apart at the seams. "Oh . . . GOD!"

She was screaming.

I shook my head.

She stopped.

I looked at the boy. I saw he had been tied with rope.

"You got any slack in those ropes, son?"

He swallowed. "No."

"Well, work them slowly," I said. "They'll give."

The woman began to shudder. She was gonna blow.

"Keep calm. You've got to lie low. You and the boy," I whispered sharply. "Keep your heads down and eyes closed."

"My . . . my husband . . ."

"Lady, we might be able to see his lungs, but at least they're moving. We have to hope for the best."

I heard El Beardo stomping back our way. I took once last glance at the Hugheses and nodded. They bowed their heads nervously.

Junior came in through the swinging doors and stood there like some sort of Cro-Mag on vacation, looking around the slaughterhouse, bobbing his head. I coughed and made sure I caught his attention.

He looked at me and let out a long, greasy fart. It sounded like popcorn going off in a wet sack. His dull eyes stayed dull, but the corner of his lip rose like an excited dog's leg. I assumed he was grinning.

"What you doing out there?" I asked.

He grunted and walked toward where I was tied on the floor.

"Forgot to lock the door," he said.

"Afraid customers will come in while you're eating somebody?"

He leaned down and slugged me so hard my lip split. Then he just kneeled down and waited for me to recover. When I looked at him like *what the fuck*, he went on.

"I ain't afraid of anybody," he spat. "Anybody comes in here unexpected, dies. Plain and simple. Paw always said nobody can tell if they ain't nobody to tell."

I raised my eyebrows. It was about all I could muster. I'd guess if there was such a thing, right at that point I was peaking on whatever concoction I'd consumed earlier.

"Too bad," I muttered. I didn't really know what I meant.

He seemed to, though. He laughed. "Too bad for you, dumb fuck!"

I walked into that one.

While he laughed I worked the cuffs around my wrists. I was fucked-up and weak, but I used my numbness to my advantage and pulled hard enough to break my wrists. I hit pay dirt. The pipe moved. Or maybe it was the room. Something moved at any rate.

His laughing turned to a raspy cough and then he was alternating glances at me and the Hughes woman. But it was the sound from his stomach that worried me most. It was loud, and rumbled. If I had to guess, I'd say the cannibal's stomach was growling hungrily. Not what you want to hear.

And then he licked his lips, catching a string of dripping saliva that slid off his yellow, fuzzy tongue.

He was hungry.

I made my move.

"You look like you need some meat, Junior."

He looked at me like I understood.

"I need strength," he said. "I need another soul."

I said slurring just a bit. "Then why don't you eat *me*?"

El Beardo went slack-jawed.

"What?"

"I'm the strongest one here. I bet I got a big-ass soul," I reasoned. "Eat me."

Junior picked up the scalpel off the table. I hadn't even noticed he placed it down.

"You know a lot about stuff, don't you?" he asked.

"I get around."

The cannibal worked his attention back to my leg. He pulled it straight, and ripped the slit a bit extra to show more thigh. He pushed away the material and cleared a large section of my flesh for his handiwork.

He placed the scalpel against the meat of my thigh just below the hipbone and slashed about a quarter inch across and *into* my leg. I closed my eyes and clenched my teeth. When he cut me, I screamed, more like a yelp. It was a stinging pain. Even with all the dope in my system, I felt it.

But that cut was just prep. He placed the scalpel down and wiped the inch-wide, inch-deep, gash with a wet rag already stained with somebody else's blood. Then he reached for what looked like a homemade cheese-cutter. It was a length of wire attached between two wooden handles.

God, I thought, this better work.

The cannibal took the cheese-cutter by the handles and pulled the thin wire taut. I tensed up, pulling hard on the cuffs until I felt my wrist bleed. I had a pretty good idea what was coming and I couldn't help myself.

It took every ounce of my strength not to lash out and kick the fucker in the face. But I couldn't risk it. I was still cuffed. I might get a good kick in, but he'd have the last laugh. I had to sit and take whatever he dished out.

He took the wire tool to the wound he'd made on my leg and pressed the taut steel under the lip of the cut. I braced. The killer pushed down, causing the wire to tuck neatly into the gash. It stung so bad I started to shake.

"Now keep still," the killer said.

And then he yanked!

The wire sliced under the flesh of my thigh fast, like a heated knife through butter, cutting an inch-thick fillet of flesh from my leg. It was the most excruciating thing I'd ever felt, but I did my best to stay still.

My eyes and teeth were shut tight trying to block the searing pain. When I opened my eyes I saw what I'd been feeling. I saw the killer, Junior, pulling as hard as he could on the handles. He almost had a slab cut off. He was bracing for the final yank.

He pulled one last time and the flap of flesh came loose.

"There!" the killer yelled like he'd achieved something.

I rocked my head. Tears ran in the corners of my eyes. The pain was unbelievable.

Junior tossed aside the bloody tool and carefully handled my strip of flesh. It wobbled and flopped in his hands. It had weight to it. I fought with everything I had not to throw up. I was dizzy, nauseous and my head spun.

In the killer's hands was about a six-inch-by-three-inch-wide flap of my leg. There was a matching-shaped wound on my thigh that glistened and bled.

I could hardly think. I craned my neck and tried to talk, but I was squeezing my teeth so hard I couldn't part them.

Then I got it out, "Now what, Junior?"

"Gonna cook and eat this here people steak," he said staring at the flesh jiggling in his hands.

"Cook it?" I spat. "You some kind of sissy?"

This upset Junior. He almost dropped the bloody slab on the dirty floor.

"What'd you mean?" he asked raising his chin defiantly.

"I mean, everybody knows when you cook people you lose all the goodness." I could hardly speak.

All I wanted to do was scream. All I wanted to do was scream at the top of my lungs and break Junior's skull open. I pictured myself beating him with a pipe, choking him with my hands, strangling the life out of him. I could almost feel his throat in my hands.

The cannibal was looking at his meat, my skin. He looked as though he was genuinely concerned with what I told him.

"Really?" he asked.

"That's what I heard."

Junior grabbed a plate from a shelf and slapped the slab of bloody flesh onto it for further examination. Behind him was a gas stove which he glanced at in between looking at me and once or twice at the Hugheses who listened to me and continued to play possum even when they heard me yell.

Between the concussion, the bleeding wound, and the near overdose, I was hanging on by a thread and I began to doubt my plan would even work. And to boot, it looked like the crazy motherfucker wasn't going to play along.

Junior poked at the hairy, bloody slab. "You sure, 'cuz Paw always taught me to cook what I eat."

I nodded, trying in vain to hide the pain. "The heat makes the soul leave the meat."

"Really?"

"Really." I had no clue.

Junior thought about it for half a second then placed the dish down and walked to a drawer. He opened it and took out, to my relief, a fork and knife. It was time to eat and time to see if I'd save the day or become the day's special.

I didn't want to, but I watched as he sliced a piece of my flesh from the jiggling chunk of thigh. He pinned the edge with the fork and sawed with the knife until he had a small, relatively hairless, piece of people meat to taste. It wobbled on the fork as he lifted it to his mouth and shoved it inside.

He chewed on me for a good minute, rolled me in his mouth, and then, finally, swallowed with a big, loud gulp. I could almost hear the last of me sliding down his gullet.

He looked around the room in that food-taster sort of manner then went back to the plate for the next slice.

"How am I?" I asked as sarcastic as I could summon. I was hurting, dizzy.

"Meat's good," he said smacking his lips. "Chewy."

I felt sick. When I looked down the fish-shaped oval wound on my thigh was bleeding so badly my leg was drenched and dripping hot gore.

Junior decided he liked me I guess because he started slicing up the fillet of McDonald on the plate into evenly cut, easy-to-chew strips. I watched him closely as he ate one strip, chewed, then moved onto the next. Each one he chewed, hair, blood, and all, and swallowed without showing any effects.

I glanced at the Hughes boy. His head was down but I could see movement around his arms. Good boy, I thought, he's working those ropes.

Junior finished the last of the meat and then licked the plate. I watched him, looking for any signs. He seemed to be acting exactly as he had before . . . until he didn't. I saw his eyes flutter and he sort of swayed as he rubbed his face.

Junior smiled and turned and as soon as he did, I saw my incredibly stupid plan had worked. I might have the tolerance built up to take a handful of painkillers, pot, and whiskey and live to tell about it, but Junior the cannibal obviously did not.

He was wasted.

Eating me had wasted him.

I was toxic.

Junior stumbled forward rubbing his face and laughed. He looked like a big freak. He just wasn't close enough yet, but it was most definitely kicking time.

"How's it going there, Junior?" I asked. "Ready for another serving?"

El Beardo Boy laughed again and looked at me like I was his best friend in the whole wide world. I tried to look pleasant but I was holding onto consciousness like a redneck gripping a greased pig. I was gonna slip any second. I had to egg him on.

"Come on, big boy," I said, "You can eat more than just one little piece of me!"

Junior laughed and then picked up the fork and knife. He was swaying erratically now and his eyes were wet and half closed and appeared to be getting worse by the second. He even tried to rub his face again and almost stabbed himself in the eye.

I laid there until he got close. When he did, I opened my eyes wide and stared him down before delivering my right, un-eaten, leg so hard into his testicles that I actually heard an audible crunching sound. He doubled over, dropping the knife and fork. The knife slashed my open leg wound as it fell.

Hurt. So bad.

Junior hit the floor in front of me. He was in a ball and vomiting foam. I looked at the Hughes boy. He and his mother's heads were up. The kid had gotten one hand free and he was working on the other. I gave him a wink.

"You two might want to close your eyes again," I said, raising my leg into the air above Junior's head on the ground.

"Don't!"

I stopped. Looked up.

The Hughes boy had freed himself. He was frantically pulling the last of the rope off of himself. I put my leg down.

I watched as the Hughes boy walked across the slaughterhouse to his father on the slab and stopped his head barely above the draining table. Nothing can describe the pain in the boy's eyes as he discovered his dad had finally passed. His exposed lungs were no longer moving.

The kid's expression changed from sorrow to pissed in less time than I'd ever seen and I'd seen it plenty. He glared at the killer rolling on the floor then at the assortment of tools.

He chose a small hammer/ax combo deal that looked like something for cutting bone, and then walked over and stood above Junior who was unaware of everything going down around him except he was fucked up and his balls were crushed. Within minutes, Junior's head would be added to the *crush* list too.

"Hey kid," I muttered.

The boy looked at me. His eyes were blank rage. "Yeah?"

"You sure you want to do that?" I said, "I can take care of it if you don't want to."

The kid slammed the blunt end of the tool down onto Junior's skull so hard his sandals, bloody feet kicked up.

The kid said, "I'm sure."

Even if I could have I don't think I would have stopped the kid. He was working out what would've turned into a lifetime of rage right there on the scene.

It took about a dozen equally hard whacks until the cannibal stopped moving. His head was pulp and hair. The Hughes kid just let the tool fall from his hand. He was done. He'd had his vengeance.

The boy's eyes cooled and he came over to me. He saw the cuff, then without asking checked the dead killer's pockets and came out with the keys. He unlocked the cuffs. My hands came free.

I didn't or rather, couldn't get up right away so I sat there waiting for the feeling to come back in my hands while the boy untied his mother.

And that was that. Case fucking closed.

I stuck around long enough to make sure the remains of the Hughes family were okay. I covered the father's body and walked them out front where they wouldn't have to look at the bodies.

Then I cleared the cash register for my pay. I made forty-six dollars and twenty-seven cents. It would barely cover gas.

I didn't stick around for the cops. What good would it do? The freak was dead. The only question remaining was how the fuck did this psycho family live off the main highway all these years without getting checked out?

Like I said, cops are retarded. They don't see what's right in front of them because they don't want to believe how bad things can get.

It's a big, dark, scary world out there as it is. Can you imagine what it would be like if they believed in monsters? You'd think they'd know. Some of the worst monsters out there are human.

STEVE NILES is one of the writers responsible for bringing horror comics back to prominence, and was recently named by *Fangoria* magazine as one of its "thirteen rising talents who promise to keep us terrified for the next twenty-five years."

Niles is currently working for the four top American comics publishers—Marvel, DC, Image, and Dark Horse. Currently ongoing at Image is the creator-owned series *Bad Planet* with co-writer Thomas Jane and *The Cryptics* with artist Ben Roman. Everyone's favorite monster hunter Cal McDonald returns in the monthly *Criminal Macabre* series from Dark Horse.

In 2002, the success of *30 Days of Night* sparked renewed interest in the horror genre. A film version of the graphic novel was released in 2007.

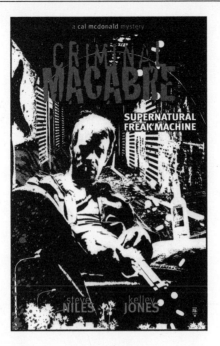

CRIMINAL MACABRE: SUPERNATURAL FREAK MACHINE

Steve Niles and Kelley Jones | ISBN 978-1-59307-731-0 | $17.95

When an old enemy Cal sent to prison escapes, his sights are set on exacting cold revenge on the guy who put him there. And it looks like he'll have to cut through everyone Cal loves to get to him . . . Cal's hardly batting an eye, though. He's already put this guy away once, right? And besides—things are looking up. He's even got a new car to brag about—a spiffy 1973 Nova. Too bad the guy who died in the car before Cal bought it has no intention of leaving!

ALREADY AVAILABLE:

CRIMINAL MACABRE: A CAL MCDONALD MYSTERY

Steve Niles and Ben Templesmith | ISBN 978-1-56971-935-0 | $14.95

CRIMINAL MACABRE: LAST TRAIN TO DEADSVILLE

Steve Niles and Kelley Jones | ISBN 978-1-59307-107-3 | $14.95

CRIMINAL MACABRE: TWO RED EYES

Steve Niles and Kyle Hotz | ISBN 978-1-59307-843-0 | $12.95

AVAILABLE AT YOUR LOCAL COMICS SHOP OR BOOKSTORE • To find a comics shop in your area, call 1-888-266-4226
For more information or to order direct visit darkhorse.com or call 1-800-862-0052 Mon.–Fri. 9 AM to 5 PM Pacific Time. *Prices and availability subject to change without notice

 DARK HORSE BOOKS *drawing on your nightmares*
darkhorse.com